John Milton – heretic, defender of the Cromwellian regicides, epic poet – holds a crucial strategic position on the intellectual and ideological map of literary studies. In this provocative and liberating study, John P. Rumrich contends that contemporary critics, despite differences in methodology, have contributed to the invention of a monolithic or institutional Milton, as censorious preacher, aggressive misogynist, and champion of the emerging bourgeoisie. Rumrich reveals the pressures that have shaped this current critical orthodoxy, and exposes the historical inaccuracies and logical inconsistencies that sustain it. Through analysis of Milton's poetry and prose, and consideration of the historical forces that informed Milton's writing, Rumrich argues instead for a more complex Milton who was able to accommodate uncertainty and doubt.

MILTON UNBOUND

MILTON UNBOUND

Controversy and Reinterpretation

JOHN P. RUMRICH

University of Texas, Austin

CAMBRIDGE
UNIVERSITY PRESS

Published by the Press Syndicate of the University of Cambridge
The Pitt Building, Trumpington Street, Cambridge CB2 IRP
40 West 20th Street, New York, NY 10011–4211, USA
10 Stamford Road, Oakleigh, Melbourne 3166, Australia

First published 1996

Printed in Great Britain by Redwood Books, Trowbridge, Wiltshire

A catalogue record for this book is available from the British Library

Library of Congress cataloguing in publication data

Rumrich, John Peter, 1954–
Milton unbound: controversy and reinterpretation / John P. Rumrich
p.   cm.
ISBN 0 521 55173 0 (hardback)
1. Milton, John, 1608–1674 – Criticism and interpretation – History.
2. Literature and history – Great Britain – History – 17th century.
3. Milton, John, 1608–1674 – Political and social views.
4. Historicism.   I. Title.
PR3587.3.R85 1996
82'.4–dc20   95–14541   CIP

ISBN 0 521 55173 0 hardback

This book is dedicated to my sisters and brother

Kathleen Mary
Patricia Eileen
Sheila Jolan
and
Joseph Bartholomew

Contents

Preface and acknowledgments

This book began in Beijing, China in 1987. My students there lent human substance to what had been previously only a hypothetical proposition: that many of us in the United States were teaching or being taught a badly skewed version of Milton. The Milton to whom the students at Peking University responded was, as Joan Bennett has described him, a radical humanist, who not only hated tyranny and superstition but who, unlike more quiescent intellectuals and artists, put himself on the line fighting against them. That last is important, since Milton's ethics, social agenda, and, I shall argue, artistic and aesthetic expressions imply each other and express an open-ended tolerance, in the societal and structural senses of that term.

My students in China, then struggling with rigorous state censorship, deeply admired *Areopagitica*. It has been argued recently that every grant of liberty rests on an implicit exclusion or limitation of that liberty. Freedom of expression is always already censorship. Yet these students understood, and brought me to understand, that while social policy may always set limits to freedom, differences in degree are of much greater practical moment than some theoretically minded Western Milton scholars seem willing to recognize. Milton, for all his idealism, was a practical man, and a practical champion of liberty. The students at Peking University revered him for that. Living under a totalitarian regime is in some ways an excellent preparation for Milton studies, especially when the government is willing to end one's life for advocating too stubbornly a larger degree of individual liberty or for challenging the absolutist ideology by which it governs. Those were of course the conditions under which Milton lived much of his life, early and late.

I therefore found myself drawn to William Empson's *Milton's God*, which also begins, though to different effect, with the culture shock of teaching *Paradise Lost* in the East. I had long been taught to view

Empson's work as occasionally brilliant, but perverse and wrong-headed – because no one could seriously think that Milton would *really* question the ways of God to men. I do not endorse Empson's ultimate position – that Milton struggled sublimely to justify the inexcusably evil Christian God but failed because the Christian God is evil from his foundations. I am not morally certain enough to feel confident in such a claim, whereas Empson came to write his book already convinced that the Christian deity was a relic of Neolithic cruelty. For Empson, Milton's heresies could blunt only the harsher edges of Christianity, a gloomy opinion that, as I argue in the last chapter, in part reflects a mistaken understanding of the poetic implications of Milton's heretical materialism.

Like Empson, however, I do believe that the struggle of Milton's theodicy is genuine and that the poet presumes no certainty as to cosmic justice. The victory of *Paradise Lost*, to the extent Milton manages it, lies instead in helping us to accept the ambiguity, doubt, and indeterminacy constitutional of our lives, without succumbing to the fear that our existence is meaningless, or worse, malignant. The epic theodicy persuades us to make use of reasonable doubt to establish a place for benevolence and grace in our lives, and it does so most significantly by virtue of the very heresy that Empson was unwilling, perhaps stubbornly so, to admit into the epic narrative. Material indeterminacy and inconclusiveness, in the formlessness of chaos, are for Milton constitutional of the cosmos, of morality, and indeed are essential to the deity himself.

This investigation is largely concerned with internal or structural logic. Hence, in assessing Milton's humanism within a seventeenth-century context, I contend that the ramifications of his philosophy of matter are salient for comprehension of his political vision and poetic practice. In the case of Milton scholarship, on the other hand, the internal logic of what I call the paradigmatic Milton may be described as a closed dialectical circuit. The dialectical structure has helped a very misleading vision of the poet to prosper – the representation of Milton as a carping didact, aggressive misogynist, and poet of the emerging bourgeoisie.

Given my intention to lay out internal logic rather than to survey exhaustively Milton's works in their historical context or contemporary criticism of them, my argument inevitably neglects exceptions and inconsistencies to its twin theses. I have tried to acknowledge such exceptions as much as possible, however. Those exceptions that are also my precursors cause even greater anxiety. Anyone who has worked in Milton studies for a few years will realize how easily others' perceptions and insights can become incorporated into one's own arguments. And like most of us, I write in dread of failing to acknowledge my debts. This dread is especially acute in the case of a book like this one, which not only has developed over a long time, but tends to be sharply critical of other work in the field and so should be correspondingly thorough and generous in acknowledgment. For the inevitable errors of omission, I apologize in advance, though I imagine that I will, quite properly, be called to account for them anyway.

Happily, there are many debts of which I am quite conscious. As I already indicated, the book began as an article, entitled "Uninventing Milton," eight years ago in Beijing, China, and I feel deep gratitude to my colleagues and former students there. I started to write "Uninventing Milton" as I was struggling to complete the introduction to my first book, which was then about to go into production. That introduction and the article make some of the same points, as indeed does this book. In general, the opinions presented in *Matter of Glory* concerning the workings of Milton's cosmos have not changed, and this study assumes and builds on that work. I hope that this overlap will be seen as continuity and development rather than as repetition.

"Uninventing Milton" was published in 1990, and I am indebted to Janel Mueller of the University of Chicago, who was then just beginning her tenure as editor of *Modern Philology* and who made the decision to publish that rather unusual piece. She also accompanied her editorial decision with generous encouragement and wise advice. In 1990–91, an NEH fellowship, in combination with a grant from the Research Institute of the University of Texas, Austin, allowed me the time to build upon the article toward a book-length study, and let me find a way to make the argument pivot so that I might offer a positive, alternative vision of the poet rather than simply criticize the existing one. Christopher Hill and John Carey read parts of the study at this point and offered encouragement and direction. Most of the crucial fellowship year was spent at the Alexander Turnbull Library, the research arm of the National Library of New Zealand. The head librarian Margaret Caldwell, her associate Philip Ranier, and the rest of the staff at the Turnbull were unfailingly generous and helpful as I drew on their extraordinary Milton collection, and were, moreover, unquestioningly accepting of an egregiously American visitor during the Gulf War. I also feel a deep sense of gratitude to Lydia Wevers,

Alastair Bisley, Brian and Ann Opie – as well as to their children – for friendship, generosity, affection, and encouragement while I was living and working in Wellington.

My greatest debt as a student of Milton continues to be to William Kerrigan. I can on occasion dissent from his published views only because his teaching, and what is more important, his passion for the truth, have set an example that encouraged me to do so. More specifically, I want to thank Stephen M. Fallon, J. Martin Evans, Wayne A. Rebhorn, and Leah S. Marcus, who all read a large part of the manuscript at an early stage and offered useful, detailed advice that helped me improve what I had already written. They also gave me a renewed sense of direction as I was bringing the work to its conclusion. Mark Womack, Dolora Wojciehowski, Joseph Wittreich, Lydia Wevers, Beth Rothermel, Maurice Kelley, George Boulukos, and Michael Bauman all read chapters and improved them with their comments. Lance Bertelsen advised me on book design and cover art and I have gratefully followed his advice. The portrait of Milton is reproduced courtesy of The Pierpont Morgan Library, New York. Research assistant Daniel Rose caught many errors at the final stage. Most telling was the abiding collaborative effort of Stephen B. Dobranski, who over several years read each chapter, made detailed comments, and suggested new sources for me to consult.

Although this book begins by citing William Empson and Christopher Hill, it also owes much to other Milton scholars. The archetype of historically reliable and industrious Milton scholarship is David Masson, whose massive biography often influences what follows. Only in comparison with Masson could William R. Parker's learned and detailed study seem somehow slight and idiosyncratic. I also am indebted to the work of James Holly Hanford, Denis Saurat, E. M. W. Tillyard, John Milton French, Don Wolfe, Helen Darbishire, Merritt Hughes, and Alastair Fowler. Finally, I want to go on record with the opinion that Maurice Kelley's work on *de doctrina Christiana* is the single most significant and underappreciated contribution to twentieth-century Milton studies. Over years of studying Milton's theological opinions, I have come to rely on Kelley as being almost unfailingly accurate and just in his conclusions. Sadly, the same cannot always be said of those who have over the years disputed them.

Abbreviations

CW   *The Works of John Milton*, ed. Frank H. Patterson, 18 vols.
(New York, 1931–38).

CP   *The Prose Works of John Milton*, gen. ed. Don M. Wolfe, 8
vols. (New Haven, 1953–82).

Masson   David Masson, *Life of John Milton*, 6 vols. (1874–81; reprint,
Gloucester, MA, 1965).

Parker   William R. Parker, *Milton: A Life*, 2 vols. (Oxford, 1968).

Citations of Milton's poetry employ standard abbreviations and are
taken from *The Poetical Works of John Milton*, ed. Helen Darbishire, 2
vols. (Oxford, 1952). These citations, and citations of the works listed
above, will appear parenthetically in the body of the text. Notes will be
used for most other references, with each chapter's initial citation of
any given work appearing in full detail.

Translations

Translations of Milton's Latin poetry are my own. Latin and Greek
words or passages will appear only for emphasis or when the argument
relies on them directly.

CHAPTER I

Introduction: the invented Milton

If you realize that Milton was really worried about the official
subject of his poem, you find the poetry very genuine.

William Empson[1]

In 1961, William Empson in the controversial *Milton's God* challenged
what he called the growing "neo-Christian" bias of scholars, blaming it
for overstatement of Milton's orthodoxy and understatement of the
sincerity of his epic theodicy. Empson claimed that the epic's "struggling" and "searching" outside the limits of the "traditional Christian"
faith is the "chief source of its fascination and poignancy."[2] In making
this claim, he was responding rather pointedly to works like C. S.
Lewis's *Preface to Paradise Lost*, which placed the epic firmly within
Christianity's "great central tradition."[3] Despite Empson's challenge,
Lewis's basic reading has increasingly dominated, though with certain
crucial refinements, and Empson's views have been dismissed and even
derided. There have been striking exceptions to this general trend,
however, most substantially Christopher Hill's historically detailed
presentation of Milton as a "radical Protestant heretic."[4]

Professor Hill introduced his study by endorsing Empson's complaint
that neo-Christian critics have attempted to "annex Milton" on behalf
of orthodoxy. He then went on to condemn the reflexive pedantry of
much recent scholarship:

There is the immensely productive Milton industry, largely in the United
States of America, a great part of whose vast output appears to be concerned
less with what Milton wrote (still less with enjoyment of what Milton wrote)
than with the views of Professor Blank on the views of Professor Schrank on
the views of Professor Rank.[5]

Empson's and Hill's complaints are in combination the basis of the first
half of this book, which, while it does not pretend to be an exhaustive

survey of recent Milton scholarship, nevertheless offers a critique of the
logic of contemporary critical practice. The arid debate to which Hill
refers – and chapter 3 argues that deflation of literary delight particularly
distinguishes contemporary criticism – diverts attention from the fact
that we Blanks, Schranks, and Ranks, despite very real differences, have
managed to agree on a basis for disagreement. The subject of that
underlying agreement I call the invented Milton, a rhetorical artifact or
paradigm foundational to contemporary Milton scholarship.

I use the term "paradigm" with the work of historian of science
Thomas Kuhn in mind. In Kuhn's analysis, a paradigm is "an accepted
model or pattern," one that serves as "an object for further articulation
and specification."[6] Such a paradigm enjoys its status because it
successfully solves problems or a problem that "the group of practitioners has come to recognize as acute."[7] By the 1960s, the "acute"
problem for "practitioners" of Milton criticism was that of Satan's
appeal in *Paradise Lost.* The old controversy over Satan's heroism had
become a worn, dead-end debate, yet it continued to consume
enormous amounts of critical energy and attention, generating a certain
amount of heat but very little light. During a period when intense
impatience with the status quo pervaded American culture, especially
in the academy, Milton scholarship was obviously going nowhere.

The invention that ameliorated this acute problem was set forth in
Stanley Fish's *Surprised by Sin.*[8] By deploying reader-response theory to
acknowledge and then defuse the problem of Satan's appeal, Fish
inaugurated a period in Milton criticism analogous to what Kuhn
describes as "normal science," a condition in which practitioners
expend their labors to extend and deepen a working paradigm rather
than rehash fundamental issues that it resolved.[9] Over the last quarter-
century, many practitioners of Milton criticism have attempted, as the
title of a recent collection suggests, to "re-member" Milton according
to the form and pressure of contemporary intellectual preoccupa-
tions.[10] The great post-Romantic impasse had been overcome, and the
practice of Milton criticism became progressive, ironically enough, at
the very moment when postmodern skeptics were calling the idea of
progress into question.

Contemporary Milton scholarship cannot be described as uniform, of
course, except in a rough way and at the most basic level. We currently
enjoy unprecedented diversity of a sort, and in conforming to Fish's
paradigm, we have, as Kuhn says, "solved problems that [practitioners]
could scarcely have imagined and would never have undertaken without

commitment to the paradigm."[11] Furthermore, as the early citation of Professor Hill indicates, the invented Milton has not monopolized critical discourse. Useful studies, oblivious to or selectively critical of the paradigm, have recently appeared and been recognized for their substantial contributions to our understanding of Milton.[12]

Also, certain works that overtly submit to the paradigm – William Kerrigan's *The Sacred Complex*, for example – have deepened our understanding of John Milton in ways that actually tend to subvert it.[13] Hence, in an otherwise laudatory review of Kerrigan's book, the late Philip Gallagher objects to the "undercurrent of profound eccentricity in [*The Sacred Complex's*] subtext ... that would seek by pathways at once subterranean and recondite to recapture Milton for the Saurats and Hills and – though Kerrigan would deny it – the Waldocks and Empsons of this world."[14] The sensitivity to an "undercurrent of profound eccentricity" is noteworthy if oddly phrased. One anticipates misgivings over the validity of Kerrigan's controversial, psychohistorical methodology. But the reference to Milton as if he were a trophy in an intellectual contest, combined with the denigration of critics like Empson and Hill (merely naming them is enough) suggests that, for some, disputes over critical methodology do not signify in comparison with what might be regarded as the cultural stakes – Milton's allegiance to an unproblematic, centrist orthodoxy.

If indeed the invented Milton has of late been ignored or implicitly challenged by some, and subverted from within by others, no one has successfully refuted Fish's main argument, not on its own terms. Nor have we found a fresh way to regard the poet, one that might displace the paradigm or at least provide an alternative to it. Though I do not deny the value of much recent Milton scholarship, or of the insights that over the last three decades the paradigm has made possible, I feel convinced that it is seriously mistaken and, what is worse, a pedagogical disaster. The purpose of the first half of this book, therefore, is to challenge the invented Milton. The second half is more constructive in its aims and attempts to demonstrate the benefit of uninventing Milton for our understanding of his works. Ultimately, I argue that Milton's poetry, though overtly patriarchal, reflects maternal influences to a greater extent than we have previously recognized, especially in its presentation of generative processes, including those of poetry and divine creation.

I thus begin with the premise that the consolidation and general acceptance of what Empson called the "neo-Christian" position derive from the crystallizing impact of Stanley Fish's *Surprised by Sin*. First published in 1967, Fish's work appealed to the more restless among its contemporary audience in part because it followed an innovative interpretive strategy – associated with reader-response theory – that placed the reader in the center of the epic action or, rather, placed the center of the epic action in the reader. The consequence was a methodologically radical update of Lewis's reading of *Paradise Lost* as a literary monument to mainstream Christianity. With the advantage of hindsight, we can appreciate the tactical brilliance of *Surprised by Sin*. Along with its appeal to freethinkers appreciative of fresh critical methods, it also pleased their customary opponents, those more traditional scholars who saw Milton as a champion of Christian essentials. In an early instance of what has since become a familiar irony, *Surprised by Sin* initiated a confederation of factions in Milton studies by putting an apparently destabilizing hermeneutics to work for traditionalist interests.

Ultimately, this book concerns itself not with the reading of *Paradise Lost* presented in *Surprised by Sin*, but rather with a corporate, almost institutionalized, view of Milton and his works. For neither reader-response theory nor the generalship of a single critic has sustained expansion of the invented Milton. This growth owes instead to a remarkable agglomeration of diverse disciplinary interests. I am none-theless committed to a refutation of Fish's seminal study, because its dexterous reading of the epic is still basic to our contemporary under-standing of Milton's works and, sadly, of the man himself.

The success of the invented Milton owes partly to epistemological skepticism over the validity of historical interpretation. Concern with scholarly accuracy and consistent use of historical evidence has come to seem uninformed and irrelevant compared with dense discussion of apparently more urgent theoretical issues.[15] Many of us have come to think that there is no such thing as an author's meaning, or indeed an author, except perhaps as negotiated within a particular community of readers.[16] Whatever interpretation best calculates and accommodates the interests of the most influential groups, and avoids positively alienating most others, becomes dominant. Given this state of affairs, I intend the term "invented" to be descriptive, not pejorative. Fish himself suggests it and means by it a rhetorically adept, and therefore politically viable (for him these modifiers are synonymous) adaptation to the features of an "interpretive community."[17] Under such conditions, as in the case of presidential politics, vague banality and dull elaboration of the status quo are often the unfortunate consequences. Lance Bertelsen has wryly observed that those in our profession who manage to thrive under such conditions are generally those we call "smart": "in other words," says Bertelsen, " 'smart' means today (with rhetorical adjustments) what 'dunce' meant to Pope – the aspiration to fulfill, through flexible and everchanging discursive practice, the will to literary power."[18]

There is no going back. Though few perhaps would push to the extreme represented by Roland Barthes, fewer still would deny the role of readers in negotiating meaning.[19] Communication is by definition a social phenomenon and literary interpretation is a special instance of human communication. But skepticism over the place of authors in determining meaning, and thus over the value of historical contextualization, derives not from a shift in focus away from authors and toward readers, who after all have no more authority than the author. Skepticism about the role played by authors (or readers) in determining meaning derives instead from assumptions about the role linguistic codes play in communication.

Philosophers from Aristotle to Derrida have studied language itself as if it were the basis of human communication. Under this assumption, communication boils down to the coding and decoding of messages between senders and receivers.[20] But, as exponents of deconstruction have argued, the upshot of post-Saussurean linguistics is that the interpretation of codes – understood as ever shifting semiotic systems of non-identity relationships – is logically without limits. And inasmuch as authors use codes, there is no way to establish what authors mean.

Human use of language, however, has developed into a conscious and sophisticated form of intentional behavior, something logically quite distinct from the codes that are typically its media. So far as we know, coding and decoding as a means of transferring information from sender to receiver does not belong particularly to humans – birds do it, bees do it, even educated machines do it. The significant difference between us and many of these other senders and receivers lies in our ability to communicate *without* the use of codes. Adam's "glance or toy / Of amorous intent," for example, can be communicative and "well understood" without any established precedent for the signs used or any conventionally agreed upon definitions (*PL* 9, 1034–35). In paradise as Milton presents it, intelligent animals, though they lack human language, still manage to communicate with humans.

If rational beings communicated solely through instinctively patterned movements or autonomically controlled, stimulus-sensitive secretions, there would of course be much less interpretive problematizing about messages or, strictly speaking, no interpretation at all – just information processing. The codes would be fixed and establishing meaning would be a function of them.

In communicating, however, most people outside the academy go beyond the limits of language use observed by a drone dancing in his hive. History and common experience tell us that, regardless of how cleverly those who trade in secrets scramble the code, they find it difficult to communicate messages to a select audience and still keep the relevant meaning hidden from others.[21] One look at the third base coach during a baseball game tells you that. Strangers utterly ignorant of each other's languages manage to make their intentions known and eventually to learn each other's codes, even without outside help. The attempt to account for human communication by obsessive resort to the code model is rather like an attempt to account for the elephant's ability to pick things up with its nose by invoking the sense of smell.[22] Those olfactory philosophers among us who might conclude that elephants therefore *cannot* pick things up with their noses are welcome to argue that pachyderms feed themselves by interpreting the odor of hay.

Chapter 2 takes up the vexed question of authorial intention, relevance, and historical context in more detail. Yet I should say that the theoretical premises of this book, per the arguments of Dan Sperber and Deirdre Wilson, are that there is no "necessary link between language and communication," and that therefore the looseness and indeterminacy of human codes do not render interpretation entirely an affair of politically or rhetorically adept invention. Intention and relevance – not the linguistic code – form the basis of human communication and interpretation.[23] A sentence like "the tank is half empty" can mean "stop and fill up before New York," or "the fish will die if we do not add water soon" or "I'm a pessimist," or "where have Corporal Smith and Gunner Jones gone?" and so on. As a matter of communication between people in particular situations, the relevant, intended meaning will generally be discernible. In line with the practice if not the theory of most Milton scholars, my argument assumes the principle that awareness of historical context allows us to attain a surprisingly strong sense of authorial intention and to discuss relevance with practical assurance. Given the relatively objective limits provided by cultural convention, we can reasonably judge particular interpretations so improbable as to be mistaken and others so probable as to be correct. And my claim is that the invented Milton is a mistake, a big one.

What are the chief characteristics of the widely accepted version of the author of *Paradise Lost?* According to Georgia Christopher's award-winning book (1982), one which Empson would have called "neo-Christian,"

Stanley Fish has shown how *Paradise Lost* is constructed for evangelical purposes so as to elicit a pattern of alternating identification with and rejection of the characters, in order to convict the reader of sin.[24]

James Grantham Turner's New Historicist study of Milton's sexual attitudes (1987) offers the substantially identical observation that Milton effects the "deliberate entrapment of the audience in fallen responses, the better to guide them toward regeneration." If Turner sidesteps language like "convict" and "sin," his citation of "entrapment" in "fallen responses" as a major feature of Milton's art conforms to the customary reading.[25] He explicitly parts company with Fish only in his insistence that fallen readers' sexual experiences do allow them to understand Adam and Eve's erotic bliss. For this particular disagreement over readers' responses, however, it is difficult to see any basis other than self-gratulatory.[26]

In the same year as Turner, Marshall Grossman steered his theoretically inventive argument, which contemplates early modern self-fashioning in *Paradise Lost*, into a similar alignment with orthodoxy. He remarks that Milton's awakening of readers' capacities for active self-awareness is especially notable in their responses to Milton's God: "the difficulty of accepting the Father is, as Stanley Fish points out, a measure of our 'crookedness'. ... It is not so much the Father who is characterized in book III as the reader's relationship to the Godhead."[27]

Judging by these three influential and ostensibly quite different works of the last decade, *Paradise Lost* instructs rather easily duped and forgetful readers by repeatedly convicting them of sin or by obtruding measures of their crookedness. True, these studies have also branched out from the standard position. Yet, each of them accepts Fish's basic position as a premise: Milton provokes an emotional response (as in the similes or the depiction of God) and then, having established fallen engagement, dominates it. That New Historicist readings like those of

Turner and Grossman should fall in so readily behind the evangelical
standard may seem surprising. Yet Fish's description of Christian
didacticism anticipates the familiar New Historicist interpretive paradigm, in which subversion is a fantasy that can never be successfully
realized. Authority, according to this model, clandestinely instigates
rebellion, or at least the thought of it, as a pretext for the assertion and
confirmation of power. Like evil and good in Augustinian theology and
its Protestant derivatives, subversion and containment constitute only
an appearance of dualism within a totalitarian system.[28]

To elicit his audience's awareness of its peccant condition and so
validate the divine perspective, Milton allegedly exploits the disjunction
between readers' fallen attitudes and standard, Protestant, ethical
doctrine – comprising what one critic calls "catechetical formulations."[29] Christopher Kendrick's Marxian study (1986) describes such
"didactic theology" as being in conflict with the epic's psychological
effect:

Theological and psychological genres appear to conflict with one another, and
... the dominant genre of the hexameron overrules affective drama, didactic
theology retroactively canceling profane psychological motivations.[30]

This mouthful does no more than "to put into generic terms Stanley
Fish's argument about the presentation of God," as Kendrick admits.[31]

When Fish comes to interpret *Areopagitica*, he returns Kendrick's
favor, noting the congruity of their respective readings of that work
too:

On one point we are in agreement, that *Areopagitica* displays a double structure
of discursive argument and anti-discursive eruptions that "uncenter" the overt
rhetorical movement of the oration .... The chief difference is that whereas I
see Milton continually undermining the forms within which he necessarily
moves in order to make his tract a (self-consuming) emblem of its message,
Kendrick sees contradictions that Milton does not control because they mark
his implication in the ideological structure of emerging capitalism.[32]

For Kendrick, Milton's use of the vocabulary of commerce and
monopoly in a tract claiming that truth is not a ware subject to such
practices betrays his social contradiction, and thus his class stand.[33]
Milton does not himself expose this implicit contradiction, says Kendrick, because of his alignment with the "revolutionary bourgeois
class." To disclose the lie of bourgeois ideology would be a betrayal.
What for Kendrick exemplifies Marx's concept of contradiction – an
economic interest profiting from ideological posturing to the contrary –

for Fish illustrates the same strategy that he finds everywhere in Milton: "it would be no trick at all, just a standard move in the repertoire Kendrick and I share with other members of the profession, to outflank and assimilate his reading."[34]

Fish's characterization of critical debate as a strategic contest seems to me persuasive, at least given the practice of the Blanks, Schranks, and Ranks of contemporary Milton scholarship. Whether one employs neo-Christian terms or New Historicist ones, whether one follows Marx or Derrida, connection with the paradigm requires only a perceived contradiction within a supposed unity. Once the possibility of a contradiction is admitted, the unified appearance can be construed as excessive and therefore significant of correction or suppression. It is a classic example of dialectical reduction and synthesis (for deconstruction, simply reverse the order of these terms). And it represents a way of dealing with complexity to which Western theoreticians after Hegel seem especially prone. Though Fish and his interlocutors can presumably go on endlessly outflanking and assimilating each other's readings, I will argue that as applied to Milton, such dialectical interpretive schemes are inadequate, and too often impositions in the service of professional or ideological agendas. What I propose is not so much a teaching as a disentangling.

As the interplay with Kendrick reveals, while Fish's interpretive theory has evolved from affective stylistics toward deconstruction, his criticism of Milton has worked to extend the consensus that *Surprised by Sin* originated. Chapter 3 takes the dialectical structure of the paradigm as its subject and eventually addresses the pursuit of dominance among Milton scholars working within that paradigm. It does so by first examining the Oedipal psychology attributed to the poet and his readers.

Kerrigan locates the psychological allure of Fish's reading of Milton not in its power to illuminate Milton's works, but in its appeal to two opposed factions among *and within* scholars:

Paradise Lost combines mythopoeic narrative with rational theodicy ... In many readers the figure of Satan generates a tension between these two poles: his mythopoeic grandeur at the opening of the work opposes his discursive condemnation by the narrator and the heavenly characters ... In claiming that the tension was deliberate, Fish healed an old division in Milton studies ... The pious reader can entertain potentially rebellious attitudes knowing that, as signs of his fallenness, these attitudes already confirm the doctrinal content of the poem and therefore have a piety all their own.[35]

According to this analysis, Fish has played a role in Milton studies analogous to that of the Oedipal ego as it attempts to negotiate a satisfactory compromise between the id's drives and the superego's laws.

For Kerrigan, Milton can also be explained through the dialectic of law and forbidden desire at the heart of the Oedipal drama: "the Oedipus complex is the generative center of [Milton's] character and his art"; "temptation remained his myth ... obedience his virtue"; "as time is a river, as God is the Father, Miltonic Christianity is the Oedipus complex."[36] Kerrigan's deployment of Oedipal analysis revitalized the paradigmatic version of the poet. The strong father of the Oedipal drama figures as the quasi-mythological figure supporting Marxian, Weberian, and New Historicist attempts to articulate seventeenth-century social and cultural history through the patriarchal particulars of Milton's life and art. Was not Milton, in Kermode's classic phrase, his father's "chief investment"?[37] Hence, while psychoanalytic criticism may seem eccentric or marginal to many, I find the Oedipal version of the poet to be central for recent developments in more purely theoretical Milton criticism. Chapter 3 reviews the Oedipal paradigm and the proliferation of dialectical interpretations it has helped to foster. Chapter 4 offers an alternative psychological model, one that is structurally integrative and indeterminate rather than dichotomous and closed. It focuses on Milton's *Comus*, which Kerrigan labels the "mask of the superego" and in which, allegedly, the severity of Milton's paralyzing Oedipal trauma is most evident. Rather than accept the portrait of Milton as a latent, Oedipally traumatized rebel, I ask in the second half of this book that we recognize the primacy of pre-Oedipal, maternally oriented aspects of his character. Uncertainties over boundaries and the extent of his powers, coupled with an overwhelming desire to achieve greatness, are definitive of the dilemma that I take to be fundamental to young Milton's developing personality.

Before indicating more about the direction that the second half of this book will take, I must first return to Fish's "thesis book."[38] I have described it as the basis of the predominant strain of Milton scholarship during the last quarter-century, but I have not yet offered compelling reasons for dissatisfaction with it, and presenting such reasons is the main business of *this* chapter. For Fish, Milton fits in perfectly with mainstream Reformation opinions on theodicy: " 'that thou may'st believe and be confirm'd' would have been a more honest – literal is the better word – *propositio* than 'justify the ways of God to men.' "[39] There is a historical basis for this opinion. Most Puritans in mid-seventeenth-century England would have condemned the presumption implicit in a genuine theodicy. Against this prevailing attitude, the stated aim of *Paradise Lost* could easily appear to be an ironic pretext designed to provoke, so as to chastise, the overweening pride of fallen humanity.

The view of theodicy presupposed by a *sincere* intention to justify the ways of God differs from the view taken by most of Milton's audience and, for that reason, the sincerity of Milton's intention may seem suspect.[40] The mature Milton's consistent assertion of free will, however, distinguishes him from the Puritan majority and, though the logic may not be immediately obvious, removes the theological need for finding theodicy blasphemous.[41] Milton invariably argues against positions – from licensing to divorce – that would imply a divine tyranny. And with free will denied, no *rational* theodicy can evade bitter condemnation of God's "justice" as tyrannical. Luther, who thought reason the devil's agent in such matters, readily admitted as much in debating Erasmus over free will: "it gives the greatest possible offense to common sense or natural reason that God by his own sheer will should abandon, harden, and damn men as if he enjoyed the sins and the vast eternal torments of his wretched creatures."[42]

Milton also agrees that reason must condemn the judgments of a determinist deity, but, for Milton as for Erasmus, in such a case reason's condemnation would be entirely fitting: "if [God] turns man's will to moral good or evil just as he likes, and then rewards the good and punishes the wicked, it will cause an outcry [*expostulatio*] against divine justice from all sides" (*CP* 6, 397). Milton's belief in human freedom is complicated and limited, more so than is usually recognized. Nevertheless, the first fact of the uninvention of Milton is, I believe, indisputable. Simply put, Milton's God does not produce rational creatures so that he can compel their choices and then reward or punish them accordingly. Humanity enjoys the freedom to choose between good and evil, and Milton's belief in that freedom renders the notion of a sincere theodicy plausible. Apart from theology and logic, it defies probability and sensible expectation to suppose that Milton would announce a theodicy simply as an ironic ruse. His practice as a poet and pamphleteer – from *On the Death of a Fair Infant* to *Samson Agonistes* – typically and prominently features

theodicy. Did the Bellerophon of poets ride a one-trick Pegasus, time
and time again ostentatiously gathering himself as if to soar, merely to
trick his readers into leaping off cliffs of presumption?

Why might an interpretation based on reader-response theory
exaggerate Milton's affiliation with ideas and attitudes characteristic of
Puritan determinism? One answer at least seems evident. A critic who
wishes to talk about readers' responses as if they were regular and
predictable must provide a criterion capable of generalizing over
individual differences. The psychological diversity and complexity of
readers, even of a single reader, would otherwise be an insuperable
obstacle. In *Surprised by Sin*, the voluntarist criterion of obedience,
according to which all humanity is the same – a miserable failure –
allows this reduction of the potential complexity of readers' psyches.
One's responses as reader, or candidate for salvation, either conform to
authorial, or divine, dictates or they do not; nothing else matters.

In pursuit of the logical coherence provided by this simple and clear
dichotomy, both Puritan determinism and reader-response theory
dismiss narrative context, or invoke it only to insist on its irrelevance:
"free will cannot be determined by forces outside it," Fish remarks;
"the point of the scenes in Paradise from book 4 to book 9 is their
irrelevance as determining factors."[43] Obedience is formulated as an
existential either-or always confronting the will, regardless of situation.
The case for a sincere theodicy and against Puritan determinism is an
argument that mitigating circumstances do matter, that the distinguishing particulars count.

The equivocal nature of human knowledge makes interpretive and
therefore moral certainty an impossibility. Although in *Paradise Lost*
Adam perceives immediately and clearly the effect of the fruit on
"defac't" Eve, he also concludes that they are so closely knit that he
cannot choose but fall with her (9, 901). This dubious assessment of the
situation, the emotional honesty of which nonetheless seems undeniable, is Adam's fortunate moment of interpretive equivocation.[44]
Plausible fallibility of human judgment allows God in turn to be
equivocal in his treatment of humanity: they must die, but then again
they must not. The ambivalent equipoise of God's doom is perhaps
more immediately apparent than its justice. Yet the aptitude of God's
response – which lies in its very indeterminacy and flexibility – is also
an aspect of theodicy. Just as neither Adam nor Eve disobeys God
exactly or entirely, so God does not punish them exactly or entirely. As
for the fallen angels, the near perfection of their intellects, together

with Abdiel's timely fulmination, renders absurd the notion of inexact disobedience on their part. As Milton remarks at one of the more chilling moments in his theological treatise, "their knowledge is great, but it is a torment to them rather than a consolation" (*CP* 6, 349).

If only the fact of choice matters, the process leading up to it can be distorted without consequence. Fish, for example, claims that Eve succumbs to temptation because she is "won to reason" and because the snake successfully initiates her "into the mysteries of empirical science."[45] She should just say no. Yet strong textual evidence – Adam's request for a mate, for example – indicates that humans are neither designed nor equipped to be so promptly and irrationally obedient. In any case, being hoodwinked by a fast-talking snake is quite distinct from being "won to reason." In fact, Eve's only attempt to answer the serpent follows precisely the recommended voluntarist course: she offers a dull recitation of the prohibition (9, 651–54, 659–63). A budding empiricist would surely have raised objections to the serpent's story, or at least required experimental confirmation ("let us feed the elephant an apple and see if it will talk"). She could have asked questions or drawn distinctions that might have established rational grounds for resistance. But she offers almost no rational resistance, appealing nakedly to divine law, and for Milton a simple no, a no not actively supported by reason, is never good enough and, according to Milton in *Areopagitica*, can be accounted heretical in its servility (*CP* 2, 543).

Milton's God in *Paradise Regained* describes the original bad choice, with customary precision, as a specifically rational failure, observing that humanity fell "by fallacy surpriz'd" (*PR* 1, 155). This tallies with his prior insistence that "Reason also is choice," an equation to which the poet had himself publicly subscribed on behalf of postlapsarian humanity – "reason is but choosing" (*PL* 3, 108; *CP* 2, 527).[46] For Milton, reason cannot be separated from or, as in Fish's discussion of Eve, opposed to obedience. Human reason is relatively slow, apt to wander according to the individual reasoner; it is, in Milton's own terminology, more "discursive" than "intuitive" (*PL* 5, 487–90). This distinction between men and angels may ultimately be only a matter of degree, but the consequence of this difference in degree – the *only* difference Milton's metaphysic admits – is that while obedience is undoubtedly essential to human virtue, it is not reducible to a Kierkegaardian either-or.

Although I will go on to argue that we must be wary of measuring humans by angelic standards, in heaven, too, reason plays a key role. This is certainly true at the very beginning of Raphael's narration, when the angels' free will is put to the ultimate test. At this the earliest point in the epic action their moral situation resembles humanity's most. In assessing this originary episode, Fish contends that Abdiel illustrates true heroism because he exemplifies volitionally pure submissiveness: "Abdiel is a hero because he says 'Shalt thou give Law to God?' (the declarative form would be 'Thy will be done')."[47] But the answer Abdiel makes to Satan is not a simple no. His defiance of Satan's illegitimate authority rests instead on an alternative construction of the revelation of the Son as God's image (5, 809–45). Abdiel himself describes his resistance as rational:

> His puissance, trusting in th' Almightie's aide,
> I mean to try, whose Reason I have tri'd
> Unsound and false; nor is it aught but just,
> That he who in debate of Truth hath won,
> Should win in Arms, in both disputes alike
> Victor; though brutish that contest and foule,
> When Reason hath to deal with force, yet so
> Most reason is that Reason overcome.   (6, 119–26)

Abdiel does not reach the extreme associated with the ancient Stoics – that one should not obey God so much as agree with him. Yet his punning judgment ("most reason is") that he *should* triumph in arms over Satan expresses a nearly syllogistic theodical expectation.

In the determinist world-view, there is little place for Abdiel's logic in contemplating matters at divine disposal or for the subjunctive mood at all – certainly not the hortatory ought or should. Abdiel goes on to deliver an unanswered blow, one that not only forces Satan to recoil but also exacts from him precisely the "knee tribute" he had insisted he would never pay the Son (5, 782). Concerning this outcome, Fish claims that Abdiel's overweening "sense of justice is disappointed." His "assumptions fail the test of experience" because neither he nor the whole angelic force defeat Satan.[48] Raphael's subsequent observation that until Satan fought Michael, he "met in Armes / No equal" confirms for Fish the hypothesis that Milton intended to render Abdiel's "military pretensions" inconsequential (6, 247–48).[49] But "met ... no equal" does not mean that Abdiel's prowess was insignificant or that he did not "win in Arms." Unlike Michael, Abdiel occupies a position hierarchically inferior to Satan's bright eminence. All the more reason that Satan is "foild" – the diction is quite precise here – by

Abdiel's stroke and the moment immediately and correctly reckoned a "presage of Victorie" (6, 200–01). That Abdiel is not Satan's "equal" underscores the dramatic impact of his unlikely triumph over his superior.

Raphael ignores most heroic actions and explicitly justifies doing so, but his magnification of Abdiel's prowess, at once military and moral, comes second only to that reserved for the Messiah, who will return alone to defeat the rebels in arms as if to exalt by counterpoint Abdiel's lone departure from them after debate. The claim that "one is not impressed ... by Abdiel" as a warrior indicates how one's reading of the poem must be wrenched to sustain an anti-theodical reading of the narrative.[50] Abdiel is Milton's new model warrior, and were he to have failed in single combat with Satan, God would, by right, have some explaining to do.

The appeal to Abdiel as an example against theodical presumption exemplifies a mainstay of the invented Milton: the ethical measurement of humanity by angelic experience and according to angelic dicta. Isolated misreadings aside, the strategy seems generally sound. Raphael and Michael preside over great chunks of the epic, after all, and the former repeatedly suggests the comparability of Heaven and unfallen Earth, even justifying the terms of his narrative history by it. Similarly, resemblance between human history as Michael relates it and the account of hell in books 1 and 2 is marked and a commonplace topic of critical investigation. The narrator himself frequently and overtly sounds the theme of resemblance, although usually to insist that while categorically the same, the "human" phenomena in hell – armies, construction methods, buildings, and so on – are "farr beyond / Compare" (1, 587–88).

Milton often represents life on Earth as darkly mirroring heavenly or hellish patterns. Yet we should see this relation as roughly similar to that between ideal and instance in Platonic philosophy. If the sharp Platonic distinction between the realm of absolute being and the realm of becoming does not hold for Milton, heaven and hell are nevertheless presented as being far more accomplished realms than Earth, less influenced by the circumstantial indeterminacy and uncertainty that lead to theodicy. Although angels, like humans, enjoy free will, their experience after the Son's exaltation is – while still governed by free will – redolent of determinism. This somewhat paradoxical state of affairs appears most clearly in the case of the reprobate rebels, who, once they disobey, are "decreed, / Reserv'd and destind to Eternal woe" (*PL* 2, 160–61).[51] Their experience of inescapable damnation is worse than it would be if they had been predestined to it. For, as they suffer, they realize that they *could* have chosen otherwise, though they did not and no longer can. This dissonance produces remorse, a self-consuming condition that cannot apply under a determinist regime. It affords Satan's soliloquy in book 4 much of its poignancy. He would be a less moving tragic figure if God had predestined him to rebel, if he had had no alternative.

Once fallen, regardless of their original condition of free will, the rebels no longer enjoy much of a choice: one way or another they will remain the "Vassals" of God's wrath, just as those in heaven seem practically certain to retain uninterrupted title to their "splendid vassalage" (2, 90, 252). In a fascinating chapter on angels in *Christian Doctrine*, Milton remarks repeatedly that bad angels are "kept [*reservantur*] for punishment," and that they know this (*CP* 6, 349). The rebels' remarks in the first two books of the poem dramatically confirm this description of their woeful state. On the other side, the continued obedience of the good angels seems, if not automatic, almost inevitable after the war in heaven. Having seen what they have seen, who could disobey? They can entertain no shadow of doubt concerning God's omnipotence or creative power, such as seems in part to have encouraged the bad angels during the rebellion, and their intelligence and knowledge are too exalted for them to be tricked into disobeying. In all things, Milton writes, they remain obsequiously obedient (*obsequentissimi*) (*CW* 15, 100).

Raphael's narrative serves as a warning because it is history, a past example of what humanity has yet to experience, and will not finish experiencing until the end of the prophetic narrative that Michael relates. That is why the human situation bears comparison to the realm of becoming in Platonic philosophy. The ethical model supplied by good and bad angels, who have in effect already had their apocalypse, does not particularly suit human beings, explicitly designed as creatures of natural and moral process.[52] For human beings more than for angels, "there still remains a meantime," as Patricia Parker has said; the "point of coincidence" between heavenly meaning and earthly phenomena is "not yet."[53]

There is never any doubt for Milton as poet or theologian that Adam and Eve would owe continuance in unfallen perfection to their own efforts. Plus, in a meritorious state of continuing obedience, they would gradually improve in knowledge and material condition. The prospect of advancement, spoken of by both God and Raphael (5, 496–503; 7, 156–59), has no equivalent in heavenly experience, where the population began having already arrived. In the context of seventeenth-century British colonialism, as J. Martin Evans has observed, Adam and Eve tilling at the behest of their "sovran Planter" bear comparison to indentured servants in a strategically vital colonial outpost (*PL* 4, 691). They are agricultural laborers whose living conditions and status are distinctly contractual, temporary, and subject to improvement.[54] The cosmic geography that nestles Earth in chaos, suspended between Heaven and Hell, bears political as well as moral and epistemological significance.

Raphael's history of certain angels' sudden change therefore links but does not identify humans and angels. The war in heaven proves simply that disobedience among rational creatures is possible. But, as compared to the cataclysmic rupture and ruin that Raphael narrates, human changes are usually less decisive, less thorough, and less abrupt. Humanity tastes nothing purely, not even disobedience. Despite the tendency of Milton criticism – encouraged by Raphael's own hints – to emphasize the similarities between heaven and earth, the Seraph does not and cannot respond very well to specifically human concerns. Raphael is called affable and sociable, but when the conversation drifts from the topics of his set task, his missionary disposition quickly becomes patronizing and his answers either abstrusely noncommittal (on astronomy) or inept and censorious (on love). The dictates of the home office come first for a diplomatic envoy, and even if they did not, Raphael's angelic nature and experience would still render him incapable of comprehending the full significance of Adam's crucial questions or of answering them with much sensitivity, tact, or understanding. The intelligence of angels is of the highest order (*eminentem ratiocinationem*), but Milton, unlike others of his time, insists that many things they do *not* know (*CP* 6, 348). The experience of being human is evidently one of them.

Human beings are rarely so coherent as good or bad angels in their attitudes, and Milton maintains in prose and poetry that, for humanity at least, the confusion will not get sorted out until the apocalypse. True, Milton individualizes the angels. For Moloch, Belial, and Mammon, as for Satan, the distinctiveness of individual identities whets the edge of their respective torments. They share, however, the clarity, solidarity, and unifying predominance of their undying hatred of God.

Moloch may wish to attack, Mammon to build, Belial to lie low, but all derive their recommendations from a single, shared, undisputed principle: God is their hated enemy. In the same way, the good angels' prevailing obedience outweighs the nevertheless sharp distinctions of character between, say, Raphael and Michael – Milton's version of good cop, bad cop – or between energetic Uriel and more complacent angels (see *PL* 3, 700–01).

Milton himself insists on the differences between unpredictable, inconsistent humans and ideologically adamant angels, even in their style of disobedience:

> Devil with Devil damnd
> Firm concord holds: men onely disagree
> Of Creatures rational.   (*PL* 2, 496–98)

Despite the rueful tone of this observation, disagreement among humans follows inevitably from the limitations of human intellect as created by God. Of the first disobedience Milton remarks in *Christian Doctrine* that Adam and Eve "did not expect for a moment that they would lose anything good by eating the fruit, or that they would be worse off in any way at all" (*CP* 6, 390). Humans characteristically lack the great knowledge ("*scientiam ... magnam*") and intuitive clarity that Milton attributes even to fallen angels (*CW* 15, 110). Regardless of the occasion, the Son's pleas for humanity seem always to boil down to "forgive them Lord, for they know not what they do." And while angels may not know everything, the consequences of rebellion are proclaimed to Satan and his followers at the very moment that they are actively contemplating it. Humanity does not enjoy the same advantage. Adam and Eve might well have chosen differently if Raphael's "warning" had come a week later than it did – as Eve wondered whether or not she should eat the fruit, for example.

Admission of angelic difference or of reason's central place in Miltonic obedience is hardly sufficient cause to abandon the invented Milton. Scholars might agree with me on these particulars without weathering any serious change of opinion. Also, I suspect that few who teach the invented Milton to their students would agree that the theodicy is ironic. Nor is it a sufficient refutation to note the coincidence of generalizing interests and common interpretive bias between contemporary reader-response theory and seventeenth-century religious determinism. Stronger than its parts, the paradigmatic Milton has achieved the transcendence ·of persona, one derived from the widely accepted reading of Milton's deceptive narrative manner and method. The punitive persona attributed to Milton seems to me the most offensively inaccurate and pedagogically injurious consequence of the paradigm. If I were a student being taught the invented Milton, I would not feel inspired and awestruck; I would feel bored and repelled. It seems to me a grave indignity that this poet in particular has for much of a generation of students been reduced to a censorious parrot.

The arguments in *Surprised by Sin* from which the *personality* of the invented Milton originated are those concerning the first two books of the poem. Even readers who demur from the consensus on some points generally acknowledge that Milton in the guise of Fish's redundant didact presides over the epic's opening. In these early books, the narrator supposedly undercuts Satan's attractiveness, first through the similes and later through the pronouncements of divine characters. In order for this to happen, the narrator must first deliberately generate sympathy for Satan and his cause.[55] Satan does hold the position of protagonist in the opening books, and reverberations of past epic heroes animate much of what he says and does. Perhaps most post-romantic readers tend to sympathize with a character occupying Satan's narrative slot – that of the noble if flawed rebel leader. Yet sympathy is distinct from moral or emotional identification. As in the case of Eve's fall and Abdiel's heroism, I wish to suggest at least the possibility of an alternative response to Satan.

As opposed to the analogous but gentler beginning to Dante's *Divine Comedy*, the descent into Milton's hell is neither peripatetic nor gradual. One begins in the midst of hell as well as in the midst of things, and surely the baroque effect of initiating the action from the very pit of the inferno, at perhaps the most intensely dramatic moment of its history, tends to overwhelm readers, effectively stunning them into at least a partial suspension of both sympathy and judgment. As Johnson remarks in one of his more reliable aesthetic judgments regarding Milton, "it is his peculiar power to astonish."[56] Theories of hell and fallen and unfallen angels were matters of heated speculation in the seventeenth century, and Milton's representations draw on this speculation and seem to assume a certain morbid fascination with what hell is like. But his readers do not accompany the hero on an increasingly riveting journey to the underworld, where, typically, extraordinary knowledge is imparted. They begin the poem in hell and leave the inferno having gained knowledge of confusion only.

If beginning with giant angels weltering on the waves of a burning lake is not enough to amaze readers, Milton quickly homes in on the uncanny epistemology of the damned. The conditional addressee of Satan's first speech never receives a more definite salutation than "if thou beest hee" (1, 84). Interrogatives consistently metamorphose into exclamations of dismay: "how unlike!" "how fall'n! how chang'd" (1, 75, 84). One hope abandoned at the gates of hell is the hope of a reliable answer. For all the similes that appear in books 1 and 2, therefore, the message seems to be that hell and its inhabitants are "not like," "farr ... beyond / Compare," "farr other once," (1, 296, 587–88, 607). We need not construe the tendency of Milton's similes to undermine points of reference even as they establish them as a device designed to instill in alert readers a distrust of *their* natural perceptions or moral values – as if the reader and not hell initiated the confusion. These self-consuming comparisons may instead express the shiftiness of a locale in which the ambiguous and peculiar prevent recognition.[57]

Aside from enduring the anguish of perpetual confusion, Satan undeniably displays his aristocratic temper. But does his anger inspire sympathy and identification? If so, it seems logical that we would take the narrator's subsequent commentary –

> So spake th' Apostat Angel, though in pain,
> Vaunting aloud, but rackt with deep despare –

as recognizing and correcting that tendency (1, 125–26). With these lines, however, Milton offers what amounts to a translation of Virgil's *Aeneid*, when Aeneas speaks to his troops following their expulsion from their native home (1, 208–09).[58] Did Virgil, like Milton, intend his description to undermine Aeneas and to remind readers of his deceptiveness?

To gauge the reaction to this passage of "the reader in *Paradise Lost*," *Surprised by Sin* cites A. J. A. Waldock. Waldock hardly qualifies as a typical reader, yet he describes the Narrator's comment as a "gentle" qualification of Satan's speech. Searching for anger and humiliation at Milton's "rebuke," Fish explains that Waldock lied:

Waldock falsifies his experience of the poem, I think, when he characterizes Milton's countermands as gentle .... We resent this rebuke, not, as Waldock suggests, because our aesthetic sense balks at a clumsy attempt to neutralize an unintentional effect, but because a failing has been exposed in a context that forces us to acknowledge it. We are angry at the epic voice, not for fudging, but for being right, for insisting that we become our own critics.

There is little in the human situation more humiliating, in both senses of the word, than the public acceptance of a deserved rebuke.[59]

Waldock allegedly falsifies his response because of a secret shame that involves resentment, fear of public exposure, and guilt. Such feelings may be easily triggered, but no matter how I read the narrator's commentary I cannot imagine taking it as a humiliating "rebuke."

As unreliable as anecdotal evidence may be, I think it worth recording that in fifteen years of teaching Milton at various universities in various cultures – including Charlottesville, Virginia; the Bronx, New York; Austin, Texas; Beijing, China; Kyoto, Japan; Wellington, New Zealand, and Montpellier, France – I have polled over fifteen-hundred students, from Freshmen and Sophomores in large surveys to Ph.D. candidates in small seminars, concerning the narrator's comment. No student has ever volunteered resentment at being corrected as a reaction. Confirmation of an already developing impression of Satan as a big talker has emerged as the most common response. Maybe they were all lying.

The aim of Milton's poetry is always, at least in part, didactic. With his experience as a teacher and sense of prophetic mission, Milton was conditioned for and eager to perform a didactic role.[60] But the didactic Milton we have come to endorse seems more inclined to inflict punishment than to teach. "We are not warned," insists Fish, "but accused, taunted by an imperious voice," one which all but sneers in passing judgment: "you have made a mistake, just as I knew you would."[61] I object to the image of Milton as a redundant pedant who already knows the truth of things, humiliates and berates his charges for their errors, and with obnoxious superiority requires conformity to traditional beliefs. It is difficult to imagine an interpretive methodology *less* appropriate to an epic so morally daring and exuberant as *Paradise Lost* than reader-response theory joined in lockstep with a quasi-determinist, catachetical didacticism.

Without denying the romantics' sympathy for Satan's cause, we may propose a more feasible response to Satan's speech and the Narrator's comment. First, readers innocent of the critical wars on this issue may reserve judgment of Satan and his claims, as they might of a loud, occasionally coherent man sprawled on the sidewalk outside some exclusive club, hurling imprecations at the (unseen) management within. At this point, at least, most would cut Satan a wide berth even if, for whatever reason, they felt sympathy for his plight. To them, the narrator's commentary on Satan's expressions of defiance would come across neither as a rebuke nor as a clumsy authorial qualification but, perhaps, as an ironic, detached observation that adds to the primary impression of confusion, astonishment, and absurdity. Confronted with the verbal fist-shaking of a supine speaker, who can barely lift his head, one may notice the incongruity between his physical and rhetorical postures. The narrator's derisive use of "Apostat" etymologically underlines this darkly comical incongruity, and his analysis of the emotional dissonance between heroic vaunting and internal despair confirms the paralyzing inconsistency of the spectacle, as well as establishing and immediately qualifying the pity of it.

My contention, then, is that as readers begin *Paradise Lost* they repeatedly find themselves surrounded by senselessness. If we sympathize with Satan, we do so because like us, though for different reasons, he is dazed and confused. Against the contemporary understanding of Milton's authorial persona as prescriptive and authoritarian, I therefore propose an alternative possibility, that at least in its first books, *Paradise Lost* inspires in readers a Christian negative capability. Keats's famous letter to his brothers defines "Negative Capability" as occurring "when man is capable of being in uncertainties, Mysteries, doubts, without any irritable reaching after fact & reason."[62] From the early 1640s until the end of his life, as the next chapter will elaborate, Milton in his prose writings consistently asked his contemporaries to tolerate uncertainty, doubt, and division in seeking truth. Evil and error, or the potential for them, he believed to be inextricably involved with human life, fallen or unfallen, and encounter with them the only path to virtue.

The theme of indeterminacy as a vital dimension of human experience and behavior underlies all the objections to the invented Milton lodged in this chapter. The theodicy must be seen as sincere because things *could* have worked out otherwise for Adam and Eve. That crucial possibility of otherness makes it of the first importance to see that postlapsarian miseries count for something and have not been inflicted maliciously or unjustly. From this theodical sensibility follows the ethical primacy of human reason in choosing – and the sometimes tragic consequences of its relatively humble limits. Furthermore, unlike the angels (again, relatively speaking), individual human beings find themselves very much in the midst of things, with matters of fearful but ennobling moment hanging, ambiguously, in the balance.

In his many writings, Milton argued for his beliefs with great power and assurance. Such power and assurance may well blind us to the fact that for him, under the dispensation of Christian liberty, human morality seemed more a matter of conscientious and charitable improvisation than mechanical prescription. I begin the next chapter by elaborating the model of communication introduced early in this chapter, one able to accommodate the play of indeterminacy within limits. The third chapter returns to the prescriptive poet of the paradigm and his putative psychological origins under the regime of a punitive father. The fourth proposes that Milton worked out of a maternally centered psychology, characterized by the confusion and uncertainty of pre-Oedipal experience. The fifth chapter elaborates a poetics of generation derived from this focus on the maternal, a dynamic poetics oriented toward what is not yet known and that assumes toleration – that crucial Miltonic word – for what cannot be foreseen. It is a poetics of feminine power, power coveted by the male poet and embodied, as I argue in chapter 6, in his conception of God and the womb of chaos.

CHAPTER 2

The question of context

This power of generalizing gives men so much the superiority in
mistake over the dumb animals.

George Eliot[1]

Heads I win, tails I burn you alive.

William Empson[2]

This chapter pursues a correlation between the tendency to depict
Milton's art as if it were determinist in its premises and the agendas,
methodologies, and interpretive strategies that Milton scholars have
brought to bear on his work. Fundamental to my larger argument is
the claim that Milton was a poet of indeterminacy who found ways to
incorporate the uncertain and the evolving into his most highly realized
works of literary art: a poetics of *becoming*. This chapter thus begins by
appealing to a theory of communication that allows for indeterminacy,
one that presents all communication, including literary art, as a means
of actively and intentionally coping with what is not already known,
with what is developing, with change. The argument goes on to assess
various attempts to pin Milton to a tradition of Christian orthodoxy or
to account for him as an expression of structurally determined aspects
of material culture. Finally, I propose an example of historical contextualization that recognizes Milton's commitment to indeterminacy
and the forward reach of his thought.

My initial premise is that communication depends not on codes but
on assumptions about what is or can be apparent to those with whom
we wish to communicate: what we think they know, explicitly or
implicitly, including our sense of *their* assumptions about *our* state of
knowledge. Dan Sperber and Deirdre Wilson, whom I follow, note that
"human beings somehow manage to communicate in situations where
a great deal can be assumed about what is manifest to others, a lot can
be assumed about what is mutually manifest to themselves and others,

but nothing can be assumed to be truly mutually known or assumed."[3] This description conveys what is commonly meant by the phrase "a sense of audience," a sense that relies on probability and calculation, not on certain knowledge of a shared code. For communication to occur under the auspices of the code model, "mutual knowledge is a necessity": both sides must have access to the same codebook and *know* that they both do.[4] If from logic and experience we regard mutual *knowledge* as an impossibility (at least outside of mystical experience), and still look for meaning under the auspices of the code model, we must conclude that communication is impossible.

While people engaged in communication cannot be assumed to possess mutual knowledge, they can be said to share in each other's contexts, to one degree or another. At least by convention, these contexts are, to one degree or another, distinct from the individuals attempting to communicate within them. If in a crowded room, with the smell of smoke suddenly noticeable in the air, a fire alarm begins to sound, communication in that room will subsequently be conditioned by what the occupants might with little likelihood of error assume about each other's mental state – i.e., a significant sound and odor have taken prominent roles in efforts at communication. As panic mounts, Van's look toward the elevator met by Ada's shake of the head, would mean something quite particular – and different from what such an interaction might have meant *before* they both heard the alarm sound. Meaning in this case as in all communication is derived by assessing behavior in light of contexts – not knowledge of a code – that are assumed, with varying degrees of probability, to be mutually manifest, or potentially so. Indeed, much of communication seems devoted to just the task of making contextual facts or assumptions more emphatic or consciously prominent and thereby increasing mutuality to a point where it approaches a state of shared knowledge. Such a state is the vanishing point of communicative endeavors, however, not their condition.

What I mean by context, Sperber and Wilson call by the name "cognitive environment," which they define as "the set of all the facts [one] can perceive or infer: all the facts that are manifest."[5] The category of "manifest" cognitive resources is a crucial innovation in communication theory. It implies both the limits and flexibility of human consciousness. We enjoy access to stores of actualized knowledge in memory as well as to sensory data, assumptions, or sets of assumptions that we are *capable* of realizing but may never have explicitly entertained – e.g., "there is a fire bell in this room" or "John Milton saw Oliver Cromwell's warts." Without the ability to filter out most data or store it as implicit knowledge or cognitive potential, the relatively narrow limits of consciousness would be continually and massively overwhelmed. For Sperber and Wilson, what is *manifest* includes not only memory and subliminal knowledge but also anything discernible or inferable by a given individual. The fact that much of what we "know" is often largely categorical shorthand or only potential knowledge helps explain the occasional inconsistencies or outright contradictions in our intellectual productions. It may not appear inconsistent to say both (1) Milton's theodicy is ironic and (2) Milton believed in free will, until we have worked out in some detail the contextual implications of these statements. Having done so, we have to decide if the inconsistency is Milton's or ours.

The notion of manifest assumptions allows for the fact that for most humans explicit awareness at any given moment is fairly narrow, but reinforced by conceptual abbreviations that can be fleshed out as the occasion arises. Consequently, although I cite "intended effects" as the primary basis for communication, I would not appeal to original authorial intention as if it were an intellectual schematic by which, theoretically, we can exhaustively determine a work's meaning.[6] This is an insupportable view of interpretation inasmuch as it assumes the possibility of achieving mutual knowledge with the author. Often, it takes time for meaning to sink in or achieve its full extent, and, also often, those attempting to communicate mean more than they immediately or specifically know that they do. Many of us spend considerable time after the fashion of Henry James's Strether "thinking what [he] meant."[7] Even the most godlike author lacks actual omniscience within his or her own mental cosmos.

For readers, too, the process of gathering meaning is typically a function of reflection and therefore duration. Too often critics deploy the notion of context as if it simply meant background, with the implicit comparison to a painting suggesting a kind of stasis and timelessness in the subject. But we communicate in time, usually in response to or as an expression of change. Moreover, sometimes we become aware of forces shaping the cognitive environment of certain sentences, our own included, only after the fact – if indeed ever at all. Communication, even with ourselves, is a matter of degree, as students of the soliloquies in *Paradise Lost* will agree. Paradoxical as it may seem, there are unconscious, preconscious, or simply unforeseen meanings that are nevertheless, at the categorical level, intended or at least *manifest*, in Sperber and Wilson's sense of that term.[8] An audience can register meaning in contexts that an author never imagined and still remain true to the author's original intention. Indeed, I contend that Milton's authorial intention was dynamic and open-ended in precisely this way.

We therefore cannot maintain, practically or theoretically, a hard distinction between meaning, a category bounded by authorial intention, and significance, a category bounded by the reader's response. Meaning for humans is social, a function of relation more than of foreconceit. As Sperber and Wilson put it, "the aim of communication in general is to increase the mutuality of cognitive environments."[9]

Yet blurring the distinction between meaning and significance does not render validity in interpretation an impossible goal, except as an absolute. The meaning of a given statement is potentially infinite; that much is inevitable. But infinities also have their limits. We can rule out the infinity of numbers between 1 and 2 when assessing candidates for the infinity between 3 and 4. Moreover, though like David Aers I agree that *"word is a two-sided act,"* I cannot accept that it is "determined equally by *whose* word it is and *for whom* it is meant."[10] Certainly, every instance of communication expresses a relationship between source and receiver, but it is not one that is, especially in literary matters, equal or symmetrical. The impossibility of mutual knowledge entails this lack of symmetry. Like ballroom dancing, communication can only be coordinated asymmetrically: one leads; the other follows.[11] This holds true even when we allow that prior experience and the musical measure sharply restrict the place of individual innovation on either's part. If when the band plays a waltz, Van leads a waltz, and Ada responds with a cha cha cha, then she has erred and communication has failed. A reader's role is thus *relatively* passive and restricted. (Please bear with this analogy a while longer before surrendering to outrage over its apparent reductiveness and implicit sexism.)

We need to steer a course between a rigid, deterministic view of meaning and one of complete randomness. Certainly, to an audience of humans, limitless information is as meaningless as no information. Nonetheless, one of the great insights of modern communication theory holds that the amount of information any source can convey actually *increases* with the degree of unpredictability about the message that source will generate.[12] As one writer on chaos theory has observed, "the more chaotic a system is, the more information it produces."[13]

For the sake of illustration, let us return for a moment to our questionable analogy and have Ada usurp the authorial role. Perhaps Van, a poor dancer, has mastered only a perfunctory and mechanical waltz and bribed the band always to play waltzes. Graceful Ada, a versatile dancer and aware of Van's plot, dances her cha cha cha out of exasperation and to convey a message to him, though in an unusual and unexpected way. She thereby introduces a little chaos into stolid Van's arrangements and opens up a world of possible, subsequent communication between them. As with music or dance, it is precisely the latitude and layers of ambiguity available within human languages – systems highly charged with chaotic potency – that permit the sophistication, subtlety, and communicative wealth that great poetry can sustain. The richest poetry is that which is most flexible, articulate, and far-reaching in its implications.[14] It has staying power, winding subtly into even the less frequently visited places of thought and maintaining its resonant power through time. A poet who always said the same thing – "you are a presumptuous sinner; repent!" for example – would quickly lose all but the dullest of his readers. The onus of cognitive relevance is on the author, and when his works no longer carry it, people stop reading. They hunger for "contextual effects" – relevance – that they are no longer receiving.[15] There is really no point in dancing a cha cha cha to the musty score of a dead man's tiresome waltz.

TRADITION AND THE INDIVIDUAL POET

The invented Milton may be described as Milton deprived of the capacity to set off the contextual effects that would make him relevant to those readers who find authoritarian narrators and repeated didactic humiliation a bore. Rather than challenge and divert his audience, Milton supposedly dictates the same lesson, repeatedly provoking and then squelching readers' evil responses. Does this punitive and tedious didacticism actually have a place in Milton's own historical context? The common practice of modern Milton criticism makes this a fair question. For scholars have consistently based their understanding of the poet on historical considerations. C. S. Lewis is representative. According to him, Milton wrote for "the ordinary educated and Christian audience in [his] time," a brief, practical assessment of audience, with its tacit rationale in authorial intention later rendered explicit by Stanley Fish: "the reader whose education, opinions, concerns, linguistic competencies, and so on make him capable of having the experience the author wished to provide."[16]

Both Lewis and Fish, like many others before and after, posit mutuality between Milton and his audience on certain, poetically influential, doctrinal assumptions.[17] The tendency to assess poetic meaning according to common religious doctrine has long been an orthodox approach among Milton scholars and other interpreters of seventeenth-century poetry. As practiced by Lewis and some others, it is an approach that promises historical fidelity yet at the same time represents Milton as the exponent of a transhistorical Christian tradition. How is this paradoxical endeavor managed?

The classic example is C. A. Patrides, *Milton and the Christian Tradition*, which uses an encyclopedic acquaintance with Christian writing to represent Milton first as an instance of "the 'characteristicall truthes' of historical and traditional Christianity" and then as an exponent of "the specifically Protestant manifestation of the cumulative Christian tradition as reflected in the current of thought contemporary with Milton."[18] The equation of Augustine, Archbishop Laud, and John Milton on the matter of prayer exemplifies the method: they all agree that God hears prayers; the Christian tradition speaks through all of them.[19] In another instance, Patrides observes that Daniel Dyke, Richard Baxter, and John Milton agree that the Christian God is the "the God of Order."[20] Focusing on such points of agreement, Patrides contends for the unity of figures whose disagreements were often sharp, practical, and significant.

Where disagreement cannot be denied, one alternative is to place on the periphery those who dissent from what is defined as the central Christian tradition. Though they hardly seem like marginal figures, St. Paul, St. Augustine, Luther, and Calvin, all, if not all with equal rigor, denied free will. According to Patrides, the Protestant Christian tradition and Milton its epic proponent endorse it; presumably, then, the reformers and the saints stand "on its periphery."[21]

Another method for dismissing Milton's singularity is to bury it in a generalization. The strict Presbyterian Francis Cheynell and John Milton, "just as emphatically," says Patrides, prescribe limits to toleration.[22] One cannot argue very effectively about degrees of emphasis, so this claim may seem plausible. Furthermore, Patrides's contention appears theoretically sound, as Stanley Fish's argument on the subject reveals: "all affirmations of freedom of expression are like Milton's, dependent for their force on an exception"; "fidelity to the original values will demand acts of extirpation."[23] Theoretically plausible or not, such arguments are unsatisfactory insofar as they scarcely allow us to distinguish between John Milton and the Grand Inquisitor.

If we compare the histories of Milton and Francis Cheynell, we find that details left unmentioned by Patrides are instructive. Milton repeatedly argued for toleration of all Christian beliefs except those of Roman Catholics. He denied toleration to Roman Catholics because he considered the Roman Church to be a foreign political power more than a religion. Milton never wrote to badger so-called heretics. On the other hand, Cheynell's chastising exhortations of the rationalist theologian William Chillingsworth in his final sickness were thought to have hastened that prisoner-patient's death. His subsequent triumphing over the dead man provoked John Locke to refer to *Chillingsworth Novissima: or the Sicknesse, Heresy, Death, and Buriall of William Chillingsworth* (London, 1644) as "one of the most villainous Books that was ever printed." In it, Cheynell describes how he threw Chillingsworth's tolerationist *Religion of Protestants* into the latter's grave so that it might "rot with its author."[24] Although Patrides never cites the tolerationist Chillingsworth as background for Milton, Cheynell, whose entry in *The Dictionary of National Biography* begins with the word "fanatic," appears four times as an exponent of the Christian tradition.[25]

Few today would follow Patrides in identifying Milton with Laud or the despicable Cheynell as representatives of the same Christian tradition. Yet Cheynell serves well as a caricature, if only to place emphasis on the generally accepted version of Milton. In *Surprised by Sin*, for example, when the subject is the reader's depraved tendency to fall under the spell of Satan's rhetoric, Fish cites Richard Baxter as the corroborating authority for the narrator's supposed rebuke:

In this case, the failure (if we can call it that) involves the momentary relaxation of a vigilance that must indeed be eternal. Richard Baxter (*The Saints Everlasting Rest*, c. 1650) warns: "Not only the open profane, the swearer, the drunkard, and the enemies of godliness, will prove hurtful companions to us, though these indeed are chiefly to be avoided: but too frequent society with persons merely civil and moral, whose conversation is empty and unedifying, may much divert our thoughts from heaven."[26]

The interpretive point of linking Milton to Baxter would be clearer if Fish had also included the sentiments that immediately precede this warning. There Baxter insists that rather than immediately "conclude [the ungodly] to be Dogs and Swine," and so shun them, one must first accept "the duty of Reproof," which "great duty," along with "exhorting those about you ... is the first step in Discipline."[27] One must reprove the ungodly before shunning them.

Baxter's recommendation of avoidance of the ungodly recalls an attitude that Milton sets up for ridicule in *Areopagitica*: "we must not expose our selves to temptations without necessity, and next to that not imploy our time in vain things" (*CP* 2, 521). Milton's reply? "We must regulat all recreations and pastimes, all that is delightfull to man. No musick must be heard, no song be set or sung, but what is grave and *Dorick*" – and so on for several pages of mockery (523–26). In his early anti-prelatical pamphlets – when he is most sympathetic to the Presbyterians – Milton does mention admonishment as one of the few duties properly performed by priests (*CP* 1, 575). Even at his most presbyterical moments, however, he never speaks of those who might resist warnings as "Dogs and Swine" and describes admonishment as a task always to be "perform'd with what patience and attendance is possible" (*CP* 1, 846–47). In his mature theology as represented by *Christian Doctrine*, Milton defines the duty of admonition in a single sentence and then cites relevant scripture. This brief definition and accompanying proof-texts conclude a chapter describing the "second class of special duties toward one's neighbor." The sentence on admonition follows a long, detailed consideration of veracity, and substantial discussions of candor, simplicity, trustworthiness, gravity, taciturnity, courteousness, urbanity, and frankness (*CP* 6, 551, 565–72).

Baxter can be considered a member of Milton's social class and lived his life under roughly similar material and historical conditions. Yet the differences between them are eye-opening. A low-church Anglican who advocated Archbishop Ussher's compromise with Presbyterianism, Baxter, albeit no Cheynell, perhaps ideally represents the "educated and ordinary" seventeenth-century Christian.[28] He argued that Christian citizens would owe obedience to a Nero, thought James I understated divine right, and, though remembered as a kind man, insisted to an audience of anabaptist mothers that hell is paved with the skulls of unbaptized infants. During the 1640s and 1650s, he had the integrity to support bishops and liturgy, disapproved of Cromwell's toleration of sects, and risked his life to speak out against the regicides.[29] He helped bring about the Restoration and was afterward offered a bishop's miter, though for reasons both principled and politic he refused it.

Milton, we recall, deplored professional clergy, defended the regicides, gloried in sectarian controversy, risked his life to propose alternatives to the Restoration, and afterward was persecuted, imprisoned, slandered, and in danger of execution. He did not believe in infant baptism, but even if he had – and Milton enjoys no special reputation for kindness – it still would be difficult to imagine him in a theological dispute reproaching mothers with visions of their children's skulls as infernal cobblestones. Baxter despised Milton's honored friend, the ardent Republican Sir Henry Vane, and begrudged Vane's bravery in facing execution with comments recalling the sentiments of those who in *Macbeth* report the execution of the rebellious Thane of Cawdor: "the manner of his death procured him more applause than all the actions of his life."[30]

Given the direct contradiction between many of Baxter's and Milton's opinions, one would expect that Milton scholars would eventually have questioned his relevance to our understanding of *Paradise Lost*. Instead, others have followed Fish, and before him Patrides, in citing Baxter as an analogue for Milton.[31] One reason for the perpetuation of this mistake is that Baxter, like Milton, struggled against a rigidly Calvinist view of human will. But Baxter's discomfort with determinism wavers and does not stem from a sense of human freedom and dignity.[32] He allowed humanity some leeway only because he felt horrified at the anarchic antinomianism implicit in a strict construction of predestination theory. The historian William Lamont depicts a Baxter almost Hobbesian in his deep pessimism over human nature and advocacy of divine right.[33] Baxter inclined to Presbyterianism primarily because of the articulate control it would allow (paid) clergy over the behavior and faith of individual parishioners. His priority, as with so many of his ministerial peers, was to maintain control over believers. His disapproval of parliamentary soldiers reading religious pamphlets is characteristic; in their quarters, he complained, "they had none to contradict them."[34]

Milton and Baxter thus disagreed about most things that mattered to them, yet Baxter is regularly accounted a member of the intended readership whose basic attitudes Milton supposedly shared. Perhaps one could argue that the virginal Milton of the late 1630s and early 1640s would have supported Baxter's admonition to avoid "the enemies of godliness" and even the society of those "merely civil and moral." True enough, in the anti-Episcopal tracts, written prior to his denunciation of the Presbyterians as the "New Forcers of Conscience," Milton attests to the purity of his youth and his abhorrence of pollution.

But by the time he writes *Areopagitica* and the divorce tracts, whatever sympathy he may have had with the Presbyterians' desire to regulate behavior and doctrine is gone. Nor does he ever revert to his former views.

Many on the fringes of Milton's ordinary audience, including those lower in the social order or in the more marginal and rigorously voluntarist sects, echo Baxter's ethical recommendations more than Milton does. Fish's reading works better for them than for Milton. For example, *Surprised by Sin* cites *Pilgrim's Progress* as a didactic analogue for the "vigilance" recommended in *Paradise Lost* – specifically, the moment when Christian flees from his family, hands over his ears, "crying Life, Life, Eternal Life."[35] But such a lesson, while characteristic of Bunyan, reverses the warfaring attitude that Milton characteristically connects with true virtue. Yet this contradiction between Milton and his ordinary audience has too often gone unremarked or unnoticed in Milton criticism.

It goes unnoticed partly because for the invented Milton there apparently is no contradiction. Milton is supposed to have adopted the narrative persona of a dictatorial teacher who leads his charges into error and then humiliates them with a traditional, authoritative reading of the action – they should cover their ears and flee from temptation. For a political Independent and proponent of toleration like Milton, however, tradition at its best was only a partial record of an ongoing search, an untrustworthy record that perpetuated many errors. Truth was a goal to be worked toward, rather than an accomplished set of beliefs. How should we reconcile the vision of Milton as a preaching narrator with the voice that, in *The Doctrine and Discipline of Divorce*, allegorized custom or tradition as the puffed-up countenance of monstrous error (*CP* 2, 223)? Milton's conviction that submission to external interpretive authority undermines true virtue was fundamental to his disenchantment with the "ordinary" Christians of his time, particularly the Presbyterians, who in his opinion enslaved themselves to tradition and authoritative interpretation of revelation. Sources often cited as background for Milton's pedagogical method and message, however, recommend automatic, habitual, unreasoning response to trial and temptation. Are we really to believe that Milton thought Adam should have run from Eve with his hands over his ears?

The argument of last resort for those who cannot make Milton fit an orthodox construction is to deny the pertinence and, most recently, even the authorship of his most heretical writing. C. S. Lewis, for one, argued that Milton's heretical beliefs seemed "private theological whimsies" that he "laid aside" in composing poetic testimonies to Christianity's "great central tradition."[36] Patrides elaborated this view, claiming that Milton, though a great poet, was an inept theologian who, dissatisfied with *de doctrina*, left it unfinished.[37] More recently, Regina Schwartz, in asserting the hostility of Milton's chaos, has denied the poetic relevance of Milton's theological insistence on matter's goodness.[38] Because Milton described *de doctrina* as his "dearest and best possession" and carefully arranged for its publication after his death, such claims seem at least questionable (*CP* 6, 121). Against this background, however, the latest attempt to nullify the heretical Milton does not seem so shocking. Despite massive circumstantial evidence to the contrary, William Hunter has denied that Milton is the author of *de doctrina*. According to Hunter, the treatise has been attributed to him through a forgery.[39]

There is of course much to recommend the search for doctrinal agreement with Milton's predecessors and contemporaries as an aid to understanding. If authors were truly singular, they would be unintelligible. Scholars such as Barbara Lewalski and Georgia Christopher, for example, have legitimately and usefully articulated in terms of a broadly defined seventeenth-century Protestantism something of the cognitive environment evoked by Lewis's "ordinary Christian."[40] Problems arise, however, when what need only be evoked as mutual awareness – actual or potential – is instead hardened into positive belief with definitive poetic consequences, or worse, a proactive didactic agenda. Too often, the scholarly effort to give Lewis's "ordinary" audience a local habitation and a place has implied Milton's identification with a fixed set of sometimes inappropriate beliefs, a construct, in other words, that cheats this theologian-poet of his distinctiveness.

Even when we limit ourselves to Milton's own century to describe his audience, Lewis's word "ordinary," though qualified by "educated and Christian," is problematic. The conventional politico-religious categories that apply to mid-seventeenth-century England (say, 1635–65) are slippery and invite caution and qualification. There were Arminians of the absolutist right (Bishop Laud and Chillingsworth, for example), and Arminians of the republican left (like the original Dutch Arminians and Milton); Independents who championed toleration in the interest of nonconformity, and Stuarts who desired it because of papist sympathies; Presbyterians who stood by the King and Presbyterians who backed Parliament against him.[41] These notorious complications of policy and faith scarcely begin to reflect the complex reality of a mid-century inhabited by Muggletonians, Monarchists, anabaptists, Anarchists, Quakers, Rosicrucians, Ranters, Republicans, Familists, Royalists, Levelers, Sabbatarians, Socinians, Rota-men, Diggers, and Seekers – to list but a few of the common labels.

For purposes of argument, the seventeenth-century English incarnation of Lewis's "ordinary" audience could be defined – by virtue of being a majority of the educated male minority – as mainly Low Church Anglican and Presbyterian, more or less convinced of the bondage of the will, and imbued with attitudes and values appropriate to what has with some distortion been called the emergent bourgeoisie. And in fact this description suffices as a composite sketch of the audience that Milton critics of various approaches have settled on over the years.

The translation of Milton as a voice of "ordinary" seventeenth-century Protestantism into Milton as a voice of the emergent bourgeoisie accounts for much of the recent success of the invented Milton. In the next chapter we will consider the settlement between neo-Christian and more sociologically oriented critics from a structuralist and psychological point of view. From the historical perspective, such a settlement assumes the Weberian mediation of Protestant beliefs into economic terms. Yet we cannot justify viewing Milton's ordinary audience as if it initiated in England the capitalist ethos whose master ideology was Calvinist Protestantism. As Christopher Hill notes, the social conditions described by Weber may have prevailed in the late seventeenth (post-1688) and eighteenth centuries, but not before, and, contrary to Weber's thesis, likely owed more to economic conditions shaping available ideology than to the reverse.[42] Our view of the Puritans is literally preposterous when articulated through the "Protestant ethic," especially given the secularization and codification suggested by that phrase. These conservative Puritans were neither a revolutionary vanguard nor radical innovators. In the context of the 1630s, they can as easily be viewed as die-hard exponents of sixteenth-century reformist agendas and longstanding, if increasingly unpopular, humanist social values.[43] Through the early 1680s they looked like anything but the new wave, which with the Sun King rising seemed absolutist and Catholic on a scale never dreamt of by a feudal monarch.

Mid-century Puritans were far from money-changers in the temple.

Many fought fiercely, suffered, and died for values and beliefs predominantly and intensely spiritual in orientation, and were especially opposed to the grasping ways of episcopacy. The emphasis on Calvinism as an ideological basis for nascent capitalism is even geographically suspect, as those familiar with the politico-religious map of mid-seventeenth-century England can attest. Calvinist determinism was strongest, not in the economically and politically innovative south, but in northern, poor, and politically feudal territories like Scotland.[44] Although usually construed otherwise, Presbyterianism, with its decentralized organization, would in the seventeenth century have looked more old-fashioned than the Episcopalianism of Laud and the Stuarts.

Whether an individual can transcend the limits imposed by the material and cultural situation is as vexed a question in recent critical controversies as freedom of the will was in the seventeenth century. Typically, Marxian interpreters, like Calvinists, make fewer allowances for individual deviation.[45] Milton fit the economic and educational profile of his ordinary audience, yet he went beyond its boundaries, or at least re-defined them, in his political, religious, and aesthetic views. In his vernacular pamphlets and Latin treatises, Milton often begins with shared beliefs, only to use them as a basis to subvert others, sometimes ones that most of his audience would call *fundamental*. Indeed, Milton was something of a contrarian, typically opposing what many in his ordinary audience believed, did, or legislated – in government, religion, education, and civil law. This is not to deny that his cultural attitudes and convictions were cultivated and bourgeois.[46] The invented Milton, however, has consistently had his attitudes explained in narrow and inappropriate terms, almost as if he were a Presbyterian divine. And despite the deterministic baggage, these are precisely the terms settled upon by those scholars concerned to preserve Milton as a champion of traditional values, as well as by those scholars interested in Milton as the exponent of a bourgeois revolution.[47]

JUMPING INTO THE WIND

The extent of Milton scholarship's deterministic bias has gone unremarked in part because it often affects critics whose political and ideological differences are otherwise so glaring. That is, thanks to Weberian theories of mediation, the orthodoxy of neo-Christian critics translates fairly easily into the orthodoxy of critics whose premises are more materialist. The more coherent and comprehensive the scholar's ideological vision, furthermore, whether idealist or materialist, the more resistant to contrary historical information the bias tends to be. Those who read Milton as a preacher of a fundamental Protestant religion, and those who read him through the supposed social and economic implications of that religion, share an interest in identifying him with the relatively stable, predictable, and yet deeply problematic "ordinary" audience that I have been describing.

It is an audience that, insofar as it has a historical basis, simply does not do justice to the complications and uncertainties that Milton wrestled with in his mature works. From the mid-1640s on, he consistently maintained that indeterminacy and differences of opinion are inevitable among imperfect creatures in an unfinished world. This tenet arose in part from a distinctively apocalyptic epistemology. Truth lies scattered in pieces and "we have not yet found them all ... nor ever shall doe, till her Masters second comming" (*CP* 2, 549). Consistent with this vision, Milton's practice in poetry and prose is often so open-ended as not to be contemporary at all. As he composed, he had in view future generations. Especially in *Paradise Lost*, he clearly intended to leave his contextual boundaries as non-exclusive, we might say as future-tolerant, as possible. I say *tolerant* with Milton's Independent convictions in mind, particularly those involving the recovery of as yet unrecognized parts of truth. The ideal of a progressive search for truth – "still searching what we know not, by what we know" (2, 551) – may be understood as a principle of dynamic coherence, one that allowed Milton room to make theodical art out of his uncertainties. A tolerance so epistemologically principled places him with contemporaries like Newton and Locke, more than it does with a saint like Cheynell.

The example of Newton in particular serves my argument in two ways. First, though Milton scholars tend to ignore him, his history brings out salient aspects of Milton's life and art better than many of the Protestant divines that we regularly adduce to set a context. Second, comparison with Newton can help us discern Milton's intellectual distinctiveness, at least regarding his heretical theology, and how some critics have worked to efface this distinctiveness.

At first glance one is tempted to leave Milton and Newton in separate cognitive boxes. England's archetypal poet, Milton cultivated perhaps the most discriminating aesthetic taste of his age. Newton, England's archetypal scientist, seems to have lacked any aesthetic sensibility, or to have suppressed any he did possess out of his stereotypically Puritan convictions. Poetry was for him a kind of "ingenious nonsense," at least insofar as it did not encrypt alchemical secrets, and the sculpture-collecting Earl of Pembroke he described, perhaps with the first commandment sternly in mind, as a "lover of stone dolls."[48] Ironically, Newton at first seems too much like the "ordinary" Christians of Milton's time – not, as one might expect, too much the Enlightenment scientist – to recommend further study by Miltonists.

Besides the gaping difference in aesthetic sensibility, no one has ever uncovered evidence of influence, mutual knowledge, or direct acquaintance to justify a comparison. Young man Milton had just entered public life when Newton was born in 1642, nor does it seem likely that the tortured young genius of Trinity College in Restoration Cambridge would later have come to the notice of the notorious, blind, old Cromwellian, crippled with gout. Yet, despite the many differences between them, we will better understand both, as well as the recapitulative ontogeny of modernity, if we come to appreciate their commonalties.

Newton's first recorded scientific experiment occurred in 1658, on the day of Cromwell's death, when great windstorms hit England. In a moment anecdotally definitive of the modern era, the scientific 16-year-old leapt into this ominous wind, otherwise variously interpreted as a sign portentous, only to measure its force by comparison to the distance he could cover in calm weather. At the biographical level, jumping into the wind also signifies the unyielding quality of Newton's most productive years of study and his highly Puritan early life in the midst of a Restoration England inimical to Puritan mores. This strength of will in adverse cultural weather, so to speak, is obvious also in Milton, who published *Paradise Lost, Paradise Regained,* and *Samson Agonistes* between 1666 and 1674, after the good old cause for which he had labored so long had gone smash. As the widely despised old man was composing and publishing these masterpieces out of the ashes of defeat – they represent his first major poetic achievements since *Lycidas* in 1637 – Newton was achieving breakthroughs in mathematics, optics, and celestial dynamics that changed the way humanity conceived of the world. Indeed, Newton's *anni mirabiles* of 1664–66 coincide with the completion and publication of Milton's great epic, which has traditionally been thought to commemorate the cosmology that Newton's discoveries displaced.

Apart from sometimes striking similarities in character and a web of shared acquaintances, the most important shared influence in the lives of Milton and Newton was probably that of Joseph Mead, a renowned tutor in Christ College Cambridge during Milton's seven years there. Mead was the only seventeenth-century writer to whose works Newton ever admitted large indebtedness. When Newton worked on apocalyptic scriptures, a far more consuming interest than any of his scientific endeavors, it was "the judiciously learned and conscientious Mr. Mede" whom he "for the most part followed." All others who had attempted the problem "botched."[49] Indeed, after the 1640s Mead's influence was pervasive for apocalyptic interpreters throughout England and the American colonies.[50]

Joseph Mead was able to bring regular, temporal order out of the bewildering chronological inconsistencies of apocalyptic scriptures, a temporal order that made them practically and currently relevant and even reliably predictive. The attribution of immediate historical relevance to scripture distinguished Mead's writings from customary allegorical interpretation of biblical prophecy, dating back to Augustine. Augustine's method dehistoricized scripture and rhetoricized it by attending to the narrative primarily as the vehicle for more salient figurative, moral, and tropological meanings. For most orthodox Christians up to Milton's time, it was always, though not literally, apocalypse now.[51]

Rather than rest content with this dispersal and dilution of apocalyptic consciousness through scriptural history, Mead, combining linguistic, historical, and textual evidence in unprecedented fashion, penetrated the apparent chronological inconsistencies that had rendered previous attempts to unlock the secrets of biblical prophecy futile. He derived synchronistic patterns out of scripture, rather than surrender to mere chronological sequence, and so brought order out of confusion. Although Mead has been called the Newton of the apocalypse, Newton might with more justice be called the Mead of celestial motions. What Newton did for the book of nature, Mead had already done for the book of scripture. The apocalyptic consciousness he helped to foster, moreover, had great significance for seventeenth-century religious politics. Though Mead himself was a diffident, studiously non-political, scholar, his ideas were deeply threatening to the status quo. One of the first acts of the Westminster Assembly in 1641, charged with reforming the Laudian Church of England, was to have Mead's work translated into English.[52] Later in that decade, the activist attitude toward the present that millenarian beliefs fostered tended to distinguish those few who favored regicide from the many who favored coming to terms with the king and resuming something like the status quo.

I will return to Newton's and Milton's apocalyptic beliefs as influenced by Mead, but before doing so it will help first to consider their Arianism. Accurate understanding of Newton's opinions about the apocalypse, or indeed his theology and cosmology generally, requires some appreciation of the crucial place of Arianism in his thought. And while Milton's Arianism does not quite pervade his thinking as Newton's does his, it is one of the pillars of his theology, vital to his logic and epic poetry. Furthermore, the critical controversy over Milton's views on this subject is deeply revealing. The following discussion of the Arian heresy thus develops in part through consideration of what Milton scholars have had to say on the subject.

Patrides's association of Milton with Cheynell as advocates of limited toleration, which seemed so egregious earlier, comes as small surprise considering his insistence that Milton was orthodox on the trinity. Cheynell enjoyed a reputation for ferocious hostility not only to rational religion and toleration, but also to antitrinitarianism. These were all evils associated with the Socinian heretics.[53] Chillingsworth, for example, was labeled Socinian because he advocated toleration and rational religion. A few years after Cheynell had hounded Chillingsworth to his grave, Parliament commissioned the "hammer of Socinianism," as Cheynell was called, to renew his attacks on the menace. This led to his publication of *The Divine Triunity* in 1650. By contrast, the very next year Milton stood before the ruling Council and Parliament for permitting publication of the condemned Racovian (Socinian) catechism. During the examination, he reportedly reminded those scandalized by his decision of the opinions expressed in *Areopagitica*.[54]

Although for many Milton scholars a subject like Milton's Arianism is a "dated controversy," it was a subject of considerable urgency in Milton's century and one of lasting intellectual consequence.[55] Many different opinions of what was essential in Christian belief existed during the seventeenth century, but most included the trinity. Those in power in church and state, whether in London, Rome, or Geneva, were even in an intolerant age remarkably unyielding on the subject. In England, at least eight antitrinitarian heretics were burned at the stake between 1548 and 1612. The last was Bartholomew Legate. In a characteristic moment of personal involvement, the scholarly King

James tried himself to convince the heretic of his error, but after listening to Legate, broke into "choler, spurn[ing] at him with his foot" and commanding him out of his presence.[56] That Legate was the last Arian burnt to death in England does not seem to have owed to a softening of official attitudes. As Thomas Fuller remarks, after Legate went up in flames, the king "politicly preferred that Heretics hereafter ... should silently and privately waste themselves away in Prison rather than to grace them and amuze others with the solemnity of a public Execution."[57] Perhaps the impulse toward demystification expressed in Arianism was dimly perceived as a threat to the ideological basis of monarchical power. If awe for the mystery of Christ's essential but unapparent divinity was lacking, what would become of the awe for kings as Christ's representatives, or indeed of any of the similarly unapparent ontological distinctions supposed to separate noble from common in a hierarchical society? Whatever it was that drove an outraged James to kick at Legate, Arianism was by no means treated as a curious relic of fourth-century Christianity. It provoked authorities in seventeenth-century Europe as no other heresy could.

The theological facts concerning Milton's Arianism are straightforward enough for summary in a few sentences. The foundation of the Arian position is the insistence that the essence of true Godhood is unique and *unbegotten* (*agenetos*). This unique essence belongs only to the paternal God, not to the Son or to the Holy Spirit. As Milton repeatedly insists, "really a God cannot be begotten at all," which "at all" applies both to figurative and literal meanings of begotten (*CP* 6, 211). For Milton, therefore, even the standard Nicene formulation "begotten not made" admits the Son's real inferiority to the Father. Arians deny the Son the essential divine attribute of unbegotteness – or eternal existence – and also deny him related attributes such as omnipotence, omniscience, and ubiquity. Inferior to the Father, the Son is not "very" or "true" God, but instead, as Milton puts it, "a God who is not self-existent, who did not beget but was begotten, is not a first cause but an effect, and is therefore not a supreme God" (*CP* 6, 263–64).[58]

No one who has written on the matter disputes that the longest (by far) chapter in *de doctrina* urges the utter uniqueness of this "supreme God," nor that it denies to the essentially inferior Son the attribute of eternal existence, as well as every other attribute definitive of true deity. It would seem then that by the definition set down at the Council of Nicea (325) and according to conventional usage, the label "Arian" is the one we should apply to Milton. The term "Arian," part of England's theological vocabulary since the sixteenth century, is the term Milton himself uses to describe antitrinitarian heresy, as early as 1641 and as late as 1673 (*CP* 1, 533, 555, 557; 8, 424). One could say it is the sole term he uses, except that in *Of True Religion* he couples it with "Socinian" in discussing those who "dispute against the Trinity." Moreover, when in this final pamphlet he describes the Arian and Socinian "dispute" against orthodox opinion, his description correlates rather exactly with his own argument in chapter 5 of the first book of *de doctrina* (*CP* 8,424–25). The only alternative to "Arian" or "Socinian" extant in Milton's time was the more inclusive "antitrinitarian," in use at least as early as 1641. Ever an elegant and precise writer, Milton himself chose fewer syllables and more exact meaning.

Despite the evidence of *de doctrina* and of Milton's customary usage scholars have for more than two decades resisted calling him an Arian – or, as would be appropriate in terms of loose seventeenth-century usage, Socinian. Instead, like Patrides, they have followed William B. Hunter in applying the term "subordinationist" to Milton's belief. The relevant entries from *A Milton Encyclopedia* are revealing:

On the basis of ... highly competent theological analyses, what had earlier been regarded by some as the Arian heresy is now generally recognized as a seventeenth-century expression of the "subordinationism" of early Fathers of the Church up to the Council of Nicea, a position that was held by many orthodox writers.

Milton's view ... has by some been identified with the Arian heresy, but this contention has been successfully questioned and corrected by meticulous and competent historical analysis.[59]

Part of the point seems to be that these theological matters are so complex that they require extraordinary expertise and analytical powers, and that ordinary readers should submit to the authoritative judgment of those few who are competent. The other implication is that those who claim Milton to have been Arian, including Maurice Kelley, David Masson, Denis Saurat, and C. S. Lewis, are comparatively incompetent.

The excerpts above do not exaggerate the general acceptance of "subordinationism" as the chosen word for Milton's heresy concerning the Son's divine status. Almost everyone who has occasion uses it, though (or perhaps because) no one seems to know what it means. The *OED* records no usage of "subordinationism" before 1843. Its chief value to Milton criticism seems to lie in the shape of its vagueness. Unlike the term "antitrinitarianism," "subordinationism" does not explicitly deny the trinity. Instead, suggesting a grammatical model, it lumps together various ways in which the Son has been considered dependent on the main clause of paternal deity. Aside from the grammatological analogy it offers those disposed to parse the godhead, "subordinationism" holds little descriptive value, no historical relevance to Milton's century, and indeed, outside of Milton studies is so obscure and technical a piece of jargon that general encyclopedias (e.g. *Britannica, Americana*) ignore it, as do various specialized sources (e.g. *The Encyclopedia of Religion* edited by Mircea Eliade). *The New Catholic Encyclopedia* does include a short entry, but contrary to the definition of the term provided by Milton studies' theological experts, it begins, "the *heresy* ... that admitted only the Father as truly God and taught the inferiority ... of the Son" (italics mine). As a heresy, however, it never existed for condemnation until the nineteenth century, and even then only taxonomically, as a forbidden category. To say, as Patrides would have it, that something called subordinationism was "upheld by the early Christian writers to the Council of Nicaea" is to perpetuate a grotesque anachronism.[60]

Obviously, Milton scholars have found this issue vexing. "Subordinationism" – with ideological evasiveness, technicality, and inaccessibility to students going for it – easily won general approval, and is still a term often used in descriptions of Milton's most carefully and completely elaborated theological position. Yet, the sole theological basis for Hunter's claim that Milton was an "orthodox subordinationist" is that for Milton the Son derives from God's own substance ("one substance [*homoousia*] with the father," according to a possible translation of Nicene orthodoxy). For the monist materialist Milton, however, *all* creatures derive from God's own substance. By this criterion, to borrow the words of John Fry, an Arian supporter of Parliament present for Charles's trial, "I might be said to be God too, as well as Jesus Christ, and the like might be affirmed of all other creatures whatsoever."[61] Milton's cosmos begins with "one first matter all" and ends when "God shall be All in All" (*PL* 5, 472; 3, 341). The Son's material being may originally be more refined and exalted than that of other creatures, but eventually parakeets and cheese fungus would also qualify as participants in the Godhead.[62]

For Milton and Newton both, Christ is a limited, localized being, not eternal but derived in time from an eternal, substantially omnipresent Father.[63] This understanding is inconsistent with the "orthodox subordinationist" category of beliefs, typically expounded by Gnostics, to which Hunter originally appealed in making his case. Newton criticized as idolatrous those Gnostics who thought it proper to worship Christ as God simply because he emanated from the substance of "the supreme God":

he that is of this opinion may believe Christ to be of one substance with the father without making him more then a meer man. Tis not cosubstantiality but power and dominion which gives a right to be worshipped.[64]

Milton is unmistakably explicit on the subject:

[God is] in a real sense Father of the Son, whom he made of his own substance. It does not follow, however, that the Son is of the same essence as the Father. (*CP* 6, 209)

As Milton repeatedly insists, "the attributes of divinity belong to the Father alone," particularly the attribute of "supreme domination both in heaven and earth: the highest authority and highest power of making decisions according to his own absolutely free will" (*CP* 6, 227).

Despite Milton's declarations to the contrary, Hunter contends that for Milton the Son is really eternal and absolute because, as the *Logos*, the Son has always existed in the mind of God. Hunter calls this the "two-stage logos theory" and traces it, too, to Neoplatonic and Gnostic speculation within the early church. Newton's meticulous knowledge of early church theological controversy sets an unmatched standard of competence, so that we can turn to his writings for historical background:

The Gnosticks after the manner of the Platonists and Cabbalists considered the thoughts or Ideas or intellectual objects seated in Gods mind as real Beings or substances.

Newton disparages this notion as crude and heathen.[65] Milton is content flatly to contradict it, insisting in his *Art of Logic* that a thing that exists only in the mind of a subject does not in fact exist at all (*CP* 8, 236). In any event, if Hunter were correct in his ontological premises, the idea for all of creation – indeed, all possible creations – would also have eternally existed in the mind of an omniscient God, so that again the Son would enjoy no special distinction.[66]

For Newton as for Milton, therefore, trinitarianism confused causes and, as a species of polytheism, was an instance of the gravest sin, idolatry.[67] Each insisted on the Arian position primarily because each viewed God as indivisibly one. As Milton wryly observes, "it would have been a waste of time for God to thunder forth so repeatedly that first commandment which said that he was the one and only God, if it could nevertheless be maintained that another God existed as well" (*CP* 6, 212). The Son, on the other hand, according to Newton's theology, "had assumed and would assume many shapes and forms ... a messenger, an agent, a vice-ruler under God, a judge" and as the "one Mediator between God and Man" acted only by voluntary reference to the Father's will.[68] Similarly, Milton suggests that Scripture calls the Son *only begotten* chiefly because he is the only mediator between God and man (*CP* 6, 210–11):

However the Son was begotten, it did not arise from natural necessity, as is usually maintained, but was just as much a result of the Father's decree and will as the Son's priesthood, kingship, and resurrection of the dead. (*CP 6, 208*)

In every guise, the contingent Son acts to fulfill the will of the one absolute being. For both Milton and Newton, this exemplary obedience entitled him to divine honors and worship, but both also thought it blasphemous to worship him as very God. For Milton, we might add, the demotion of the Son to finite if still divine status reflects again the insistently theodical point of his theology. In *Paradise Lost*, the Son's freely made decisions function as a striking counter-example to those of Satan and Adam, his angelic adversary and human predecessor respectively. Through his *voluntary* obedience both God's ways and the human race are justified.[69]

Some might object that, regardless of Milton's own usage, the label "Arian," deriving from a fourth-century controversy, is as inappropriate to the seventeenth century as the nineteenth-century label "subordinationist." Especially later in the seventeenth century, Arianism undoubtedly reflects a historically specific inclination to apply reason and logic to religious belief and an associated tendency to rigorously scrutinize doctrinal and scriptural history. It also manifests the growing conviction among secular, educated men that the individual conscience alone must dictate in matters of faith. This distinctly early modern profile, retrospective though it may be, certainly fits figures like Newton, Locke, and the surprisingly large number of their intellectually eminent circle who held Arian opinions. Arguably, it is a profile that fits Milton as well. It does not of course fit fourth-century Arians, and in that sense the label "Arian" seems misleading. Yet we should consider another side to the intellectual-historical picture. These agents of the Enlightenment formed their consciously Arian opinions deliberately and knowledgeably in the vocabulary of fourth-century church history, a century for various reasons considered highly relevant by many educated and forward-looking men in seventeenth-century England, early and late.[70]

Newton, for example, more explicitly and personally than was ever true of Milton, thought in terms of fourth-century trinitarian controversies even as he expressed through them concerns specific to his own era. At the most fundamental level, Newton firmly believed that a properly monotheistic understanding was the heart of true religion and inseparable from a correct understanding of God's works. His understanding of celestial motions, backed by empirical observation and expressed mathematically, also reflect his Arian convictions. Hence, the design of the Mosaic temple, according to his biblical research, seemed "anciently contrived to represent the frame of [the] Universe as the true Temple of the great God."[71]

By the early 1670s, Newton's massive and what would be sustained efforts in biblical and historical analysis centered on early church history, and especially the trinitarian controversies of the fourth century.[72] He repeatedly and variously builds the case for Arius while construing Athanasius as a vile politician symbolic of humanity's evil inclination to substitute man-made intricacy and superstition for the unity and singularity of divine truth. Regarding Athanasius as "his personal nemesis," Newton dwelt repeatedly and at length on the injustice he felt had been done to Arius, with whom he came to identify both intellectually and emotionally. Well before 1675, claims Richard Westfall, "Newton had become an Arian in the original sense of the term."[73] Newton convinced himself that "a universal corruption of Christianity had followed the central corruption of doctrine," Westfall continues, a corruption especially evident in church government, where the former polity was replaced by "concentration of ecclesiastical power in the hands of the hierarchy."[74]

Thus, finally, we see where Newton's Arianism meets his apocalypticism. The triumph of trinitarian doctrine at Nicea and its civil sanction under the Holy Roman Empire became for him the focal moment – the "great apostasy" predicted in scripture – when state-sponsored superstition and ignorance had overthrown true religion. For Milton, too, Christianity had been "defiled with impurities for more than thirteen hundred years" – that is, since the time of Constantine and the institutionalization of Christianity as the state religion (*CP* 6, 117). Like Milton, Newton also refused to take orders in such a church – "accept ordination he could not" – though he became a Fellow, ironically, of Trinity College. Westfall also observes that the doctrine of the trinity had for Newton "fouled every element of Christianity," and "the Protestant Reformation had not touched the seat of the infection." Hence Newton's neglect of "minor diversions such as optics and mathematics" in favor of theology proceeded from a consistent and lifelong commitment to a "reinterpretation of the tradition central to the whole of European civilization."[75]

Arianism never became for Milton the unifying explanatory principle – a kind of religious theory of gravitation – that it was for Newton. Yet their opinions concerning the corruption of the Christian tradition by state churches are similar. Furthermore, their opinions similarly reflect the influence of Joseph Mead on a point that in Milton's time was of enormous political consequence and marks another key characteristic of Independent thought.

Presbyterians and Independents agreed that some apocalyptic history had passed, though more was to come. But while Presbyterians typically sought to institute an order defined by historical and legal precedent, Independents tended to see the imminent future as precipitating an ideal order, one that would transcend previous laws and institutions. Representative of Presbyterian belief on the subject, Richard Baxter supposed that the paradigm for the millennium had already occurred, under Constantine, and that Christians should work toward a return to the ideal represented by the Holy Roman Empire.

Hence, amidst the many vacillations in Baxter's writings, one consistent theme, as William Lamont has shown, is his yearning for the reign of a godly prince, one who would use civil authority to promote the interests and discipline of true religion – under the guidance of divines like Baxter.[76] This ideal, and an associated adherence to preexisting forms of scriptural and national law, was the basis for Presbyterian allegiance to the monarchy and outrage at the regicide. Independents like Milton, on the other hand, tended to look back not to the first thousand years of the Holy Roman empire, but forward to an unprecedented millennium when the true King, Christ, would return and rule.[77] The expectation of a new and just order – Augustine's invisible city of God made visible on Earth in real time – had the effect of rendering the institution of monarchy, as well as ecclesiastical policies and even civil law, less sacred and more open to question.

For Milton as for Newton, according to Mead's chronology, the papist anti-Christ originated in the fourth century, not the fourteenth, and it was a product of the union of civil and ecclesiastical powers. Hence, as Newton would, Milton disapproved of the institution of Christianity as a state church and of the hierarchical exaltation of its clergy. His malediction of Constantine in 1641 – featuring, ironically, a slighting reference to the emperor's Arian inclinations – indicates early on his skeptical attitude toward supposedly sacred rulers (*CP* 1, 554–59; see also 1, 420). Opposed to Baxter in his millennial beliefs, Milton berated Constantine for promoting prelates to luxurious lives and giving them authority over matters better left to individual believers. His aversion to the mixture of civil authority and religious concerns is thus of a piece with the millenarian, tolerationist, historical perspective evinced by the opening argument of *Areopagitica*. For it was under the "Roman *Antichrist* ... bred up by *Constantine*" that religious persecution, and with it pre-publication censorship, waxed strongest (*CP* 1, 559).

In stressing Milton's similarities to Newton on issues that some see purely as matters of dusty doctrine or weird apocalypticism, I have tried to present additional evidence that emphasizes Milton's reach into the future. This poet cannot be resolved into a punctilist background of religious doctrines or fixed within the silhouettes of such doctrines' sociological implications. Any unifying generalization, whether doctrinal or methodological in emphasis, is an obstructive fiction insofar as it limits interpretation according to its own artifice, as if "all must be supprest which is not found in their *Syntagma*" (*CP* 2, 550). Milton was not prone to the catechetical formulations and admonitory posture characteristic of Presbyterian clergymen or of various other contemporary writers, like Bunyan, for example. Yet, much of Milton scholarship has suffered from a tendency to treat his works as if they were messages susceptible to decoding according to a traditional knowledge or faith that he shared with his contemporary audience.

The theoretical premise of this chapter has been that acts of communication, including literary art, work to affect, alter, or respond to their contexts – or cognitive environments. While inevitably they resort to the known in responding to what is unknown, they do not inevitably represent an attempt to reduce the future to the past. Milton believed that the future would produce an order for which past kingdoms and laws had no precedent. What was coming would be different, not a repetition. Hence he insisted on the inevitable provisionality of human understanding: "the light which we have gain'd, was giv'n us ... by it to discover onward things more remote from our knowledge" (*CP* 2, 550). He did not suppose that his works were messages to an audience "under a perpetuall childhood of prescription," an audience that already knew or could know the contents and needed only to decode them (2, 514). The wisdom contained in books is "a potencie of life" and "vigorously productive," not a transcription (2, 492).

By reading Milton as if he were a determinist Presbyterian, Milton criticism errs in ways that Milton supposed the Presbyterians themselves did. It is one of the odd doublethinks of Milton criticism that though he is widely *read* as if he were a censorious Presbyterian minister, he is nevertheless generally recognized to have been Arminian and Independent. How then do we explain the acquiescence and active development of Milton as an admonitory pedagogue when, as was argued in the first chapter, the text of *Paradise Lost* does not require it, and when, as this chapter contends, such a version of the poet contradicts what we know of his place in history? There is more to this problem than can be accounted for by an implicit political compromise between those who wish to reduce Milton to a religious orthodoxy and those who wish to reduce him to a structurally predictable expression of class consciousness. It is time to follow this double-edged investigation into the field of psychology, where recently the poet has been the subject of illuminating psychohistorical analysis.

CHAPTER 3

Responses and their vicissitudes

This man of the bad conscience ... apprehends in "God" the
ultimate antithesis of his own ineluctable animal instincts; he
reinterprets these animal instincts themselves as a form of guilt
before God (as hostility, rebellion, insurrection against the
"Lord," the "father," the primal ancestor and origin of the world)
... In this psychical cruelty there resides a madness of the will
which is absolutely unexampled: the *will* of man to find himself
guilty and reprehensible.

Friedrich Nietzsche[1]

Frank Kermode's classic assessment of young Milton as "his father's
chief investment" was more prescient than historically accurate.[2]
Prescient, I mean, of the now common critical tenet that the scrivener's
investment yielded a poet who still produces spiritual profit – by
entrapping sinful readers and inculcating standard Protestant doctrine.
The description of Milton senior as a "ruthless" businessman, however,
simply does not bear scrutiny.[3] Also problematic, as noted last chapter,
is the common assumption that he ruled his family according to a
Protestant ethic that allegedly prevailed on young Milton's native
Bread Street. The notion of a Protestant ethic makes better sense when
applied to the late seventeenth (post-1688) and eighteenth centuries,
the period from which most of Weber's evidence derives. It was then
that values like those for which Milton and his contemporaries risked
their lives had become imbued with a certain complacency: less
intensely spiritual, more secular, in short, constituent of the dominant
ideology. Yet the dubious bit of Miltonic biography prospers.[4]

This chapter ultimately will ask what the common representation of
this father–son relationship says about *us*. It prepares to do so first by
examining the psychology we attribute to Milton and his father and
then by assessing the plausibility of that attribution considering the
historical record. My claim will be that the construction of the father as

a profiteer who commodified and so dehumanized his son, tells us more about the psychological tendencies and interpretive tools of contemporary Milton criticism than it does about the poet and his father.

As mentioned in chapter 1, William Kerrigan has contended that staggering Oedipal trauma led Milton to forsake the consolations ordinarily associated with sexual maturity and to seek instead second-hand pleasures born of self-denial and resentment. More specifically, the claim is that Milton during the 1630s found himself at an Oedipally evocative crossroads of parental expectation and contrary vocational desire.[5] In response, the would-be poet adopted an unconscious strategy at once regressive and revisionist, as he settled into a long period of studious isolation and extended latency. The original paternal "no" forbidding access to the mother was, retrospectively at least, undone by the poet's categorical repudiation of sexual love – in the form of a secret vow of virginity, alleged by various scholars to have occurred sometime in the 1630s.[6] Such a transformation of fearful submission into renunciation restored to the poet a sense of agency. Moreover, on the assumption that a commitment to virginity insinuates that all sexual intimacy is a defilement, it would have included an implicit "indictment of progenitors."[7] Dedication to virginity so construed, in a textbook instance of *resentiment*, would also hold the unconscious appeal of turning the tables on his father – penalizing him for sexual defilement while preserving the son unscathed.

Traditions celebrating virginity were common in the Renaissance, and Milton knew of them. But Protestant authors routinely criticized the deliberate failure to breed as aggression against one's ancestry and as self-defeating self-love, which in its refusal to continue the family line destroyed one's own image too. "Peevish, proud, idle, made of self-love," virgins were conventionally represented as implying the guilt of parents: "to speak on the part of virginity is to accuse your mother," as Shakespeare's Parolles says.[8]

Supposing that Milton did manage to avert his conscious attention from contemporary, Protestant opinion toward sexual abstention, he would still have had to contend with classical attitudes toward male virginity. Plutarch, for instance, records that many Greek cities accounted celibacy an offense against society and cites the laws instituted by Lycurgus to penalize "confirmed bachelors" (*hoi agamoi* – the term also used by Paul to describe himself in 1 Cor. 7:8, 32).[9] The Greeks agreed with Parolles: "it is not politic in the commonwealth of nature to preserve virginity."[10] Milton and his parents were simply too well informed not to recognize the possibility that an "indictment of progenitors" might lurk in the heart of the most unspotted virgin.

The self-aggrandizing twist and vengeful profit supposedly enjoyed by the virginal Milton places too great an emphasis on repression and interiority in the formation and activity of an early modern psyche. The notion of a celibate Milton's *unconscious* desire for revenge depends on the Cartesian assumption of a sealed-off mind and the Freudian proposition of a psyche that unwittingly organizes present experience in terms of its childhood development. At certain moments, especially in his two final poems, Milton may reflect the increasing tendency toward the modern contraction, opacity, and internalization of psychic life. But overall, this trend in early modern intellectual history, unlike so many others, he did *not* notably advance or anticipate. Although he figures as perhaps the greatest English poet of *individuality*, he did not have much to say about *interiority*, though these distinct notions are often confused. We find more definite intimations of the walled-off self in Shakespeare's poems and dramas, Spenser's allegories, or, for that matter, in Chaucer's *Troilus and Cressida*. With the exception of a few moments, mostly involving Satan, Milton's interiors sound relatively inauthentic, at least according to post-romantic expectations for representations of inner life. In Milton's art, even private speech tends to sound public, rhetorical; the "secret furious inviolacy" that Kerrigan posits of him was more furious than secret.[11]

If Milton seems at times incapable of keeping things bottled up inside, therefore, it was not from lack of self-control but from lack of a bottle. He recalls a highly educated Othello or Lear more than a reflective, latent, and symptomatic Hamlet. One of the least appreciated consequences of Milton's heretical materialism is that for him community was ontologically inescapable, the necessary condition even of existence felt as difference. Individuality for him primarily meant going one's own way against or in agreement with the group or other authority – but out loud and not in a state of reflective detachment within it. His "personal" triumphs and anguish break through his "public" utterances even when, as in the divorce tracts, he seems to try to choke them back.[12] In *Areopagitica* he embraced the chaos of the sects: their ongoing search for, and community of disagreement over, the still undiscovered shape of truth. If we may usefully apply any dialectical scheme to Milton, it is not that of opposition versus identification – the individual "no" against the dominant "yes." Rather, as befits the son of a musician, it is one of discord versus harmony, the goal being articulation of difference within a substantial sameness. Being oneself secretly, beyond the reach of the thought police, is not even a temptation for this poet, nor would he have considered the effacement of self in multitudes of uniform, obedient creatures a virtue.

Any meaningful consideration of Milton's character ultimately must involve the particular historical conditions in which his personality was formed. Kerrigan recognizes the significant cultural differences between modern domestic conditions and those that shaped personality in the Renaissance. Yet, he observes that many Puritan families apparently fostered unusually close emotional ties within a clearly defined family unit.[13] While conceding that Milton matured within an affectionate and relatively focused Puritan family, we should still remember that he was subject to diverse and diffused interpersonal forces, perhaps more so than the limited geometry of an emotionally intense Oedipal triangle can adequately calculate. By Freud's time, the increasingly exalted and unquestioned status of fathers, heightened sexual repression, and ever smaller family groups had magnified the likelihood of patriarchal intimidation.[14] Although the cultural trends that justify the stress placed on Oedipal trauma in the analysis of nineteenth- and twentieth-century psyches had already commenced in the seventeenth, even in Milton's case they would probably have been relatively inchoate and diluted.

A succession of influential and sometimes beloved tutors and teachers populated Milton's youth. A maidservant attended him as he studied late. Apprentices and servants shared family life in the rooms over the scrivener's place of business. Milton's own adult style of living in households crowded at various times with immediate family, resident in-laws, servants, live-in students, amanuenses, friends, professional and familiar acquaintances suggests a continuing breadth of intimacy and affection, a wealth and diversity of quasi-family relations, that should not be ignored in measuring the determinative force that any particular relationship might have had to fix his character. While the father and mother who presided over young Milton's large and busy household undoubtedly influenced him, we cannot consider this influence in isolation. A larger personal, professional, religious, and even recreational community shot through every facet of his ordinary family life – to an extent that most today would find quite extraordinary.

One thinks of *Samson Agonistes* and the character of Manoa, who has often been tied to Milton's father by those who find autobiographical meaning in the drama. The consistent presence of the Chorus of Danites contextualizes and to some extent negotiates relations between father and son, relations mediated typically, even after Samson's death, through the larger community, including the Philistines. More importantly, the example of the solicitous Manoa suggests that the emotional tenor of the relation between Milton and his father has been misconstrued. I think it unwarranted to assume that the young poet was driven with a "sometimes heedless rigor" by "rod-wielding schoolmasters of the Renaissance."[15]

The contention that an Oedipally traumatized Milton found paternal figures profoundly threatening therefore seems at least debatable. Yet, structurally, as I will later show, it is a hypothesis that fits well with current approaches to literary interpretation. A cowed Milton's hypothetical chastity can easily be converted into a displaced expression of emergent capitalism. If the poet represents his father's chief investment, after all, would not the investor's attitude toward his son mediate Protestant patriarchal rigor in an emerging capitalist society? Such rigor would of course also shape the son's sexuality. Yet, the harsh character attributed to Milton's father does not suit the biographical and literary evidence we possess. It is to this evidence that I now turn.

A POET BEGOTTEN

he would be chearfull even in his Gowte fitts; & sing

John Aubrey[16]

A close contemporary of Shakespeare, Milton's father followed a similar trajectory from agricultural life to newfangled, disturbingly cross-categorical and morally suspect, urban occupation. He prospered in the London of the late 1580s and 1590s and became a prominent citizen in that city of 200,000. Like Shakespeare, with whom he could have been acquainted through Thomas Morley, he succeeded in part because he was in the right place at the right time and was innovative.[17] The primary fact of the senior Milton's biography was not his career as an investor, however, but his rebellion against his recusant father. The prominence of the story in the first four lives of Milton – it is the first fact to appear in John Aubrey's notes toward a biography –

suggests that the poet himself stressed this bit of family history, that it represented a key to his sense of family identity.[18] Adherence to the principles of such a father could easily result in disobedience to him or, more likely, feeling able to disagree with him freely and openly in matters of conscience.

The comparison of Milton's father with Shakespeare, a dramatist known for his real estate investments and also the son of a recusant, is instructive. Milton senior was a real estate investor known for his musical talents. If Shakespeare's characteristic vision was meta-dramatic, the senior Milton's was meta-monetary. Economic relations having to do with land deals not only dominate Shakespeare's biographical record but consistently figure in his poetic and dramatic expression of nature and culture. Yet we do not typically think of Shakespeare as a ruthless businessman invariably looking to squeeze out a profit, even in human affairs. None of the early biographies so much as hint that Milton senior was a grasping man – quite the contrary: "[he] acquir'd a Moderate Estate by his Profession," says John Richardson, "was Content with it, and Retir'd into the Country."[19] Although he did not completely retire until he was approaching 70 (about 1631), his involvement in business declines progressively throughout the preceding decade. In the abundance of records concerning his business, though many concern litigation, nothing justifies a charge of ruthless profit-mongering. Parker concludes that "we have ample evidence about Milton ... to be confident that he was honest and fair in his business dealings" (pp. 17–18).[20] Ironically, the contemporary tendency to see him as a rigorous and demanding patriarch, who drove his son for at least spiritual profit, appears to rely on a medieval ethic already outmoded in the seventeenth century – that usurers are grasping and avaricious by definition.

In our attentiveness to his money-lending, we tend to note and then sequester the fact that Milton senior was also a well-regarded composer. The early biographers set a different course, with Aubrey's background notes again pointing the way:

he came to London, and became a Scrivener ... and gott a plentiful estate by it & left it off many yeares before he dyed. he was an ingeniose man, delighted in Music, composed many Songs now in print especially that of Oriana.[21]

One early biography attributes the scrivener's retirement not only to "a moderation not usual with such as have tasted the sweets of gain," but also to his being "inclin'd rather to a retir'd life by his addiction

to Music."[22] Nor was this addiction fed solely by somber religious
dirges:

> Fair Orian, in the morn
> Before the day was born,
> With velvet steps on ground,
> Which made nor print nor sound,
> Would see her nymphs abed.
> What lives those ladies led!

Ernest Brennecke, Jr., the author of a useful but neglected book on
Milton's father, cannot with certainty say if the paternal musician
wrote the lyrics about this *alter ego* for Elizabeth, who, like Sabrina in
Comus, walks with "printless feet" (line 896). But the scrivener definitely
composed the "rollicking" music for them.[23]

Brennecke maintains that Milton senior reached a high point in
his art when he set to music David's lamentation over the death of
Absalom:

When David heard that Absalom was slain, he went up to his chamber over
the gate, and wept. And as he went, thus he said: O my son Absalom, would
God I had died for thee, O my son Absalom, my son, my son!

It is well worth the effort to follow with the mind's ear what Brennecke
says of the composer's effort:

Milton's composition is laid out for five voices and is in the Dorian mode. The
three middle voices begin the narrative quite unpretentiously – almost casually
. . . With the words, "he went up to his chamber," a rising scale is introduced
in the low registers, working up to the limits of the vocal range. There is a
moment of complete and breathless silence after the words, "and wept"; and
with the anguished cries of the king the music develops more and more
intense feeling, the high notes of the bass portraying the very extremity of
despair. Near the conclusion the tenor's lowest register is masterfully used to
indicate a complete and subdued abandonment to woe.[24]

Milton's father achieved his greatest artistic success on the subject of an
indulgent father mourning the death of his rebellious son (a rebel who
appeared in popular culture, ironically, as long-haired, artistic, and, if
we can rely on Chaucer's Miller, squeamish). The music suggests that
imaginatively at least the composer sympathized with the father who
found that loss nearly insupportable.

The evidence usually cited by those who argue that Milton's father
pressured his son is *ad Patrem*, which evidently addresses some dissatisfaction over the choice of poetry as a vocation. Nor can we hear Milton

speak of his indebtedness, as he does in *ad Patrem* and elsewhere, without also hearing echoes of Satanic rebellion: "so burdensom, still paying, still to ow" (*PL* 4, 53). A carefully nurtured sense of indebtedness may be the most effective coercion of all, and is notable for feeding the glow on smoldering coals of resentment.

Yet Milton's expression of gratitude for what he considers his greatest debt, his education, leaves an entirely different impression:

whatever the heavens hold, the subjected earth breeds, or the flowing air bears between them; whatever lies beneath the waters and excitable waves of the sea – through you it is permitted for me to know, through you, if I want to know. From behind a cloud science comes visibly and uncovered bends her clear features for kisses: if I do not choose to flee; if the touch is not distressful.[25]

His gratitude pivots at the junction of his father's freely chosen bounty and his own unforced volition: "through you it is permitted ... through you, if I want" [*per te nosse licet ... per te, si nosse libebit*] (line 89). The father procured access to universal knowledge for his son, but unless Milton is merely adopting a rhetorical posture, his father neither forced him nor had a specific return in mind. Milton enjoyed the right to refuse an unwelcome intimacy. If anything in this scenario makes him uncomfortable, it is prospect of Lady Science's embrace.

The poet's attitude toward his human father conveys such confidence that it appears as if his mature son loved him as an equal rather than as one to whom subordination and obedience were owed:

Now, why marvel that you happened to have begotten me a poet when we, closely knit by flesh and blood, incline to sister arts and allied interests?

> [*Nunc tibi quid mirum, si me genuisse poëtam*
> *Contigerit, charo si tam propè sanguine iuncti*
> *Cognatas artes, studiumque affine sequamur?*]   (lines 61–63)

Always in medieval Latin and often in classical usage, *gigno*, the root of *genuisse* (line 61), suggests divine agency. A key term in Christological controversy, it appears frequently in Milton's *de doctrina Christiana*. In chapter 5 of the first book, both Sumner and Carey translate *genuisse* (the same active past infinitive as above) as if it were passive (e.g. *CP* 6, 205, 210; *CW* 14, 180–81, 188–89). In Greek, its etymological source, *gignomai*, is an intransitive deponent verb and means "to come into being, to become, or to assume a certain status or function," which exactly covers the range of meaning that Milton the theologian gives to "beget" (*CP* 6, 205–06).

Had he wished to avoid these non-biological associations or to attribute agency to his father unequivocally, Milton would have known to use a verb like *genero*, one more redolent of biological contexts (among its synonyms is "to secrete").[26] Grammatically, the original Latin makes the father an indirect "you" (*tibi*, a dative split between *mirum* and *contigerit*) and from that dative the weakly implied subject of *genuisse*. The son himself (*me, poetam*) stands on either side of the crucial infinitive, a poet begotten, if not self-begotten. Were clarity desirable concerning responsibility for the begetting, would not Milton have replaced the redundant and confusing *me* with *te*? The father's role in these lines is reduced to wonder at providence.

In short, Milton speaks of his begetting as a matter beyond his father's control, with a hint that the son's poetic career is a matter of divine disposition. Oddly, his arguments anticipate those Jesus uses to answer Satan in *Paradise Regained*, though in a much more affectionate register. The implication is that the begotten poet's duty to God takes precedence over any owed to his earthly father. The subsequent parallelism strengthens this implication by generalizing away from the father–son connection – "closely knit by flesh and blood" – and ends by explicitly putting them on the same plane. Just as they are tied by blood (*sanguine*), so are their respective arts literally of the same birth (*cognatas*). And just as they are tied by flesh (*charo*), so their studies are in a sense one flesh, or wedded (*affine*). Like Milton's angels, the composer and the poet are equally sons of the same God. And just as Milton senior disregarded his father's wishes when it came to the welfare of his soul, so the young poet would presumably feel compelled to do the same in an analogous situation.

The next three lines make the meetness and complementarity of father and son explicit as Milton in an etiologic myth somewhat reminiscent of Aristophanes's in Plato's *Symposium* insists that Phoebus divided himself between father and son (lines 64–66). As poet and musician they, together, possess all of him. This well suits with Kerrigan's identification of the musically inclined Attendant Spirit in *Comus* as a paternal figure. Henry Lawes, a noted musician and friend of Milton's father, filled the role. In his guise as Thyrsis, "whose artful strains have oft delaid / The huddling brook to hear his madrigal," the Spirit speaks of the mutual affection between him and "a certain Shepherd Lad," whom Kerrigan, like others before him, identifies as one of the versions of the young poet in the masque (lines 494–95, 619). The shepherd shares poetic knowledge contained in "his leather'n scrip"; Thyrsis enchants him with music (line 626). Of Milton's own musical gifts, Aubrey writes that "he had a delicate tuneable Voice & had good skill." Aubrey also records that "his father instructed him."[27] As *At a Solemn Music* suggests, Milton throughout his life cherished the soothing paternal inheritance of music, and, like the fallen angels (*PL* 2, 552–55), took comfort in it as refuge from pain: "he would be chearfull even in his Gowte fitts, & sing."

The relationship portrayed in *ad Patrem* was multi-faceted and psychologically complex, a complexity belied by the claim that Milton's Herculean labors as a student came at the insistence of a harsh father.[28] The early biographers insistently stress his own "insuperable Industry," and mention discipline only to suggest that in his case none was necessary.[29] The anecdotal evidence we possess concerning his relations with the indeed intimidating and rigorous William Chappell indicates that young Milton readily defied rod-wielding representatives of the Renaissance superego rather than bow in secret resentment before them. (Chappell was famous for his relentless "logomachy and logical weapons"; in a debate before King James, his opponent fainted before Chappell's relentless assault.[30]) The quiet assertiveness and independence beneath the surface of *ad Patrem* suggests that far from averting wrath or even securing permission, Milton meant to ameliorate discontent over a decision that lay outside his father's will. Whatever encouragement and support he may or may not have received, young Milton – like his father before him – felt entitled, even bound by a higher obedience, to choose for himself.

As in the case of his mitigation of biological indebtedness, Milton's protestations of liberty could indicate denial of a quite different situation. It by no means stretches credibility to suppose that Milton might have defensively "chosen" – as a form of rebellion – extreme versions of the sexual virtue and religious calling that he may have felt pressured to follow. Yet more apparent in many of his writings is the confidence that he will be allowed to do as he thinks right, that others will attend to his reasons. It is not merely stubbornness that leads him to knock his head repeatedly against the wall of unsympathetic public opinion, as for example in the four divorce tracts.[31] Milton's rhetoric often implies a deep conviction that once he explains, his audience will eventually come round to his way of thinking or, as his father unfailingly did, allow him to do as he wishes. Milton sustained many bitter defeats without losing that assurance. Indeed, I would argue that such assurance is a psychological prerequisite for sincere theodicy. The stronger the assurance and the more bitter the defeat – no defeat could have presented a harsher challenge than the Restoration – the more searching and honest the theodicy would likely be.

THE DOCTRINE AND DISCIPLINE OF MILTON CRITICISM

Why read a poem that treats its reader so badly? Why continue to suffer an experience that is unpleasant?

Stanley Fish[32]

This chapter began by questioning the applicability of the Oedipal model to a psyche shaped in early seventeenth-century London and has gone on to question the representation of young Milton as the anxious "investment" of a daunting father. Yet the dubious likeness has won widespread approval. I want now to suggest that the steady critical elaboration of this now customary portrayal depends on a common dialectical structure.

The paradigmatic Milton, as defined in chapter 1, is at bottom a didactic poet who in *Paradise Lost* entraps and humiliates fallen readers to inculcate traditional doctrine. How did a reading that renders the experience of Milton's poetry "unpleasant" become so successful? Kerrigan's analysis, observed in the first chapter, holds that within readers the "yes" of desire and the "no" of prohibition are *both* registered in scenes of temptation and (dis)obedience: "the pious reader can entertain potentially rebellious attitudes knowing that, as signs of his fallenness, these attitudes already confirm the doctrinal content of the poem and therefore have a piety all their own."[33] In other words, when readers consciously recognize their forbidden desires (thesis), they do so under the category of negation (antithesis): leaving the individual psyche in ambivalent equipoise (synthesis). A similar process of division and resolution characterizes the interplay of Oedipal desire and paternal authority in Freudian theory.

Psychoanalytic principles thus seem to justify an interpretation that reconfigures literary delight according to the imperatives of instruction. Or collapses it, rather, for while reader-response interpretation may afford rebellious desire its place in the sun of consciousness, the spot resembles that which Shakespeare's Henry V allots his conquered passions when he compares them to "wretches fettered in our prisons."[34] When we recall that in Fish's reading, rebellion means *any* diversion from the focus on God and salvation – whether it be Satan's rhetoric or the temptation of plot – things start looking pretty grim. In an ideologically rigorous commonwealth, the emphasis on fettering of such pleasures would also have civil repercussions, as it did, for example, when Cromwell's regime became more conservative and thorough. Henry's simile, with its icy edge of post-Falstaffian, monarchical rigor, is quite pointed, therefore, and depends on a classical analogy between the individual psyche and the state, an analogy often exploited to justify totalitarian discipline. The same basic correlation has its contemporary exponents, of course, who in building from individual psychology to cultural ideology further illustrate the general utility of the dialectical structure I have been describing.

John Guillory and Christopher Kendrick illustrate the ease with which psychohistorical analysis can be converted into theoretically sweeping, dialectical formulations. Kendrick, for example, puts Kerrigan's account of *Comus* as a masque of the superego through Weberian, Foucauldian, and Marxian paces, describing the young poet's resentful chastity as a sexual displacement of the bourgeois commodification of his authorial labors.[35] Guillory, on the other hand, reads *Samson Agonistes* as a historically specific expression of the Freudian death instinct, mediated in terms of the Protestant ethic and triggered by Milton's conflict with his father over vocational and sexual choices: murder *is* a guilty Samson's business.[36]

Derrida, too, can be made to conform to this theoretical reduction of life, as the latter-day Fish has demonstrated in venturing to identify "the dilemma to which Milton's entire career is a response":

One sees it in *Lycidas* when the first person voice struggles against the traditions that claim to have already spoken him. One sees it in *Paradise Lost* when the prospect of merging in an undifferentiated union with a God who shall be "all in all" (3, 341) turns into the horror of a uni-verse in which all distinctions will have been effaced and the landscape will be reduced to a "universal blanc" (3, 48). And one sees it ... in *Of Prelaticall Episcopacy* and *The Doctrine and Discipline of Divorce*, when the scattering touch of interpretation and woman is at once courted and pushed away.[37]

For Milton, self-assertion allegedly equals rebellion, whereas the simultaneous but opposed drive for obedience threatens dissolution of individual identity. Derrida's notion of "différance" thereby becomes a bridge for adapting the paradigmatic Milton to the reverse dialectics of postmodernism: "it is simply not possible to affirm the diacritical nature of one's being without betraying that affirmation in the very act of producing it," observes Fish of the deferrals of submission inhabiting every Miltonic sign of obedience.[38] That is to say, given a system of non-identity relationships, autonomous individuality and self-abnegation imply and even, at a sufficiently abstract level of analysis, constitute one another.

Milton scholarship of the last decade has in many respects gone beyond the asceticism of *Surprised by Sin* and its unusually pure illustration of what Nietzsche in the epigraph to this chapter calls "the *will* of man to find himself guilty and reprehensible." Yet recent readings of Milton still retain the accent on discipline and punishment. The urge has been imputed to Milton himself and to the ideology or the episteme of the historical moment that spoke through him. Hence, in Guillory's reading, *Samson Agonistes* mediates the death instinct through the (erotic) Weberian category of vocation, and *Comus*, in Kendrick's reading, represents through sexual abstention the pinch-fisted and ultimately destructive self-interest of possessive individualism.

The structural affinity that allows for such easy converse among these distinct critical approaches might be traced back to Hegelian philosophy (with special reference to the master–slave dialectic), and from there to Augustine and ultimately to various Hellenic philosophers (e.g. Heraclitus, Parmenides, Plato). This habit of the Western mind works to organize non-identity relations into apparently dualistic oppositions that actually partake of a larger whole. These oppositions are then susceptible to hierarchical synthesis within that comprehensive system. Rather than attempt a detailed genealogy of this intellectual strategy, however, I wish to consider the antipathy to pleasure that, in Milton scholarship at least, has become associated with such dialectical thinking.

In the case of reader-response interpretation, Milton is seen to be effecting a gratifying psychological balance that reconciles rebellious impulses with law. If readers cooperate with the didactic plan, they will see their guilt exposed, accept harsh authorial rebuke – and *like* it. For, as Fish insists in response to the questions that serve as epigraph to this section, "for the seventeenth-century Puritan and indeed for any Christian in what we might call the Augustinian tradition, the kind of discomfort I have been describing would be paradoxically a source of comfort and the unpleasantness a source of pleasure."[39] Pleasure that arises from "discomfort" and "unpleasantness" *is* something of a paradox, though hardly one limited to Augustinian Christians.

Participation in the aesthetic of pain requires only a theoretical model that construes conflict and tension according to what might be called a *managed* dialectic or a bi-polar organization. I observed in chapter 1 that the New Historicist dialectic of subversion and containment exhibits the same false appearance of dualism. Like good and evil in Augustinian ontology (or Nietzschean ethics, for that matter), subversion and containment only seem separate, independent forces. They in fact occur within a single, closed system. Subversive desire, like Satanic evil, can never be successfully realized but is nonetheless useful for the display of power, a display that generally involves inflicting anguish on some victim – in Satan's case, more extreme anguish than can be imagined.

Once established, this structural dynamic tends to replicate itself, particularly at the level of the critical investigation that uncovered, or, as I think more likely, imposed it. The isomorphism among the investigators' methodologies allows for the formation of a basic consensus (e.g. Milton was his father's chief investment) and then interdisciplinary competition over its significance. Of Kendrick's rival reading of *Areopagitica* Fish claims, as noted in chapter 1, "it would be no trick at all, just a standard move in the repertoire ... I share with other members of the profession, to outflank and assimilate his reading."[40] To outflank and assimilate another's interpretation, and to do so as an exhibition of professional mastery concerning an agreed upon subject – can there be any doubt that this too represents a kind of pleasure?

The association of the structure I have been describing with the Oedipus complex perhaps makes it seem more civilized and judicial than sadomasochistic in character. Not all readers of Milton would admit to enjoying pain and humiliation, perhaps, but no one will deny having been a child subject to parental or religious authority, or an adult subject to governmental power. Within the Oedipal triangle as presented by Freud, father–son relations *do* smack of sadomasochism. The son finds the father threatening and himself puny, the penalty proposed irrevocably contrary to desire, the desire itself – at least retrospectively – shameful, so that the intimidated child renounces sexuality altogether and retreats into latency. The way is prepared for him to identify with his great forbidder.

For Freud, however, subjection of desire by the superego ordinarily marks a *deferral* rather than a *source* of satisfaction, a deferral that permits "unreproved pleasures free" (*L'Allegro* line 40). Such deferral is tactically distinct from mere surrender, in which a weak ego caves in, betraying desire as it were and leeching strength from the superego at the price of its own experience of shame. If we insist that the Miltonic ideal of obedience requires surrender of the ego, we should at least admit that such surrender is a survival strategy characteristic not of normal ego psychology but of masochism.

To read *Paradise Lost* as if the epic itself were a rod-wielding school master is to collapse Horace's classic dichotomy: the subjunctive wanderings of literary pleasure are inexorably channeled into the entrenched imperatives of painful instruction. We are left no way out, a state that Milton, who consistently associates pleasure with freedom from such totalitarian discipline, deplores: "[we] have need of som delightfull intermissions, wherin the enlarg'd soul may leav off a while her severe schooling; and like a glad youth in wandring vacancy, may keep her hollidaies to joy and harmles pastime" (*CP* 2, 597). Yet we seem to wish to reduce the pleasurable variety and plenitude of his verse, as well as his endlessly provocative narrative, to temptation, and the same one over and over: instead of sitting astride a "flying Steed unreind," we are allegedly victims of a jade's trick, and, if we are pious, are required to take a wretched sort of pleasure in the discovery (*PL* 7, 17).

I would not deny that a sadomasochistic dialectic holds a place in *Paradise Lost*, or that over the centuries, various readers – Pope and Johnson come to mind – have responded to it. But it applies to the angelic realm, *not* to the play between narrator and reader. Michael Lieb observes that God places the good angels in "absurd and humiliating predicaments" to test and educate them.[41] Fish himself euphemistically construes "God's *insensitivity* to the angels' feelings" (my italics) as "a compliment" because such insensitivity, what Empson preferred to call God's "usual grinding contempt," presumes their loyalty.[42] God deprives the loyal angels of any chance to make an effective contribution to the war in heaven, Fish observes, but allows them many opportunities to display obedience through patient endurance of humiliation.

If these commonplace observations among Milton scholars are accurate, Milton's God can hardly be considered "insensitive" to angels' feelings. Effective humiliation obviously requires considerable sensitivity, of a certain sort. Before the war, Satan had interpreted the Son's exaltation as the beginning of the angels' degradation (5, 800–02). Subsequent events do not refute his prophecy. God diminishes the good angels' wonted powers during the war, deprives them of an expected (and traditional) victory over the rebels, and, as per Satan's oracle, reduces them under the command of the solely triumphant Son.[43] Furthermore, the armor of the good angels' faith apparently includes the tactical disadvantage of obtuse innocence in the face of subterfuge, rendering them ridiculous victims of Satan's martial resourcefulness. Later, Gabriel implicitly allows that the angels' adoration of God is fawning, cringing, and servile, which is a troublesome if tacit admission, though of course it can be explained away (4, 959–60).[44]

Masochism as a sexual practice is primarily a Western cultural phenomenon and it appears to have begun to achieve a degree of popularity only in the seventeenth century. This chronology may reflect an increasing emphasis on the independent self in the early modern era and the suitability of masochism as a means of flight from its burdens. In Western society, the humiliations sought out by sexually masochistic males include status loss, degradation, deprivation of control, and, in extreme cases, reduction to the category of sexually dysfunctional object.[45] Evidence suggests that this profile applies especially to those males who occupy positions of power and authority and presumably wish to escape from carrying off the demanding illusion of their exaggerated selves.[46] The good angels, consistently described as powerful males occupying high positions, endure all but the humiliation of sexual dysfunction or objectification, a punishment reserved for the fallen angels.[47]

It will surely be objected that love of a superior (God) that is equated with obedience and involves humiliation and acts of submission will *seem* like masochism to unregenerate readers, incapable as they are of seeing beyond their own corruption. Usually in Milton studies, however, denigration of unregenerate interpretation comes with an explanation of how the poem encourages pious readers to doublethink their way through their fallenness to reconstruct a pure version of fallen perception. I find no basis for such encouragement concerning this fallen perception, however, except perhaps God's promise of an apocalyptic literalization of the masochistic impulse to identify with the dominant partner – when "God shall be All in All" (3, 341).

If the humiliations of the good angels intimate something like masochistic experience, the case of the fallen angels allows no doubts. In conformity with the most common expressions of masochism, the rebels characterize themselves as God's "thralls": slaves without names, things without social identity (1, 149, 361). Satan can easily be construed as a prime example: obsessed with status, desirous of escape from the unrealistic obligations that his presumption of authority imposes, and subject to repeated humiliations, deprivation of control, incessant ontological degradation, consciousness of sexual impotence, and, of course, unending torture. Indeed, what is perhaps most specifically masochistic in the story of the bad angels is the peculiar version of pain invented for them. Pain usually signifies physical damage. Masochists, however, seek intense pain without real injury, just the sort of pain conferred upon the rebels (6, 430–36).[48] Such pain may be regarded as symbolic or fictional – pain removed from its ordinary physiological implications and accepted, even desired, as the expression of one's place in a relationship.[49] That is precisely how Satan repeatedly represents his fortitude.

The problem of pain has always made masochism a puzzle. At a time when he sought to explain psychological economy according to the pleasure principle alone, Freud tried to account for painful gratification through crossing subject–object identifications and variable active–passive positions.[50] For him, the pattern of sadism–masochism epitomized these "vicissitudes" of sexual instinct: "masochism is actually sadism turned round upon the subject's own ego."[51] The assumption is that the pleasure derives from causing suffering, even when inflicted on oneself. Freud thus considered sadism the originary behavior and masochism its passive reflection. Here, too, we find the appearance of opposition within an encompassing system of mutual dependence. Masochists identify with their torturers and sadists with their victims.

Although Freud's account of passive–active reflexivity in sadism–masochism has proven broadly influential, few follow him in tracing the outcroppings of such behavior to underlying Oedipal trauma. Alternative explanations focus on pre-Oedipal experience and on biological and cultural influences that transcend the nuclear family.[52] The psychological structure consistently appealed to in such accounts is that of narcissism, with its characteristic, bi-polar shifts between feelings of lofty grandiosity and utter worthlessness.[53] In the case of what seems to be angelic sadomasochism, I would speculate that Milton's representation is partly a legacy of Christian doctrine and partly an expression of an emerging culture – modern culture, with its distinctive ideology of autonomous selfhood. This combination of cultural depth and specific, contemporary relevance would explain why ideologically sensitive critics like Guillory and Kendrick seem drawn to the most overtly sadomasochistic scenes in Milton's poetry and read them as Christian mediations of nascent capitalism: in *Comus*, the self-possessed, disdainful Lady bound to a chair before the herdmaster enchanter, and, in *Samson Agonistes*, a blinded Samson, undone by Dalila, about to destroy hordes of Philistines and himself in a violent peripetia of active-passive subject positions.

If the prophetic Milton did indeed anticipate the downside of the coming bourgeois Protestant ethic, as such criticism suggests, we should not suppose that he did so unconsciously or uncritically. I believe that he struggled with narcissistic pressures from his earliest days and that these struggles appear in his works. I would further claim that as he grew older, he became more aware of darker consequences associated with his ambitions for greatness, and repudiated them. His theological modifications of Augustinian Christianity suggest that he was particularly sensitive to the sadomasochistic potentialities of his faith and found them inimical.[54] Though the crucifixion is the central Christian story, the image of God as a cruelly tortured son crying out to an unrelenting father who is also God, was never represented in his completed works. Intimations of the passion that occur in *Paradise Regained* indicate that Milton found Anglo-Saxon traditions of the joyously brave and triumphant Son more to his taste than late medieval representations of Christ as the tortured and spat upon man of sorrows.[55] Empson argues, convincingly, that Milton's heresies, especially his Arianism, consistently undermine the religion's sadomasochistic appeal: "Milton has cut out of Christianity both the torture-horror and the sex-horror, and after that the monster seems almost decent."[56]

As we have seen, however, modern Milton scholarship has since mid-century worked to mitigate Milton's heresies, especially his Arianism. This example aside, the proclivities of late twentieth-century Milton studies appear regularly, and more insidiously I think, in its tendency to appeal to the angelic realm as the moral standard by which to judge human behavior. As we saw in chapter 1, Milton takes care to distinguish angels from human beings. Insofar as they are relevant to human experience, they represent principles and behaviors of a concentration that humanity simply cannot support – Satan's power to maintain steadfast hate, for example. We taste nothing purely; in comparison, angels are unmixed and extreme. Certainly, the sadomasochistic dialectic has relatively little to do with human beings in the epic. Adam and Eve, for whom more literal pain is invented, are neither angels nor devils, and Milton's often harsh and derisive God does not treat them as if they were. Yet modern Milton criticism has tended to identify more with the simple extremes of the angelic than the ambiguity of human experience and to judge the latter according to the measure of the former.

If Milton tried to undo the submission–dominance dialectic of Christianity, why then do at least certain Miltonists insist that the didactic Milton instructs and delights members of his "fit" audience by entrapping, exposing, humiliating, and punishing them? The basis for an answer may lie in Robert Adams's observation that "the Christian humanist majority ... has [long] held the strong right-center position in Miltonic criticism ... against ... many antagonists."[57] The division on which the paradigmatic Milton depends is a fact not of individual psychology but of reception history. Over the centuries some readers have sympathized with Satan or sided with God and made that choosing of sides the central issue of the poem. But I suspect that few, at least few before our time, have first sympathized with Satan and then immediately felt badgered by the narrator for having done so. The best that can be said of the reader-response version of *Paradise Lost* is that a very longstanding and sometimes acrimonious conflict among readers of Milton was made susceptible to a synthesis imposed on the poem and passed off as the poet's own didactic therapy for individual minds.

According to Wilhelm Reich, such pleasure as masochistic submission allows rests in its prevention of a more severe punishment (castration, for example).[58] Another theorist has hypothesized that the evolutionary logic of this strategy may be seen, for example, in a dog's willingness to bare its throat and so assume a defenseless posture to save its life.[59] In Milton studies, the extreme punishment spared pious readers seems to have been visited upon the once eminent critical faction – from Blake and Shelley to Waldock and Empson – who found Satan's complaints aesthetically pleasing and worth pondering, and Milton's God aesthetically problematic and perhaps tyrannical. Their rebellious responses were characterized as having first been piqued by Milton and then harshly condemned – though these readers, unlike *us*, were too dull to recognize the condemnation. They refused to submit. The derision and dismissal that over the last generation has met Empson's *Milton's God*, for example, suggest that the "healing" of the Milton community has required drastic measures. Those who disagree with the penitent community's reading are, like Satan, perceived as defeated and as objects of contempt, without their knowing how this humiliation has occurred. They have been transformed and left to wonder at themselves, after the fashion of the rebel angels in book 10. The pious on the other hand are allowed to look on in scorn. If there is no explicitly sexual satisfaction involved in condemnation of evil interpreters, we should suffer no illusions regarding the appeal that critical dominance has for some.

CHAPTER 4

"Comus": a fit of the mother

Artemis and Hecate are one

Marija Gimbutas[1]

It is appropriate that a psychoanalytic assessment of Milton should stand at the heart of this book, despite the vulnerability of such methodology to speculation and anachronism. To address the invented Milton adequately – to account for the egregious didactic persona *we* have imposed on his poetry – it seems obligatory to work at the interpretive place where the ineffable phenomenon of personality has been extracted from the textual record and synthesized for conversion into contemporary theory. That interpretive place lies in the domain of psychoanalysis. My argument thus far has been that undue stress on the Oedipus complex – the Freudian drama of law and desire – validates our mistaken reading of Milton as the punitive voice of Christian didacticism. I want now to take that argument in a more positive direction.

The clearest case for the Oedipus complex as an interpretive key for Milton and his works appears in Kerrigan's reading of *Comus*. Much about the masque recommends such a reading. For Freud, a child's internalization of parental authority – the installation of the superego – is the developmental consequence of the Oedipus complex. In Milton's masque, the Earl of Bridgewater's children appear in the forest alone, at night, away from parental authority, and with only the light of their own consciences to guide them. The Lady's temptation by an enchanter who brandishes an astonishing wand is nevertheless "secretly" witnessed by an audience that includes her parents, particularly her father enthroned with his "new-entrusted Scepter" (line 36).

It is not merely the theatrical conditions that make an Oedipal reading seem plausible, but also the pertinence of the masque to the particulars of young Milton's life. For Kerrigan, the Lady, positively,

70

and Comus, negatively, each signifies an aspect of the poet's psyche. The Lady's climactic seizure while under Comus's control suggests Milton's prolonged paralysis within the Oedipal dilemma, while the evil enchanter's desire for the Lady indicates the ordinary, final resolution of Oedipal frustration – mating with a woman reminiscent of the mother. It seems quite telling that Comus should register the resemblance between Circe and Lady Alice the moment he hears his victim sing (lines 252–65). The presentation of the "normal" Comus as the *villain* of the piece thus apparently signifies Milton's unusually stubborn and self-righteous response to Oedipal trauma. Through regressive denial of desire and renunciation of sexuality the poet allegedly transmuted forbidden desire and filial vulnerability into a hidden spring of artistic virtue: the sacred complex.[2]

The last chapter maintained that Oedipal anxieties did not dominate Milton's personality, poetry, and religion. This chapter offers an alternative reconstruction of the poet's personality, as well as an alternative reading of the masque, one that suggests a different set of conditions for his poetic creativity.[3]

The portrait of Milton at age 10 reveals a delicate, sensitive face over a fine, lace-frilled collar. The gold-trimmed, black doublet wraps him tight and signals a pampered gentility and almost aristocratic luxury strikingly inconsistent with the severity of his properly Puritan, close-cropped hair. Parker's assessment is tantalizing:

The mother who dressed her son in such a charming costume may have surpassed her neighbors in piety and charitable works, but she was also an Elizabethan woman, a merchant-tailor's daughter, who loved rich and beautiful things. (p. 8)

Parker suggests that the two sides of Sara Milton found a synthesis in the distinctive personal style of the son she dressed so lavishly: "he grew up to be always careful of dress and speech, hypersensitive concerning his personal integrity, nice of manners and of morals" (p. 8). Subsequent criticism has ignored Parker's too brief speculation, however. I want to investigate further the divergent maternal impulses that make the little boy in the portrait seem so at odds with himself.

In an Oedipal reading of *Comus*, Sara Milton figures only as a negated object of desire – the biographical source of the Lady's devotion to chastity. Even in a patriarchal culture, however, early relations between mother and child form the basis of all future

Figure 1   *Portrait of John Milton at the Age of Ten*. Attributed to Cornelius Johnson,
1593–1661/2

psychological developments.[4] The mother means practically everything
to the newborn child. Later, the modified configuration of the Oedipus
complex and particularly the male child's fateful competition with the
father are thought to circumscribe and skew her significance. Hence,
for Freud, a main consequence of Oedipal conflict is that the father
replaces the mother as the external focus of mental life.

The mature Milton's description of his deceased mother associates her with charity: "my mother [was] a woman of purest reputation, celebrated throughout the neighborhood for her acts of charity" (*CP* 4, 612). It would appear that *charity* represented Sara Milton's characteristic virtue, at least from the poet's perspective. And, as Kerrigan points out, Milton would have remembered Spenser's allegorization of charity as a mother (*Charissa*) overflowing with the milk of human kindness, inexhaustibly nursing her babes.[5] In *Comus*, such intimate, maternal love is a virtue conspicuous in the Lady for its displacement by cool chastity. The diagnosis is that the Oedipal poet, cowed by his father into repudiating desire for the mother, negated her characteristic virtue of charity and instead established chastity as his heroine's signature trait.

Unfortunately, the standard translation of Milton's testimonial to his mother has proven misleading. *"Matre probatissima, & eleemosynis per viciniam potissimum nota"* is more precisely rendered "a mother of approved character, and noted throughout the neighborhood for *almsgiving"* (*CW* 8, 18; my translation and emphasis). In light of the official, quasi-oratorical context of this description in *The Second Defense*, Milton's phrasing seems deliberately modeled on Cicero's formulaic testimonial to a deceased woman of good reputation as *"probatissimam feminam."*[6] *Probatissima* derives from the passive participle of *probo*, "to regard as good or right" and, like the rest of the sentence, insistently places Sara Milton in public view; she was *seen* to be good. *Eleemosyna*, on the other hand, derives from ecclesiastical usage. Its classical antecedent (*eleos*) is Greek for mercy, that least Roman of virtues, and from church Latin it had infiltrated medieval English as "alms." It occurs a number of times in *de doctrina*, where both Sumner and Carey translate it as "almsgiving" or simply "alms" (*CW* 17, 372–73; *CP* 6, 789).

Had Milton wanted to identify his mother with the comprehensive virtue of Christian love or charity in general, he would surely have used *caritas* instead of *eleemosyna*.[7] But in the eulogy of anyone less than divine the use of so exalted and comprehensive a term would have fractured decorum. In his theological treatise, Milton, orthodox for once, analyzed charity as the divine wellspring of all moral good, encompassing both neighbor-directed virtues like almsgiving and self-directed ones like chastity. Chastity in Milton's analysis does not stand *opposed* to charity, in other words, but, like almsgiving, is an instance of it: chastity is charity directed toward the self, though it expresses social responsibility; almsgiving is charity directed toward neighbors, though it expresses personal abundance (*CP* 6,726–27, 789–92). An esteemed

woman could perform an act of charity just as well by refusing sex with
a lecherous neighbor as by giving an impoverished one alms. In
describing his mother as well regarded and openhanded, therefore,
Milton probably intends a rhetorically conventional depiction of her as
a modest exemplar of both aspects of charity, with *probatissima*
suggesting the matronly version of chastity. An upstanding woman, she
donated money to the needy. That is all. The voluptuous image of
Spenser's Charissa nursing her babies overwhelms the nice limits of
Milton's Latin diction and iconographically insists on those tender
mercies of maternal love that his official description excludes.

In *Comus*, the association of motherhood with physicality and
domestic intimacy belongs solely to the enchanter. Yet his words do not
evoke an image of the mother as an object of desire, as would seem
logical in an Oedipal context, but rather as a lavish source of life and
provision. Like Sara Milton, Comus's Mother Nature takes special care
to "deck her Sons," though doing so requires the labor of "millions of
spinning Worms" (lines 717, 715). When the enchanter speaks of her in
sexual terms, it is her excessive fertility that fascinates him rather than
the warmth and tenderness of her love.

> in her own loyns
> She hutch't th'all-worshipt ore, and precious gems
> To store her children with   (lines 718–20)

Her generative depths are figured forth as a treasure house dedicated
to her progeny.

The reproductive geology by which the maternal Earth generates
precious metal and gems is no freak of Comus's fancy. Milton
consistently worked it into his fictional premises and in so doing
exploited the alchemical science of his day to elaborate the metapho-
rical motherhood of Earth. Just as he believed that the sun ripened wits
within the womb of the mind, so he portrayed gems and minerals as
conceived of moisture by light and born out of the earth.[8] In *Paradise
Lost*, the sun is characterized as "Arch-chimic," its light capable of
producing subterranean effects by its "vertuous touch" (3, 609–12).
Satan's production of gunpowder by interference in underground
elements' gestation, as I further argue in the next chapter, epitomizes
evil artifice in the epic. In *Comus*, Circe, mythographically regarded as
an offspring of sunshine and water, is elementally related to gems that
gestate underground.[9] Her elemental associations may explain why

Comus becomes so elaborately maternal and reproductive in his imagery when he speaks of blazing riches below.

Comus's speech thus plays off a common seventeenth-century model of geological processes as procreative. He imagines that the virtue of reflected starlight emitted by a blazing surfeit of underground jewels will encourage the birthlike emergence of a monstrous, subterranean race from the deep "so bestudd with Stars" (line 733).[10] The light emitted by neglected underground gems would temper those creatures who ordinarily live beneath the surface and they, like the "materials dark and crude" "temper'd" by the touch of "Heavens ray," would venture forth into "the ambient light" (*PL* 6, 478–81). Note that in this context *temperance* is not a static moral virtue but a natural, developmental process. Unless creatures of the sea and air are indulged in, Comus insists that they, like underground gems, would breed without check and transgress their elemental limits. Nature would everywhere produce offspring beyond the limits of her capacity to support them. The inference? Children who refuse to consume nature's procreative bounty verge on matricide, leaving her to teem herself to death, "strangl'd with her waste fertility" (line 729). This anxious vision of nature's prodigious fertility discloses a nexus of Milton's life and art. A more wholesome but still burgeoning version of the theme influences his descriptions of Eden and provokes Adam and Eve's concern, climacteric to the epic narrative, over the Garden's "wanton growth . . . / Tending to wilde" (9, 211–12).

In contradicting this vision of an incessantly procreative nature, the Lady takes a cooler attitude, one reminiscent of Milton's testimonial to his mother:

> Imposter do not charge most innocent nature,
> As if she would her children should be riotous
> With her abundance, she good cateress
> Means her provision onely to the good
> That live according to her sober laws
> And holy dictate of spare Temperance:
> If every just man that now pines with want
> Had but a moderate and beseeming share
> Of that which lewdly-pamper'd Luxury
> Now heaps upon som few with vast excess,
> Natures full blessings would be well dispenc't
> In unsuperfluous eeven proportion,
> And she no whit encomber'd with her store. (lines 762–74)

As the illuminating Leah Marcus observes, the Lady represents a temperate mean between unacceptable extremes. Politically, she takes a middle position between those Puritans who argued against festivity altogether and the coercive governmental prescription of festive ritual as a communal opiate. The Lady sings ravishingly and dances too; her objections are to "ill manag'd Merriment," "wanton dance," "swill'd insolence" (lines 172, 176, 178).[11]

Similarly, were the Lady in charge of sober Nature's modest provisions, the economic extremes of crushing poverty and miserly wealth would be quickly mitigated. Almsgiving would quickly translate into a general redistribution of wealth – at least among the good and just. Yet the Lady's recommendation of temperance is itself somewhat extreme, at least rhetorically. In striking contrast to Comus's bent for reproductive figures as he advocates luxurious indulgence, the Lady completely avoids generative imagery. For her, nature is not so much a mother as a *cateress* – a buyer or purchasing agent in the original sense of the word. What better epithet for Nature so described, or for the Lady herself, than "*probatissima & eleemosynis nota*"?

Both Comus's and the Lady's visions of maternal nature are Milton's, and I wish to consider the possibility that they reflect a deep-seated, ambivalent fascination with feminine procreative power. In certain respects, the Lady's rehabilitation, or sterilization, of Mother Nature recalls the history of those prominent classical deities with whom the Elder Brother identifies his sister – Diana and Minerva. Philip Slater has argued that the classical Greeks' antagonism toward matriarchal figures moved them to redefine and narrow the original import of Artemis (Diana) and Athena (Minerva).[12]

In my opinion, pressures analogous to those Slater sees shaping the culture of fifth-century (BC) Athens also affected that of seventeenth-century England. If it nevertheless seems vagrant to draw on a sociological analysis of classical Athens to illuminate a Renaissance English poet, we should recall that the culture of ancient Greece captivated young Milton. Basic to *Comus* is the same Platonic eroticism that dominates his self-conception in the 1620s and 1630s, as his correspondence with Charles Diodati amply demonstrates.[13] Deep sympathy and intimate knowledge drew Milton to classical Athens, despite the intervening centuries.

The patriarchal Greeks of the first millennium, BC, suppressed the orgiastic and procreative aspects of the old goddesses. Yet traces of

Artemis's past remained, at least through Roman times. The Christian world knew that she held sway at Ephesus as a mother deity and birth goddess whom "all Asia and the world worshippeth" (Acts 19:27). Early myths about Athena, a figure who seems to have descended from a Cretan snake-divinity, portray her as the mother of Athens' first king, Erichthonius (or Erectheus) – half-man and half-serpent. As early depictions of her aegis corroborate, he was supposed to have retreated into its snaky folds before he became king of Athens and instituted his mother's cult. Although the Athenians ultimately denied Athena's maternity and reworked the myths concerning Erichthonius, serpentine vestiges of the original story and the matriarchal cult remained, even in Athenian religious life. In her role as protector of heroes and cities the goddess also retained a maternal aspect. Athena herself, however, like Artemis, was transformed into a forever youthful virgin – at least as worshipped in Athens.[14]

The origins of these goddesses were probably largely unknown to Milton. Nevertheless, in a moment of uncanny fidelity to the patriarchal Greeks' revisionism, the Elder Brother chooses precisely those artifacts that preserve traces of ancient fertility cults to symbolize the power of chastity. Diana's "dred bow" (line 441), cited by the Elder Brother as an armament of chastity, once stood for the new moon, the phase during which dark rites like those Comus commences in honor of Cotytto and Hecate might be performed (lines 128–44). As Marija Gimbutas has claimed, "Artemis and Hecate are one."[15] The paralyzing power of "that snaky-headed *Gorgon* sheild / That wise *Minerva* wore, unconquer'd Virgin," the Elder Brother interprets as an effect of "rigid looks of Chast austerity" (lines 447–48, 450). Yet "wise *Minerva*" received the Medusa's head in her aegis from the grateful hero Perseus, whose story may obliquely record an early triumph (during the second millennium BC) of Indo-European invaders and their patriarchal religion over a goddess-worshipping indigenous population.[16]

According to Ovid's late retelling, Medusa had been a virgin devotee of Minerva until Neptune raped her. The victim was then punished for the pollution she had undergone. Minerva transformed her beautiful hair into writhing snakes (*Metamorphoses* 4, 795–803). Later, Perseus, equipped by the virgin goddess and acting on his mother's behalf, decapitated Medusa to crown her punishment. Milton alludes to Perseus's divine armament when in one draft of his *Letter to a Friend* he characterizes his scholarly seclusion during the early 1630s as a Neptune's helmet of invisibility (*CP* 1, 319). (We will return to this point later.) Stealthy Perseus used his Neptune's helmet to elude the vengeance of the Gorgons after he had decapitated Medusa.

This is not the place for extensive consideration of the Medusa myth or its cultural implications.[17] Yet the story of her origins does highlight one of the more perplexing problems in *Comus*: whether it is possible to be an innocent victim. Mythological victimizations, including abductions, rapes, and dismemberments, figure prominently in *Comus* and throughout Milton's writings. Yet, the philosophy elaborated by the Elder Brother and the presence of the Attendant Spirit suggest that evil agents cannot harm virtuous maidens. Sabrina's death by drowning, however, and the Lady's own continued paralysis indicate that matters are more complex than the Elder Brother allows. Ironically, Medusa's rapist, Neptune, is presented in *Comus* as responsible for the installation of the Earl of Bridgewater as Lord President of Wales (lines 18–36). Furthermore, relevant local contexts for *Comus*, according to Leah Marcus, include rape cases that reflect on the Earl's concern that justice be done on behalf of such victims.[18] Yet the theodicy-minded Elder Brother, quite in concert with the classical Greeks, perceives in the mythological sign of a rape and subsequent murder – the Medusa's head in Athena's aegis – the power of virginity to protect itself.

The punitive transition of Medusa from beauteous maidenhood to snaky-headed rape victim, moreover, was typically interpreted as the consequence of her unchastity, and not Neptune's. George Sandys, for example, took her as a representation of "lust and the inchantments of bodily beauty."[19] Her fate recalls that of Skylla, who also appears both in *Comus* and, by way of Sin, in *Paradise Lost*. Despite Ovid's insistence on her innocence, Sandys construed Skylla's metamorphosis, inflicted by a jealous Circe, also as the consequence of unchastity.[20] For Milton, significantly, it is Sin's transition to motherhood that directly causes the terrible distortion of her "nether shape" (*PL* 2, 784). Her first-born, Death, tears his way through her entrails and his thronging Cerberean progeny repeatedly return there to torment her from within.[21]

Procreation brings death. The common Renaissance association of maternity and death found expression in Milton as early as his *Epitaph on the Marchioness of Winchester*, where he imagines that "*Atropos* for *Lucina* came," killing an unborn son in the womb and his mother with him: "the languisht Mothers Womb / Was not long a living Tomb" (lines 28, 33–34). If the link of womb and tomb was already commonplace, Milton nonetheless added a twist of his own. In *Comus*, we have seen, mother nature threatens to teem herself to death, writhing with life even in death – like the Medusa's head. Sin's conjunction with Death similarly produces the manifold confusion and stunning noise of the hellhounds that fix their mother in her fate. They are "hourly conceiv'd / And hourly born" (2, 796–97). The same connection appears even in the laudatory verses on Shakespeare, where a master spirit's potent natural genius bereaves the reader's womb-like fancy of itself. Paralysis sets in as astonished readers with swarming imaginations freeze into "marble with too much conceaving" (line 15).

One possible explanation for Renaissance authors' fascination with and reversals of the plain meaning of the Medusa's head – that she is the victim not the agent of violence – depends on the psychoanalytic interpretation of it and the paralysis it produces. Freud took the Medusa's head to be symbolic of female genitalia, and the immobility it caused he interpreted as terror of castration brought on by the male's presumed conception of women as castrated men.[22] Others have argued, however, that the male's response to female genitalia reflects a more complex set of attitudes toward sexual difference than that proposed by Freud. These attitudes include fascination with and envy of woman's procreative power as well as dread at the prospect of being enveloped by the mother, after the fashion of Erichthonius hidden in Minerva's aegis.[23]

Otto Weininger described the ambivalent prospect of engulfment as "the alluring abyss of annihilation," reflecting a morbid obsession that in *Paradise Lost* Milton's rebel angels frequently exhibit, especially Belial. It is Belial who inspires the mobs "that night / In Gibeah, when the hospitable door / Expos'd a Matron to avoid worse rape" (1, 503–05), an allusion to the astonishingly violent and troubling biblical story in which a "matron" is surrendered to preserve her husband. The next day he finds her corpse left on the threshold and later dismembers it, sending the pieces throughout Israel as a cry for vengeance (Judges 19:11–30). It is insistently "when Night / Dark'ns the Streets" that Belial inspires his "Sons" in Sodom and Gibeah, and it is Belial who publicly expresses the fear of being "swallowd up and lost / In the wide womb of uncreated night" (1, 500–01; 2, 149–50).[24] Satan exploits this dread of the dark abyss in recounting the dangers that must be passed on the way to the new world: "the void profound / Of unessential Night receives him ... / Wide gaping, and with utter loss of being / Threat'ns him, plung'd in that abortive gulf" (2, 438–41; see also 10, 475).

If the masculine response to the Medusa's head seems often to involve castration anxiety, it may therefore proceed as much from the prospect of the mother as the *agent* of castration – by envelopment – as from the spectacle of her as victim.[25] Such paralyzing anxiety could also represent a paradoxical, concurrent wish to resemble the mother *through* castration. Bruno Bettelheim argues in recounting common themes of initiation rituals that such simultaneous envy and fear of the opposite sex are often a psychological basis of adolescents' rites of passage into adult sexual roles.[26] In these rites, symbolic castrations are performed on young men, as if by resemblance they could lay claim to feminine procreative power. Moreover, as Bettelheim notes, "castration as an institution, appeared comparatively late in history among relatively sophisticated peoples and ... it was performed to please or to make the castrate more like overpowering mother figures."[27]

Yet why should Milton's relationship with his mother have been fraught? Although I wish to suggest that the Lady's paralysis in *Comus* reflects maternal influences more than paternal, Sara Milton herself grew up in a patriarchal society, one in which male supremacy and the restrictive denigration of women were already becoming systematic. Yet, women nevertheless held real if theoretically limited power. Within an early-modern productive household like Milton's, as Christopher Hill reminds us, "the wife had a position of authority over servants, apprentices and children, though in subordination to her husband."[28] (A similar arrangement shaped mothering in classical Greece.[29]) Parker worries that "perhaps Milton as a boy spent too much time in the company of a doting mother and an older sister"(p. 8). What was the tenor of her "doting"?

A long-awaited male child may have represented the means for realizing dreams of consequence that Sara Milton as a woman in seventeenth-century England would not ordinarily have been permitted outside the household, even as she held sway within it. In such a situation, an intense narcissistic involvement with one's child is often the result, a type of psychological entanglement characterized by Freud in terms that recall the Lady's aspirations in *Comus*: "the laws of nature and society shall be abrogated in [her] favor; [she] shall ... be the center and core of creation." She becomes a repository for the fondest wish of all, "the most touchy point in the narcissistic system, the immortality of the ego."[30] Along with those high aspirations, a mother in Sara Milton's position might also have communicated a certain resentment to her first son. Sara Milton and her husband waited a long time before she conceived that first, precious, male child. In accordance with scripture, his birth would surely have been taken as a spiritual validation of her – simply because he was a boy.

Although most parents have a degree of narcissistic interest in their children, the stakes seem to have been particularly high for young Milton. His modern biographers unanimously depict him as the focus of his parents' attention, hopes, and even religious ambitions. For children molded under such circumstances, the pressure can seem unendurable: "they [seem] pivotal in their families – the only child, the brilliant child, 'the genius' – and thus [carry] the burden of fulfilling family expectations."[31] In contrast to the prohibitions of the punitive superego, the grandiose expectations that heralded the birth of the young poet would at least have been positive, if exaggerated and burdensome.

On the other hand, the child absorbs and incorporates a mother's unrealistic hopes and any ambivalence almost as nourishment. The consequence can be a deep uncertainty over one's own boundaries coupled with the conviction that one must – almost as a condition of this uncertain self's existence – fulfill great expectations. Such a dilemma seems to me exemplified in young Milton's development. As Freud observed, newborn infants do not recognize any distinction between themselves and the mothers on whom their existence depends.[32] Indeed, in the pre-Oedipal scenario, a strong paternal presence can aid the male child in forging a separate, gendered identity and protect him from the threat of absorption by the mother.[33] Without the separation from the mother that a father can help establish, the narcissistic child takes the idealized version of itself, derived from the time of its original, oceanic union with the mother, as the pattern by which to define itself and all other objects of desire. At every stage of development, of course, reality denies the child this omnipotent, omnipresent, immortal version of the self, though the child always retains a nostalgia for it.

In terms of psychoanalytic theory, I am arguing that Milton's personality reflects a narcissistic, pre-Oedipal problematic more than an Oedipal one.[34] As I noted at the beginning of this chapter, early relations of a child with its mother form "the phylogenetic foundation" for all future developments.[35] Considering typical, middle-class, domestic practice in seventeenth-century England, we may suppose that the maternal psychological foundation would have been firmer and more influential in Milton's historical milieu than in Freud's or our own. Though they had no effective place in masculine affairs outside the household, mothers like Sara Milton oversaw their children's training and discipline usually up to the age of 7, and in Milton's case later if, as Parker supposes, Sara Milton was responsible for the charming costume worn in his early portrait.[36]

In societies where mothers are boxed in simply because they are women, Slater remarks, "the mother does not respond to the [male] child as a separate person, but as both an expression of and a cure" for her own frustration. The consequences for the child are intensified if the box in which the mother is kept includes compensatory control over her husband's children. Hence, Freud's claim that mother–son relations are typically least "liable to disaster" and largely uncomplicated by egoistic motivation may well be the most sentimentally inaccurate statement that the father of psychoanalysis ever made.[37]

Mother–son relations certainly do not run smoothly in the mythology of patriarchal Athens. Hera (Juno), unlike Artemis and Athena, underwent no transformation to virginal youth but instead became the often deceived wife of the father of the gods. To avenge herself, she vindictively pursued male heroes, usually Zeus's bastards – her mortal step-children – and set an example for the legendary mothers whose anger at a husband meant woe for *his* children. Classical tragedy, so intimately known and honored by Milton, teems with mothers dangerous to heroes and their sons, ax-wielding Clytemnestra and barbarian sorceress Medea, most famously. The story of Orestes, a father-avenging matricide, far overshadows that of the incestuous patricide Oedipus as a central cultural myth among the Greeks. Key to the defense of Orestes from his dead mother's avenging furies is the denial by Apollo, supported by Athena, that mothers have any procreative entitlement, shaping influence, or legitimate expectation of special loyalty from the children they carry for their husbands.[38]

The corpus of Milton's poetry, too, is more remarkable for the number and the troubling emotional impact of its mothers than of its fathers, especially mothers of dead or doomed children: the mother of the Fair Infant, the Marchioness of Winchester, the Muse that bore Orpheus, the poet's late espoused Saint, Eve, Mary, and of course, Sin. Milton early and apparently easily sympathized with the unalloyed grief, the "sorrows wild," of a mother bereft of her daughter; it occasioned his first sustained moment of poetic power in English.[39]

The search of Ceres for her lost daughter, moreover, lived powerfully in his imagination.[40] The emotions that might greet the loss of a son never came so easily to Milton, and in their complexity and inconsistency were perhaps always "above his years." Even Mary's anguish in *Paradise Regain'd* arises from more complex emotions than simple sorrow at the dimly foreseen loss of a beloved child:

> O what avails me now that honour high
> To have conceiv'd of God, or that salute
> Hale highly favour'd, among women blest;
> While I to sorrows am no less advanc't
>
> . . .
>
> This is my favour'd lot,
> My Exaltation to Afflictions high.   (2, 66–92)

Inseparable from Mary's concern for her son is an injured, almost bitter, consciousness that she has been misled by the promise of exaltation and favor. Patience eventually prevents this ironic murmur, but the tinge of recrimination and resentment lacks scriptural basis.

The immediate literary precursor of Mary's speech occurs in Spenser's story of Marinell, who in book 3, canto 4 of the *Faerie Queene* receives an apparently fatal wound from chaste Britomart's spear and is mourned by a mother who calls her son her image:

> Dear image of my selfe (she said) that is
> The wretched sonne of wretched mother borne,
> Is this thine high advauncement, o is this
> Th' immortal name, with which thee yet unborne
> Thy Gransire *Nereus* promist to adorne?   (st. 36, 1–5)

If Milton does recall this passage from Spenser in depicting Christ's mother, his recollection characteristically differs from the original. Marinell's mother bemoans her son's loss of a grand destiny; Mary laments the "favour'd lot" she thought due *her* through her son's greatness. I suspect that for the young Milton, it may sometimes have seemed that maternal affection would have been more certain and less conditional, life itself less perplexing and burdensome, if only he had been born a female.

As intriguing as psycho-biographical speculation can be, we will never know the real situation in the house on Bread Street. We can, however, ascertain the situation in *Comus*. There, though men are nominally in charge, they are functionally irrelevant. Male authority appears mainly as a passive point of reference – a locus for praise:

> if all the world
> Should in a pet of temperance feed on Pulse,
> Drink the clear stream, and nothing wear but Freize,
> Th'all-giver would be unthank't, would be unprais'd,
> Not half his riches known, and yet despis'd,
> And we should serve him as a grudging master,
> As a penurious niggard of his wealth,
> And live like Natures bastards, not her sons.   (lines 720–27)

Like Lear, whose *hysterica passio* and "fit of the mother" are provoked by the ingratitude of his children, Comus insists that to reason needs is also to ration recognition, cheating generous superfluity of acknowledgment.[41] The wealth Comus refuses to slight, though, is that of a master, not a father. The shift in line 727 away from the masculine "giver," in whose service "we" belong, registers us not as "th'all giver's" offspring, but nature's.

Comus recommends conspicuous consumption and surfeit as expressive behavior – praise through too much. On the other hand, the Lady, complaining of "ill manag'd Merriment," ruefully observes that excessive harvest celebrations "thank the gods amiss" (lines 172, 177). These tones of regret yield to harsher accents when she responds to Comus. Anticipating Milton's later attacks on "canary-sucking and swan-eating" prelates (*CP* 1, 549), she insists that spare temperance would leave "the giver ... better thank't" (line 775)

> His praise due paid, for swinish gluttony
> Ne're looks to Heav'n amidst his gorgeous feast,
> But with besotted base ingratitude
> Cramms, and blasphemes his feeder.   (lines 776–79)

Despite their opposition, the Lady and Comus agree in defining the masculine "giver" as one toward whom we must behave gratefully, rather than as one who is the source of life. The facts of nativity leave little room for mother–child equivocation. It is an indisputable, material relationship, and relation stands. The recipient of gifts, on the other hand, can behave in any way that can be construed as grateful.[42] And when that kind of rhetorical framing was called for, Milton never seems to have been coy or tongue-tied, no matter who he was addressing nor how counter-intuitive his argument.

Flexibility in interpretation decreases markedly, however, when the issue of debate becomes the Lady's own connection to and expression of the natural realm. Comus recognizes her exorbitant beauty as a natural symbol of excess, "nature's brag" (line 745). His orthodox and familiar argument holds that the Lady would express miserly self-love were she to withhold her physical charms from currency or deny the significance of these insignia: "there was another meaning in these gifts" (line 754). It generally goes unnoticed that although Comus wants the Lady to participate in the natural world of her origins, the rhetoric of his request downshifts with a lurch from his preceding representation of Nature as feverishly prolific. His recommendation of "mutual and partak'n bliss," though it may be a posture adopted solely for the purposes of his temptation, is hardly incompatible with temperance (line 741). Consistency calls for him to speak in terms a little less tame.

Whereas Comus moves from recommendation of excess to a plea for moderate indulgence, the Lady follows a reverse trajectory. After splashing the cold water of nothing-too-much on Comus's equation of opulence and praise, she heats up while refusing to explain her transcendence of nature's ways. The enchanter's moment of modera-tion she opposes with an inexpressible devotion to abstinence. An audience of Milton's contemporaries (and most moderns, too) would surely applaud the aristocratic lady's rejection of the lecherous en-chanter.[43] The propriety of a 14-year-old girl struggling to preserve her virginity is not at issue. The concern here is with the transcendental significance that attaches to virginity in the masque: virginity registered as a physical means to spiritual exaltation. There is after all something disproportionate in *how* the Lady rejects her tempter:

> Yet should I try, the uncontrouled worth
> Of this pure cause would kindle my rapt spirits
> To such a flame of sacred vehemence,
> That dumb things would be mov'd to sympathize,
> And the brute Earth would lend her nerves and shake.
>
> (lines 793–97)

The Lady's potential for "vehemence" – expressed by threatening silence – is as defiant of "sober law" as the natural profusion to which Comus had so amply and lavishly given tongue earlier.[44]

By turns, then, the Lady and the enchanter are in their speeches excessive and moderate, moderate and excessive. Yet this chiasmic inconsistency is more apparent than real. For both, moderation is prone to slide into excess, not the other way round. At first, Comus marvels at the Lady's singing and wishes to make her his queen. In the end, he offers no coronation but tempts her with the "lushious liquor" that would transform her into another one of his herd (line 652). What room for moderation among those who "roule with pleasure in a sensual stie" (line 77)?

On the other hand, Comus is quite right to see the Lady as "scorning the unexempt condition / By which all mortal frailty must subsist" (lines 685–86). If the Earth may be described as a "pin-fold," escape from the society of "ougly-headed Monsters" requires more than moderation (lines 7, 695). The only way to be distinguished from the rest of the herd is to live the life removed and refuse even to "strive to keep up a frail, and Feaverish being" (lines 7–8). "*Spare* Temperance" shades into oxymoron, as if "a moderate and beseeming share" in practice meant "the lean and sallow Abstinence" (lines 767, 769, 709; italics mine). With defilement defined as contamination from the outside, seekers of eternity would be wisest simply not to partake of any produce "of this Sin-worn mould" (line 17). For both Comus and the Lady it is an all-or-nothing world, with no place left for temperance. The opposition between them is characteristic of the all-or-nothing paradox of narcissism, in which "total fusion and stratospheric isolation become equally essential and equally terrifying."[45]

While I agree that Comus, like the Lady, may be seen as a possible version of young Milton, it seems to me that he represents not an Oedipally normal offspring, as in Kerrigan's analysis, but a son entirely subsumed by his mother's influence. The specifics of his vocabulary, his festive attitudes, his charming cup, as Leah Marcus has shown, amount to a devastating portrait of clerics in the Church of England, the Mother Church whose service, I would guess, Sara Milton, perhaps more than John Milton Sr., desired her son to enter.[46] In describing the extraordinary rage that animates Milton's anti-prelatical tracts, Kerrigan imputes it to the poet's prolonged and difficult Oedipal trauma.[47] Yet it may have been the *probatissima* mother, more than her husband, whose fondest dream was for her precious first son to join the church, thereby magnifying her "approved character."

According to this scenario, when the young poet stuck at playing his part the resultant tension could well have brought on the long hiatus in his parents' country home, where he voluntarily became a "helplesse, pusilanimous & unweapon'd creature," as he admits in his *Letter to a Friend*, adopting the delaying tactic of a bookish stasis as his Neptune's helmet of invisibility against maternal vengeance (*CP* 1, 319). Milton was twenty-five when he wrote the masque as well as the revealing letter.[48] Heavily revised, it reflects the poet's troubled awareness that he has entered the "tyme of a mans life" when "the desire of house &

family of his owne" should motivate him (1, 319). In light of his use of "weapon'd" in *The Doctrine and Discipline of Divorce* ("weapon'd to the lest possibilitie of sensuall enjoyment"), it appears that Milton's years of study in the English countryside may have been felt by him as a kind of self-imposed castration (*CP* 2, 236). Whether or not we accept the speculative notion of Milton's vow of virginity, he clearly was struck by the notion that one might make oneself a eunuch "for the sake of the kingdom of heaven," (Matt. 19:11–12; 1 Cor. 7:7–9).[49]

By doing nothing active with his life, and thus in a patriarchal society becoming like his mother, he could ward off the emotional consequences that visible, definite opposition to her ambitions for him might occasion. He froze, or rather, like Erichthonius, he hid within the maternal aegis. That Medusa represented for Milton a paralyzing power over one's destiny is consistent with the role he assigns her in hell where "with *Gorgonian* terror" she refuses to allow the devils their only hope of change – the alluring waters of oblivion (*PL* 2, 611). Unwilling to be what they are supposed to be, the devils are not allowed to become anything else either, though they are ceaselessly tantalized by the possibility of an exit from their fix.

It was not until several years after Sara Milton's death that Milton found himself in a historical situation that allowed overt opposition to the church. He leapt into anti-prelatical controversy with barely controlled anger, but not I think of an Oedipal cast. He explicitly objects to the prelates' rhetorical use of "the awefull notion of a mother" to force those who wish to reform the church to submit blindly (*CP* 1, 728). Indeed, he at one point compares himself to Electra in disputing against the prelates: "a wise Virgin answer'd her wicked Mother" (*CP* 1, 905).

Though wicked, Comus is of course no mother, even if he does confront a wise virgin. Yet his prelatical history begins with maternal desire:

> This Nymph that gaz'd upon his clustring locks,
> With Ivy berries wreath'd, and his blithe youth,
> Had by him, ere he parted thence, a Son
> Much like his Father, but his Mother more.   (lines 54–57)

Bacchus represents merely a passive means to Comus's begetting, as indeed Milton's own father does in *ad Patrem* (lines 61–62). Circe shapes the enchanter in her own image and likeness. The "charms / And ... wily trains" he hopes will stock him "with as fair a herd as graz'd /

About [his] Mother" are a maternal inheritance (lines 150–53). He is "deep skill'd in all his mothers witcheries," indeed, "excells his Mother at her mighty Art" (lines 523, 63). The deities the enchanter calls upon – Cotytto, Hecat' – are feminine (lines 129, 135). The setting of "thickest gloom" he requires is, in a remarkably malignant but vigorous choice of verbs, "spet" by "the Dragon woom / Of Stygian darknes" (lines 131–32). Despite his much remarked wand, therefore (which Circe also classically and prominently employs) the sexual overtones of his enchantment are in fact both masculine and feminine: "[I] wind me into the easie-hearted man, / And hugg him into snares" (lines 163–64). He is a hermaphroditic serpent.

If we look past *Comus* for a moment, we find that intimacy with women in Milton's poetry often involves a maternal aspect, and when it does, it consistently sets up an emotional predicament. Nor does this predicament appear to bear any relation to paternal law. It rather reflects a dread that once such intimacy is entered, it will become an inescapable snare and a kind of death. Sexuality is the area of life in which this fear, one of boundary violation, is most frequently registered.[50] The fact that humans are not hermaphroditic, and are therefore incomplete, is the foundation on which narcissistic anxieties over sexual desire build.

As Adam observes, the male needs a partner to "manifest / His single imperfection" (*PL* 8, 422–23). On the other hand, any illusion of completeness would of necessity be shattered by the sexual act. If Milton did entertain the intention to remain a virgin, I would argue that it was on this psychological ground. Moreover, this anxiety over boundaries may explain something about his marriage choices. Men whose relations with the mother are problematic tend to place a high value on virginity, a condition that is seen to mitigate the peril of being swallowed up by a mother figure.[51] Richardson was more insightful than precise in recounting Milton's stated preference for virgins: "he would never think of taking a Widow."[52] Hence, the imagined approach of women, as in the prospect of embraces and kisses from naked Lady Science in *ad Patrem*, or even the attempted embrace of his dead wife in Sonnet 23, arouses uneasiness in Milton, or at least diffidence. In the case of Lady Science, as we saw last chapter, he contemplates flight: "From behind a cloud science comes visibly and uncovered bends her clear features for kisses: if I do not choose to flee; if the touch is not distressful" (*ad Patrem* lines 90–92).

Similarly, in Sonnet 23, his dead wife's approach inspires a sudden bolt of activity: "But O as to embrace me she enclin'd / I wak't, she fled, and day brought back my night" (lines 13–14). Milton's description of his late wife by reference to post-partum church rituals – "Mine as whom washt from spot of child-bed taint" – has often exercised critics debating which of Milton's first two wives is meant (line 5).[53] In either case, however, it fits with his characteristic inclination to represent and address women as mothers. Gerald Hammond notes that Milton in the sonnet is "almost entirely passive"; "his one act is to wake up." This one act may be understood as "heroic resistance" against the temptation to let death take him, rather than face each cold dark morning so as to deliver an epic conceived in the realm of dreams.[54] No one can doubt that this is a sonnet of poignant love and loss, but it is also one of heroic resolution to go on living in the darkness of this world rather than relax into the next.

Rude awakenings and failed embraces are standard topoi of heroic literature. Achilles, Odysseus, and Aeneas qualify in one way or another as Milton's precursors.[55] Indeed, when it comes to telling the tale of paradise, Milton will, though with important differences, place Adam, too, among his antecedents:

> She disappeerd, and left me dark, I wak'd
> To find her, or for ever to deplore
> Her loss. (8, 478–80)

Yet the sonnet's characteristic variations on received traditions operate in significant contrast to the classic situation. In the case of Milton's antecedents, the visionary hero attempts the embrace and fails; the sonnet reverses these roles. The failed embrace nevertheless establishes, as it does in the antecedents, the cost of commitment or re-commitment to a heroic enterprise definitive of the hero's identity. If, as seems likely, the reference is to his second wife, the maternal associations may reflect Milton's concurrent efforts as mother of a great poem. To complete the labor of a heroic enterprise, Milton seems to have followed a pattern of pushing away from a maternal presence and appropriating her role for himself.

In Milton's major works perhaps the clearest instance of this pattern appears in *Samson Agonistes*. Admitting that he is helpless and blind, "in most things as a child," Samson describes as "perfet thraldom" Dalila's offer of "nursing diligence" (lines 942, 946, 924). The richly dressed Dalila is Samson's Comus. Having once succumbed to them, Samson now despises her "trains," "ginns," "toils," and "fair enchanted cup" (lines 932–34). He fears her more than he does Harapha, with whom he eagerly desires to come to grips: "let her not come near me" (line 725). Justifying her betrayal of him, Dalila claims that she "feard lest one day [he would] leave" (line 794).[56] Although she characterizes this as a lover's jealousy, it is of a strangely protective kind: "I knew that liberty / Would draw thee forth to perilous enterprises" (lines 803–4). In prison at least he would be safe from danger, Dalila says, and "I should still enjoy thee day and night / Mine and Loves prisoner" (lines 807–08).

"Still," combining stasis with prolonged duration, and therefore expressive of a kind of paralysis, is one of the hardest-working small words in Milton's poetic vocabulary, and routinely features in his descriptions of unendurable or paradisal conditions. In this case, Dalila's bliss would be Samson's hell, so that her request that he allow her "redoubl'd love and care" to "ever tend about [him]" is met with revulsion (lines 923, 925). What he rejects is not a sexual temptation, at least not in the usual sense, but her desire to dominate him through caretaking. Rejecting her lightest touch, Samson ends as he began: "at distance I forgive thee" (line 954). The drama concludes by famously comparing the dead Samson to a Phoenix, that "self-begott'n bird," suggesting that in his death he has become his own mother: "From out her ashy womb now teemed, / Revives, reflourishes, then vigorous most / When most unactive deemed" (lines 1699, 1703–05).

The Lady is comparable to Samson, who rejects the childish life offered him by both Dalila and Manoa, but remains enslaved, without a real option, until "rouzing motions" – his Sabrina – plant in him the seed of a heroic rebirth and death (1382). In the Lady's case, Comus, representing complete maternal dependence and a derivative version of the self, is rejected. Circe's nonetheless enviable powers are distributed among other, more independent, versions of the self. In Ovid's *Metamorphoses*, Circe "the vertue knew / Of every simple" (14, 268–69), a quality to which Comus's memory of her "potent hearbs, and balefull drugs" attests (255). Milton endows his shepherd boy alter ego with botanical counter-knowledge: he knows "simples of a thousand names," "their strange and vigorous faculties" (627–28). In Ovid, when Circe chants her spell, "Earth grones, dogs howle, rockes horcely seeme to rore" (14, 406–10). A similar potency to confer a kind of voice on the speechless through the power of words is possessed by the Lady, as we have seen: "dumb things would be mov'd to sympathize, / And the brute Earth would lend her nerves, and shake," if she chose to speak (796–97). Finally, the musical power to soothe that Comus attributes to hers and the sirens' song is transferred to and transformed in both Thyrsis and the Lady.

The pattern followed by the good characters in *Comus*, therefore, is to reject scornfully the maternal dependence represented by Circe's son while nevertheless assuming powers like Circe's. On the one hand, maternal support – generalizable to nature itself – is absolutely necessary; on the other, enveloping care and affection threaten with oblivion one's identity and sense of self-determination. The history of Sabrina, who enables the fantasy of *autonomously* possessing maternal powers, is instructive:

> Sabrina is her name, a Virgin pure,
> Whilom she was the daughter of *Locrine,*
> That had the Scepter from his father *Brute.*
> She guiltless damsell flying the mad pursuit
> Of her enraged stepdame *Guendolen,*
> Commended her fair innocence to the flood.   (lines 826–31)

In the case of Sabrina's victimization, the mythical precedent of Apollo and Daphne, cited by an inflated Comus, is replaced by a more appropriate analog. Sabrina flees not a would-be lover, but a mother figure who would destroy her. Guendolen's rage, moreover, proceeds from the fact that she, like an English Juno, is *not* Sabrina's mother.[57] I would suggest that Sabrina can act as an intermediary and undo the Lady's paralysis because she was herself a victim of a menacing maternal figure, though innocent even of having been born of her.

Comus exemplifies a literary genre more given than most to fantasy. The grandiose autonomy desired by the Lady may have no more realistic appeal than the total fusion represented by Comus, but the supernatural intervention of Sabrina ameliorates her situation, and rather decisively if magically. As we read further in Sabrina's history, the narcissistic dream she manifests becomes clearer. The drowned virgin, taken to Nereus's hall, is bathed

> In nectar'd lavers strew'd with Asphodel,
> And through the porch and inlet of each sense
> Dropt in Ambrosial Oils till she reviv'd,
> And underwent a quick immortal change.   (lines 838–41)

As we recall from the Elder Brother's speech, this is much the same infiltration and metamorphosis, though more gradually accomplished, that the Lady can expect should she maintain her chaste ways and "oft convers with heav'nly habitants" (line 459). Sabrina is particularly noteworthy for her power "to help insnared chastity" and undo paralysis: "she can unlock / The clasping charm, and thaw the numming spell" (lines 909, 852–53). The drops she sprinkles from her "fountain pure" and the other rituals she performs allow the Lady to establish her independence from the natural realm while at the same time retaining the enchanting powers that derive from maternal nature (line 912).

Instead of reading *Comus* as a masque of the superego, therefore, I am arguing that we should view it as a performance reminiscent of one of the initiation rites described by Bettelheim, who observes that such rituals reflect participants' ambivalence "about accepting the societally prescribed adult sex role," not "fathers' jealousy of their sons" or paternal desire "to create sexual (castration) anxiety and to make the incest taboo secure."[58] Appropriately, the work of Spenser's to which Milton is most indebted in *Comus* is book 3 of the *Faerie Queene*, which features a hermaphroditic Knight of Chastity seeking her sexual destiny, her triumph over a wicked enchanter who has imprisoned a beautiful maiden, and the allegorical tableau of the Garden of Adonis. Nowhere is the pertinence of this Spenserian context more evident and generally recognized than in the Attendant Spirit's epilogue. Also directly relevant to the epilogue, and one of Spenser's major sources in book 3 of the *Faerie Queene*, is Apuleius's tale of Cupid and Psyche.

Apuleius' narrative tells of maternal Venus's indignity over the attention Cupid pays the beautiful mortal Psyche and the eventual triumph of their love despite Venus. The son must plead his case and wins the gods' "free consent" to Psyche's translation into an immortal (line 1007) before Apuleius' intensely status-conscious Venus will relent. Allegorically, Milton's closing image of Venus's "fam'd Son advanc't" – advanced over his mother – holding Psyche "sweet intranc't" suggests the linguistically inevitable equation of Psyche with the soul (lines 1004–05). Concerning Milton's situation in the 1630s, the allegory suggests a preference for his own feminine psyche over other involvements – despite the contrary wishes of a status-conscious mother, who perhaps cherished hopes of more tangible advancement for her son.

That still leaves us with the Spenserian Adonis, who, if wounds are mouths, testifies rather conspicuously on behalf of an Oedipal reading. Yet, on closer examination, the placement of Adonis in a paternal position relative to Cupid (or Milton) simply does not work, mythologically or allegorically.

Adonis, like Psyche mortal and like Psyche unconscious, is in myth always and inevitably an astonishingly beautiful boy, even as Psyche is an astonishingly beautiful girl. Milton knew the story of Adonis in many of its forms.[59] His history as a dying god had already led Spenser to identify him with "the first seminary of all things that are borne to live and dye."[60] Milton, like Spenser, knew that Adonis was associated with fertility cults. His relation to Venus in the epilogue and his position parallel to Psyche suggest that he represents the painful cost of participation in the natural realm and, more specifically, the road not taken by Milton. Far from representing Oedipal vengeance turned back upon the father, therefore, the figure of Adonis stands for the natural cycle of life and death that Milton's Lady aspires to transcend.

Milton's masque may be taken to reflect his wish to renounce compromising involvement with identity-threatening maternal powers, whether in the guise of a fatally prolific mother nature or of a Circe-like church. Hence the Lady coolly resists acquiescence in a natural world that would efface her spiritual singularity. The autonomy she desires, however, hearkens back to the hallucinatory perfection of infancy, one that subsists, paradoxically, in utter if unrecognized dependence on the mother. If in his later poetry Milton transcends this nostalgic devotion to an illusion and manages to celebrate "the genial Bed," his old discomfort with the sometimes messy excessiveness of nature, even with the "enormous bliss" of Eden, still breaks through (*PL* 8, 598; 5, 297). As in *Comus*, though, it would be erroneous to account for the epic poet's discomfort by reference to father–son jealousy. It is time we recognized that Milton's response to female creative power amounts to more than our bias toward the superego and its punitive didacticism can allow.

CHAPTER 5

The art of generation

Like to a chaos, or unlick'd bear whelp
That carries no impression like the dam

Richard III[1]

Comus, I have argued, reflects young Milton's wish to renounce a compromising involvement with identity-threatening maternal figures, whether in the guise of a fatally prolific nature or a Circe-like church. The Lady resists acquiescence in a natural world that would efface her spiritual singularity and seeks instead the lofty autonomy described in the Attendant Spirit's epilogue. The rejection of Comus's debauchery may seem to us – as it surely would have to an audience of her contemporaries – proper and justly contemptuous. The extreme terms of the rejection, however, imply an unrealistic dread of entanglement and aspiration for self-sufficient exaltation – the cleaving emotional aftermath of a lost paradise that never was. The grandiose material transcendence enabled by "the sage / And serious doctrine of Virginity" is nostalgia for an illusion (lines 786–87). Hearkening back to the hallucinatory totality of infancy, it recalls not a state of transcendence but one of complete dependence on the mother.

Paradise Lost also reflects a desire for self-sufficient totality, primarily sexual totality, though in a genre less given to fantasy than the masque. If Milton's narcissistic yearning for a sense of completeness was subject to continual renegotiation, it nevertheless continued to influence his poetry, not least the great works of his maturity. The poetic benefit of being sexually complete, female as well as male – like Tiresias – was a share in or at least consciousness of total creative power, such as that experienced by Adam in the creation of Eve.[2] Unlike *Comus,* the epic masterpiece of Milton's maturity does not hinge on the quixotic desire to bypass the mother while covertly appropriating what she represents. It instead discloses the manifold

94

generative force of maternal nature in a way that allows the poet to participate in her realm of power.

Recent attempts to transform Milton from a champion of cultural misogyny (which he was not) into a seventeenth-century feminist (which he was not) are understandable. Such a strategy may even seem warranted in view of the fact that Milton has on occasion been unjustly condemned by feminist critics. Yet these condemnations do respond fairly to the institutionalized misreading that I have been criticizing – that is, the portrayal of Milton as a belligerent preacher of traditional doctrine. Anger directed at this Milton simply registers an antagonistic orientation to the same old invention. The refusal to defer to the catechism of this domineering, patriarchal voice as if it were sympathetic and progressive seems to me both reasonable and refreshing.[3] What should be recognized in the poet's defense, however, is that the overbearing Milton disdained by feminist readers is the construction of a *de facto* alliance of twentieth-century critical and professional interests, and not the seventeenth-century poet proposed here.[4] I am not trying to rehabilitate Milton according to contemporary standards or reinvent him as a feminist. For the most part, he shared the masculinist assumptions of his age. Adam and Raphael speak always of sons, never of daughters (only Cain seems to have daughters) (e.g. 5, 389; 10, 760, 819), and the narrator includes no women in the familial charities "Of Father, Son, and Brother" that he says spring from wedded love (4, 755). Rather than defend Milton according to contemporary standards, I intend to investigate the unstable and complex significance of gender in his works, particularly in light of seventeenth-century theory and practice in matters of generation.

ATROPOS AND LUCINA

They plaid the hasty midwives, and would not stay the ripening, but went streight to ripping up.

(*CP* 3, 391)

Milton is often considered to be the chief poet of a patriarchal, Oedipally conflicted literary tradition – one in which poets create out of a competitive response to other poets. Harold Bloom describes this tradition in almost Anglo-Saxon cadences while introducing his theory of anxious poetry: "battle between strong equals, father and son as mighty opposites, Laius and Oedipus at the crossroads; only this is my subject here."[5] (Though one assumes Bloom has read Swift, this sentence appears to have been written without ironic intent.) In such a view of poetic creation, women are practically irrelevant, except perhaps as poetic subjects and signs of relations between male authors. While this model of authorship may not be entirely anachronistic, it does seem to me incapable of comprehending a great deal in early-modern culture and in Milton's writings. Female creative power was the subject of intense controversy in the seventeenth century, and it both fascinated and repelled Milton. Expressing one side of this ambivalence, the horrifying, quite precisely misogynist vision of Sin with a clamorous kennel for a womb should by itself awaken sympathy with the feminist wrath directed at Milton in recent decades.[6] Yet this revolting allegory also has a mitigating historical context. In what follows I will consider both the practice and theory of generation in the seventeenth century and argue that Milton, despite his ambivalence, consistently represented creation of all kinds according to the feminine model of reproduction.

What husbands and sons knew of childbirth was, in the early seventeenth century, typically limited to dire sounds from behind closed doors. Robert Baillie's politically motivated report of monstrous births to antinomian heretics in New England assumes the absence of men and a consequent danger of spiritual corruption. From a religious perspective like Baillie's, these congregations of women, focusing on the ministrations of the midwife or "wise woman," presented a perfect opportunity for devilish manipulation.[7] Despite this revealing fear, the absence of men seems to have been customary and was enforced, at least in part, as a matter of decorum. In 1658, for example, a Dr. Willoughby, asked to consult with a midwife on a tricky delivery, was required to crawl into the patient's dimly lit room on all fours, examine her while she remained covered, and crawl out again into the hallway to confer with the midwife.[8] Pious mothers in labor kept men out of the room and relied on the kindness of neighbors.

Neighborhood women who attended did so in part to assist the midwife but also to witness the birth, particularly in the case of stillborn children who might otherwise be thought victims, if not of Satanic intervention, then of more mundanely inspired infanticide. Christopher Hill records that in 1624, Parliament put the burden of proof that a newborn had not been done away with on the mother.[9] A woman like Sara Milton, noted among her neighbors for probity and charitable works, was just the sort of reputable witness to be summoned.

Deliveries would normally occur in the bed where the child was conceived, and while childbirth was a common event, it was poorly understood and fraught with largely unameliorated pain. Mothers were counseled to endure labor as an ultimately merciful expression of divine justice, one that offered some purchase on the steep climb to redemption. Yet the raw agony of the ordeal devastated some. Lucy Hutchinson notes, for example, that the torturous delivery of twins drove one of Colonel Hutchinson's ancestors insane, and "all the Art of the best Physitians in England could never restore her understanding."[10]

Aside from being so excruciating as to usurp the sovereignty of reason, difficult childbirths often brought fatal consequences for mother and child. Lawrence Stone calculates that 45 percent of aristocratic women died before reaching the age of 50, and, though these women presumably obtained the best care available, a quarter of these deaths came as a consequence of pregnancy and childbirth.[11] Milton's poem lamenting the "travail sore" of 23-year-old Jane (Savage) Paulet, the Marchioness of Winchester, offers a case in point (line 49). As Milton put it, "*Atropos* for *Lucina* came," slitting thin-spun lives instead of umbilical cords (*Epitaph* line 28).[12] This mythological substitution occurred terribly often. Most will recall, if only from controversies over the dating of "Methought I saw my late espoused saint," that Mary Powell and Katherine Woodcock died soon after childbirth.

Given that so many women died bearing children, and that under the Stuart kings about a quarter of all children died before reaching the age of 10, we may suppose that people in the seventeenth century were somehow steeled to such losses, that they did not feel them as we would.[13] "On the Death of a Fair Infant," with its attempt to console the "sorrows wild" of the young mother – probably Milton's sister – suggests that mothers' feelings of loss were not insignificant, despite the spiritual rewards promised those who bore their anguish patiently (line 73). One suspects that mounting apprehension during pregnancy would have been emotionally wearing for all involved, perhaps especially for other children in the household. From ages 4 to 7, young Milton, still a few years shy of the fastidious little boy who looks out of his childhood portrait, watched as his prim, middle-aged mother each year became pregnant and was ultimately seized with the pangs of childbirth. Only one of three potential siblings – Christopher – survived infancy (Masson 1, 39–40). The bifurcated image of mother

nature that unfolds in the debate between the Lady and Comus –
rational cateress versus convulsively prolific source of threatening life –
was not without a basis in the poet's childhood experience of his own
mother.

At least the women in Milton's life were spared the worst of what
childbirth in the seventeenth century could mean. Descriptions and
drawings in Jacob Rueff's sixteenth-century Latin treatise on human
generation show the ghastly tools of last resort employed in stubborn
deliveries. Perhaps because the person who ordinarily performed such
a service would also have worked as a dentist, Rueff compares these
deliveries to pulling teeth (*si postulaverit necessitas, huic instrumento forcipem
qua dentes eruuntur adhibeas ...*).[14] The verb chosen to describe the
operation, *eruo*, is typically used with reference to plant life and means
to remove forcefully, to uproot or tear out, though it also commonly
appears in descriptions of mining for gold or gems. Both strains of
imagery imply the maternity attributed to the Earth and, as we will see,
both occur in relevant portions of Milton's works, reflecting the poetics
of generation with which this chapter is concerned.

An effective and humane obstetric forceps had been developed by
the 1630s or earlier, but well into the eighteenth century, at a cost of
untold thousands of lives and immense suffering, the inventors and
their descendants jealously guarded their singular innovation as a trade
secret.[15] More often than would otherwise have been necessary therefore, midwives took drastic measures, calling in "Chirurgians, Medici-
ners, and Barbars," as one writer ruefully observed,

to dismember the children and pull them out by peeces, and sometime it
behoveth to open the poore innocent mother alive, and put yron tooles in hir
bodie, yea to murther hir, for to have hir fruite.[16]

Milton's Ovidian condemnation of men inspired by Satan who with
"impious hands" rifle "the bowels of thir mother Earth" had a vivid
microcosmic reference in the everyday life of seventeenth-century
Londoners (*PL* 1, 686–87). Such butchery was common enough that
Charles I, complaining of "tumults" that forced Parliament to enact
certain measures, compared them to "midwifery ... whose ... impatience was such that they would not stay the ripening" of mature
counsel "but ripped up with barbarous cruelty, and forcibly cut out
abortive Votes."[17] Milton scornfully replied, in effect, that if such
legislation was like Macduff "untimely ripped" from the parliamentary
womb, it was similarly destined to quell a tyrant.

The nightmarish depiction of Sin in *Paradise Lost* may therefore be understood as a hellish exaggeration of conditions that were all too often hideous in fact and must have caused anxiety and terror to match the jeopardy and pain. Sin's horrible situation is graphically physical, yet the hellhounds "that with ceasless cry / Surround" her and "with conscious terrours vex [her] round" cause constant psychological anguish to accompany the physical torment (2, 795–96, 801). Samson comments bitterly on such conformity of physical pain and mental turmoil:

> My griefs not onely pain me
> As a lingring disease,
> But finding no redress, ferment and rage,
> Nor less then wounds immedicable
> Rankle, and fester, and gangrene,
> To black mortification.
> Thoughts my Tormenters armd with deadly stings
> Mangle my apprehensive tenderest parts.   (lines 617–24)

Like Samson, Sin finds that her tormentors, though "within unseen," still bark and howl as they mangle her insides (2, 659). The physical distress inflicted on her bowels suggests an etymologically literalized remorse, and at an anatomical site where the symptoms of *gutta serena* caused Milton, too, considerable anguish.[18]

Other similarities allow us to relate the suffering of Sin to that of the blind poet, and I want to suggest that they darkly reflect Milton's strong if ambivalent identification with what I will call feminine poesis. Milton the despised Restoration fugitive, reportedly "in Perpetual Terror of being Assassinated," gives voice to vexation similar to Sin's when he describes himself "in darkness, and with dangers compast round," and requests the protection of his muse from the "savage clamor" of enemies who threaten to dismember him (*PL* 7, 27, 36).[19] According to our best knowledge, he was at the time deep into the composition of his epic. Richardson reports that amidst the riotous celebrations of Charles's return, an anxious and melancholy Milton "would lie Awake whole Nights."[20] Nor were the poet's fears groundless. The political cause for which he had labored so long had gone smash; many wished him dead or contemplated his sufferings with relish. More specifically, on the anniversary of Charles's execution in 1661, there was rioting in Holborn, especially around the Red Lion's Inn, near Milton's residence. The corpses of Cromwell, Ireton, and Bradshaw, untimely ripped from their graves so that they might suffer posthumous dismemberment, had been temporarily deposited there. "The vicinity [was] mobbed," says Masson, "for a day and two nights" (6, 215).

Thereafter in Milton's works, the sense of being surrounded by the noise of a crowd of enemies is consistently a feature of personal trial, as in the case of Abdiel, "encompast round with foes" who make no secret of their "hostil scorn" (*PL* 5, 876, 904). Usually such trial precedes triumphant delivery, if in unexpected fashion. Enoch, whom "old and young / Exploded," is miraculously "snatcht" from "amid the throng" before violent hands can seize him (11, 668–71). In *Paradise Regained*, the Son as he tries to sleep before Satan's final temptation, is "environd" with howls, yells, and shrieks of ghosts and furies (4, 423). Manoa's shattered hopes of ransoming Samson from slavery amid "the popular noise" of the Philistines are expressed in terms of a false or abortive pregnancy: "What windy joy this day had I conceiv'd / Hopeful of his Delivery, which now proves / Abortive" (lines 1574–76).[21] Instead, surrounded by the sound of his captors' "clamouring thir god," "with these immixt," Samson brings destruction on all and through death delivers himself, "like that self-begott'n bird ... / From out her ashie womb" (lines 1621, 1657, 1699, 1702).

Some may continue to feel indignant about Milton's depiction of Sin suffering in the throes of a perpetual and savage labor, and accuse him of vengefully multiplying the pangs of childbirth to express his hostility toward women. But we should take into account that in creating this allegory Milton may have been calling on remembered family trauma, as well as on the more immediate trauma of his experience as a vatic poet in the midst of delivering an epic composition. His depiction of Sin is a representation of hell, after all, and few events even in seventeenth-century England had more potential for expressing the pains of hell than a childbirth gone bad or, for that matter, a hated, blind poet at the mercy of what Charles called the hasty midwifery of a "tumult."

I want to take this inquiry a step farther and consider the extent to which Milton understood his poetic imagination, his "apprehensive tenderest parts," as if it were a womb.

First, what part did his blindness play in that understanding? Although the invocation to book 3 permits us to construe the poet's blindness as a kind of castration, I am not persuaded that such a wound should automatically be interpreted as the penalty for transgression into the father's sexual domain.[22] Kerrigan observes that

Milton probably considered his blindness an inheritance from his weak-sighted mother, a plausible notion yet one that seems inconsistent with the construction of blindness as paternal vengeance.[23] I wish to suggest on the contrary that Milton registered his loss of sight as a physiological alteration akin to what Bettelheim entitled a symbolic wound – that is, a wound that endows the male bearer with envied feminine power.

Consider the similarities between the conditions created by Milton's blindness, as described in the invocation to book 3, and the womb of chaos. He explicitly relates the "ever-during dark" he inhabits to the darkness of chaos, and, like that cosmic womb, he awaits the "piercing ray" of "Celestial Light" (3, 45, 24, 51). The imagined introduction of celestial light into Milton's mind thus recalls the dynamics of creation, which figure into the same invocation. The light that "as with a Mantle didst invest / The rising world" can also invest Milton, or at least the poetic world being born in his mind, with the mantle of inspired poetry (3, 10). His capacity to emit rays of physical vision may have been "cut off," therefore, but he suggests that this wound has enabled him to experience the gestation of an epic within his mind (3, 47).

The conditions that characterize Milton's composition of the epic – as if in a dream, during sleep, with the cooperation of a supernatural agent – fall into a pattern that characterizes not only the creation of our world but indeed every moment of authorship, innovation, or substantial change of status in the poem. Adam's narration of his own creation, for example, is punctuated by God casting him into dreams during which each new stage of his development occurs: first, the awakening to existence, then, the installation in the Garden, and finally, the birth of Eve (8, 287–311, 452–78). Raphael's revelatory account of creation is delivered to a similarly rapt Adam, who afterwards is described "as new wak't" (in one of the eight lines freshly added to the 1674 edition – 8, 4). On a different note, rousing themselves from a "grosser sleep," Adam and Eve arise "as from unrest" to find themselves fallen (9, 1049, 1052). God subsequently assures Eve of restoration through her seed and does so during a sleep that Michael himself compares to Adam's during Eve's creation (12, 610–14; 11, 369).

The strikingly recursive association of creativity with the womb of darkness, with sleep and dreaming, holds also, though with significant variation, for the innovations produced by the author of evil: "sleepst thou Companion dear" are the words that begin Satan's original temptation of his unwary associate (presumably Beelzebub) (5, 673); the next night, with heaven in repose, Satan invents gunpowder for his sleepless followers, using crude materials torn from the bowels of a previously inviolate terrain (6, 511–23). Once in hell, he pursues the same method, first disturbing the confounded Beelzebub and then the other rebels. Indeed, the narrator compares Satan's stricken troops to guards "sleeping found by whom they dread," who "rouse and bestirr themselves ere well awake" so that they can plot afresh (1, 333–34). Here, instead of tearing up the ground to invent gunpowder, they do so to build *Pandemonium*. Later, in the Garden, "squat" by sleeping Eve's ear, Satan disturbs her rest by attempting to inspire venom and engender pride (4, 800–09). He invades even the serpent, and inspires him "with act intelligential," in darkness and under the veil of sleep (9, 190). The initial act in Satan's various evil inventions thus tends to involve intrusion on and sometimes violent disruption of rest. God follows the reverse course, as evinced not only by his relations with Adam and Eve as cited above, but also by the cosmic paradigm of divine activity: "Silence, ye troubl'd waves, and thou Deep, peace" (7, 216).

A blind poet at rest in the dark, Milton thus represents himself as able to respond creatively to light, like calmed chaos, and possessing a similarly womblike power. Though it was not at all unusual for a Renaissance poet to compare fancy to a womb, Milton's concern with feminine procreative power goes beyond convention. Hermaphroditism is pervasive in *Paradise Lost*, and I take it to be a sign of Milton's yearning for transcendence of limitations imposed by gender.

Comparisons between mental and physical conception were commonplace in the Renaissance and authorized by the philosophy of erotic sublimation originally set forth in Plato's *Symposium*. Furthermore, in Western culture at least, human generation has historically been a hub for relations to other areas of knowledge, and perhaps never more controversially so than amidst the epistemological perplexity of the seventeenth century. Aside from its obvious biological centrality, the development of new human beings incarnated for many thinkers, as Charles W. Bodemer has noted, "such fundamental concerns as the basis of being, actuality and potentiality, and the nature of change."[24] Ironically, while massive practical ignorance and nascent professional avarice made motherhood appallingly perilous, the development of new life in women's wombs was the focus of lively philosophical debate and theoretical disputation.

HARVEY'S FABLE

> Least I might seem made up of nothing but the *subversion* of other
> mens *Doctrines*; I have chosen rather to propose a feigned [fanciful]
> Opinion, then none at all.[25]

Physician William Harvey, best known for discovering the circulation
of blood, was one participant in this debate who had considerable
clinical experience and empirical data to back up his theorizing.
Harvey, whom his follower Walter Charleton named "the true
Oedipus in all abstrusities of this kind," specialized in both obstetrics
and neurology, believing these specialties to be closely related.[26]
Methodologically, Harvey's first allegiance was to his own observations,
though he proceeds from clearly Aristotelian premises. Where Aristotle
insisted that "the nature of the semen is similar to that of the brain,"
for example, Harvey's clinical experience led him to insist that the
more consequential resemblance lies elsewhere. For, as the uterus nears
conception, it "groweth more *tender*, answering in *lubricity* and *softness* to
the internal ventricles of the *Braine*" (p. 542).[27] He thus asked the
following question:

> [If] the substance of the *Uterus* ... ready for *Conception*, doth ... neerly resemble
> the Constitution of the Braine: why may we not imagine that both their
> functions are also alike; and that something like, if not the selfe same thing
> that the *phantasme*, or *appetite* is to the *brain*, is excited in the *Uterus*? (pp. 542–43)

Finding no evidence to exclude the possibility, he proposes that the
womb is "a no lesse admirable Organ then the Braine, ... framed ...
of a like constitution to execute the office of Conception," and designed
by nature "to a like function" (p. 544).

From Plato on, mental productions had typically been described as
if they were physical births, not the other way round. The physical
was made to symbolize the higher reality of the ideal, as one might
expect in a culture dominated by philosophical idealism. The
assumed priority of the brain over the womb manifested itself in
common beliefs that evinced the mind's profound influence over
reproduction. Deformities and other undesired traits were often
traced to the mental and emotional condition of the parents at
conception.[28] The assumption of the mind's priority appears also in
the widely believed report, glanced at already in this chapter, that
antinomian heretics Anne Hutchinson and Mary Dyer bore children
resembling their mothers' heresies:

God visibly from the Heavens had declared his anger ... punishing Mistresse *Hutchinson* with a monstrous birth of more then thirty mis-shapen creatures at one time ... and Mistresse *Dyer* her principall assistant, with another monstrous birth of one creature, mixed of a Beast, of a Fish, and a Fowl.[29]

The description of the nativity symbolized the intellectual deviance of the mothers (many of whose heresies Milton shared) and vindicated the author's more orthodox beliefs.

What is remarkable about Harvey is that his "feigned Opinion," which he at least recognized as a fabrication, makes the womb the equal of the brain, rather than merely a physiological vehicle whose operations were suited to reify ideological errors or, more commonly, to express the labor of poetic composition:

As we, from the Conception of the Form, or Idea, in the Braine, do fashion a form like to it in our works, so doth the Idea or *Species* [form] of the *Genitor*, residing in the *Uterus*, by the help of the formative facultie, beget a *Fœtus* like the *Genitor* himself; namely by implanting that *Immaterial species* which it hath, upon its Workmanship. (p. 543)

Without benefit of adequate magnification in his dissections of deer and other animals, Harvey believed that "there is nothing to be found abiding therein [i.e. in the uterus] after *coition*: for the *geniture* of the *Male* doth either suddenly fall out againe, or vanish away" (p. 541).

Considering this evidence, Harvey denied that an agent contained in the sperm directly or materially influences formation of the fetus. Though mistaken, this was Harvey's most intrepid deviation from the classical tradition, with its nearly uniform insistence on the male seed's formative virtue. Harvey argues instead that the uterus possesses the capacity to conceive an immaterial idea, transmitted to it by semen, just as the brain conceives images, transmitted to it by sensory spirits. The ramifications of the womb playing so active a role in reproduction were, at least from a seventeenth-century patriarch's point of view, intolerable. No less of an authority than Aristotle had observed that "the female always provides the material, the male that which fashions it"; "this is what is meant by calling them male and female."[30] The action or passivity of one's contribution to reproductive processes was thus considered *definitive* of gender, according to Aristotle.

Well before Aristotle wrote about the generation of animals, Apollo's speech in Aeschylus's *Eumenides* (delivered on behalf of the matricide Orestes) anticipated and put dramatic point on his influential analysis: "The mother is not the true parent of the child / Which is called hers.

She is a nurse who tends the growth / Of young seed planted by its true parent, the male." Deciding the case in favor of Orestes, Athena endorses Apollo's claim: "No mother gave me birth."[31] In the seventeenth century Nathaniel Highmore attacked Harvey and, like Aristotle, insisted that "the reason why there are distinct Sexes, is, because one of them must supply the part, and office, that the Earth doth to Vegetables; which is, to contain, preserve, and supply it with fitting nourishment; which is done by the Female."[32]

To his credit as a scientist, Harvey knew that he lacked sufficient data to substantiate his explanation for how conception occurs. Rather than pretend to scientific demonstration, therefore, he compared himself to a story-teller, his theory to a fable:

Since I plainly see that nothing at all doth remain in the *Uterus* after *coition*, whereunto I might ascribe the *principle* of *generation*; no more then remains in the *braine* after *sensation*, and *experience*, whereunto the *principle* of *Art* may be reduced; but finding the *constitution* to be alike in both, I have invented this *Fable*. (p. 546)

If having babies and having ideas involve organically similar processes, he reasoned, might he not propose a unified theory, or fable, concerning the "dark, obscure business" of conception (p. 539)?[33] Though Harvey's theorizing was misinformed, the fable he constructed is nonetheless culturally significant.

In brief, what he denied to the male seed, Harvey attributed to the womb, that is, a plastic power – or "formative faculty" – to produce a copy of the masculine ideal once it has conceived it.[34] Pregnancy thus became as much a process of artistic *mimesis*, of "*plastical Art*," as poetry, music, or painting (p. 544). For Harvey, the "*Univocal Agent*" of all generation, artificial and natural, is imitation of a form: "*Natural*, and *Artificial Generation* are after one and the same manner ... for both are first moved by some conceived form, which is immaterial, and is produced by *Conception*" (pp. 549, 554). Hence he compares the womb's shaping of a baby not only to an artist's work but also to a bird's natural artistry, which allows it after winter's silence to reproduce a song "learned the *Summer* before" – "onely by meere *phansie* [by means of an imaginative faculty]" (p. 545). That conception and generation should occur in the womb without sperm being present does not strike Harvey as any more mysterious than natural phenomena like birdsong or the power of the "*brain* of the *Artist*, or the *Artist* himself by virtue of his *brain*, [to] form things which are not present with him, but such as he only hath formerly seen, so much to the *life*" (p. 545). The attribution of artistic power to the womb represents another crucial deviation from Aristotle, who also frequently compares the process of generation to the process of artistic shaping, but always identifies the male's seed as the artist.[35]

Harvey's attempt to arrive at a univocal theory of conception exalted the status of the womb in an unprecedented way and thus tended to elevate the status of women and threaten that of men. Given an analogical habit of mind, moreover, the threat reached into the heavens. It was Aristotle, again, who specified the cosmological counterpart of woman's seed (the menses or catamenia): "the catamenia have in their nature an affinity to the primitive matter."[36] In the final chapter we will consider in some detail the cultural implications, especially with regard to orthodox Western cosmological hierarchies, of Milton's implicit deviations from classical embryology. Yet there are even more fundamental concerns at stake in Harvey's embryological fabling than those tied specifically to one's position within a patriarchal, social hierarchy.

Harvey's theory and empirical evidence sanctioned what appears to be widespread and longstanding masculine anxiety over gender identity and reproductive superfluity: "for the *geniture* of the *Male* doth either suddenly fall out againe, or vanish away."[37] Aristotle himself mentions the problem, if only to dismiss it: "the question may be raised why it is that, if indeed the female possesses the same soul and if it is the secretion of the female which is the material of the embryo, she needs the male besides instead of generating entirely from herself."[38] The philosopher decides this issue by begging the question, that is, by citing the formal incapacity of women to generate active seed.[39] But Harvey, in his limited way and without any obtrusive ideological consciousness, refuses to participate in what had by his time become a doctrinaire "subordination of the female to the male," at least with respect to generative agency.[40] And so again he parts company with Aristotle, and we see the millennia-old plant metaphor boomerang. When the womb begins to exercise "the *plastick generative power*," according to Harvey it "*procreateth* its own like, no otherwise then *plants* doe, which we see are impowered with the force of both *Sexes*" (p. 540).[41] As Pagel notes, Harvey's theory of generation involved "no coming together of the male and female components, but an almost parthenogenetic generation."[42]

Nicholas Culpeper in his *Directory for Midwives* testifies to his era's concern with the extent of women's role in reproduction. Among the most hotly disputed topics within the subject of generation, he lists prominently: (1) whether or not women have seed; (2) if they do, whether or not it "act in Forming" the child; and (3) "whether the active power of forming lie in the Womb or not."[43] Nathaniel High-more, though he had no data to prove Harvey wrong, insisted on principle that "if nothing be found in their wombs then; we may as safely and conclusively argue, that either that Female never coupled with the Male, or never retained his seed [and thus would not be pregnant, despite Harvey's representations to the contrary]."[44] The intangible action of the man's seed, as if by contagion, was too close to no action at all, at least in Highmore's opinion: "we must needs acknowledge something more then an irradiation, or faecundating quality, imprest on the womb by the Masculine seed."[45]

As if in compensation for the artistic efficiency he grants women in human reproduction, Harvey undercuts the categorical difference between mental and physical generation. That is, at the same time that he practically excludes men from any direct role in shaping the fetus, their seed merely transmitting an image for *mimesis*, his univocal theory of conception nevertheless affords a quasi-scientific basis to masculine claims of real, if mental, participation in what would otherwise be an almost exclusively feminine realm. To return to Bettelheim's notion of symbolic wounds, one might almost say that Harvey performs a brain-based subincision to compensate for the male's anatomical shortcom-ings. Within his patriarchal setting, however, it is the womb he conforms to the mind, not the other way round – as if to say, men have always possessed a real power to reproduce, at least mentally. For all the stress placed on the agency he allows the womb, therefore, one very important consequence of Harvey's theory is the generative entitlement it allows men in a culture where, by and large, men alone were allowed the dignity of mental labor.

Without arguing for any line of influence between Harvey and Milton, I wish to argue that the poet after his own fashion weakened the distinction between womb-based and brain-based conception and generation, and thus the distinction between female and male. We recall, for example, that after juxtaposing poetic creation with the birth of the world from the womb of chaos, the invocation to book 3 describes versifying in terms of birdsong associated with the change of seasons (lines 38–40). As in Harvey's example of the songbird remem-bering a song learned the summer before – "onely by meere phansie"

– the distinction between natural and artificial poesis is effaced. Milton, too, tied the annual resumption of his poetic powers to the change of seasons. Furthermore, the Miltonic nightingale, if not quite "swallowd up ... / In the wide womb of uncreated night" so as to be entirely subsumed by the maternal, does sing "darkling," and, in the mytholo-gical person of the raped and mutilated Philomela, is feminine (2, 149–50; 3, 39).[46]

Autobiographical passages aside for the moment, descriptions in *Paradise Lost* of various types of generation – which we may for now designate with Harvey's phrase as the "plastical art" occurring after conception – evoke a process similar to the *mimesis* described by the physician. To describe cosmic generation, for example, Milton mixes figures from art and nature. The "Omnific Word" deploys "gold'n Compasses" to measure off the part of chaos subject to further creation (7, 217, 225). Immediately thereafter, the "Spirit of God," his "brooding wings ... outspread," infuses this fluid mass with "vital vertue" and "vital warmth" (7, 235–37). Although the artistry and procreative virtue of the operation seem predominantly masculine, "brooding" implies femininity. Yet, the effects of this brooding – infusing virtue and warmth – were usually associated with the mascu-line side of reproduction.

The confusion of customary gender roles continues as "the Womb ... / Of Waters" is represented as impregnating the Earth, herself "the Great Mother," through a process of fermentation in "warme Prolific humour" and "genial moisture" (7, 276–82). Harvey never entertains the possibility that Milton depicts here, that of one womb impregnating another. But fermentation was one category of causation that Harvey favored as an explanation of how an immaterial idea present in the sperm might be conveyed to the womb without a material vehicle (p. 547). Later in Milton's creation scene, the womb of the Earth, having emerged from the womb of fermenting waters, opens at the divine command and brings forth the "perfet formes" that have been shaped within her (7, 455). "Answering his great Idea," material creation takes form according to the design of a masculine, artistic, paternal God, yet the generative process of "answering" God's relatively immaterial Word occurs within wombs of water and earth that themselves derive from the greater womb of chaos (7, 557).

Milton's mixing of traditional gender roles is perhaps clearest at the microcosmic level, in the depiction of the creation of Eve by God and Adam. It is of course God, not a womb, who shapes Eve, but he does

so according to Adam's "wish, exactly to [his] hearts desire" (8, 451).[47]
If we may say that the Creator here "answers" his creature's great idea
of an equal partner, it would seem to place God in the role of efficient
cause that Harvey assigns to the plastic art of the womb. And if Adam
possesses no womb of his own in which to shape Eve physically, he does
possess imagination or fancy: "Mine eyes he clos'd, but op'n left the
Cell / Of Fancie my internal sight" (8, 460–61). Fancy in *Paradise Lost*
Milton personifies as feminine and a mimic, which is consistent with
the identification of imagination as the womb of the mind (5, 102–11).
Hence, the effort to generate Eve seems collaborative and mutual: at
the same time that God's hands shape Eve, Adam's imitative fancy also
forms her "exactly to [his] hearts desire." Though it is not overtly
alluded to, the situation recalls the Pygmalion myth, with both Adam
and God enjoying some claim to the status of sculptor. And if God
alone plays the part of Venus by endowing the sculpture with life,
Adam is the masculine source from which the idea of Eve – the
feminine ideal – originates.

Milton's poetic representation of cosmic and microcosmic creation
does not contradict Harvey's unprecedented valorization of the womb
and seems to correspond in particular with his theorizing concerning its
artistic virtue. But Harvey, in accord with most seventeenth-century
natural philosophy, would have rejected the notion of a feminine ideal.
Though Harvey attributed unusual artistic force to the womb and
opposed the traditional denial of woman's generative agency, he did
not deviate from the general, masculinist premise basic to Aristotelian
thought concerning the female of the species.

Aristotle insists that "the female is, as it were, a mutilated male," in
some sense a "monstrosity" because of her deviation from the nominal
human form – that of the male – and consequently defined in relation
to the male "in virtue of an incapacity." And by "mutilated" Aristotle
does not refer simply to the absence of male genitals, as is clear from
his later discussion of eunuchs, "mutilated in one part alone."[48]
Similarly, Harvey assumes that the immaterial species retained by the
womb as a model for its generative art is masculine because the male is
the "more *perfect Animal*" (p. 543). That the ideal human form is
masculine, claimed Harvey, is confirmed also by sexual desire. A
woman's uterus conceives in conformity with her natural desire for the
male (p. 543). If the developing embryo becomes female, it represents a
deviation from the womb's original conception of and desire for the
masculine human form.

In Milton's presentation of Adam's request for a mate, of course, the situation is just the reverse. Eve is conceived in conformity with Adam's natural desire for the female. The implicit presence in *Paradise Lost* of so radical a notion as the feminine ideal could be explained as an unintended outcome of Milton's fidelity to scripture, in combination with his rationalizing narrative strategy. But no scriptural precedent justifies a scene in which Adam requests a mate, nor the participation of his imagination in her formation.[49] And when we recall the spiritual import that Milton the divorcer assigns to Adam's loneliness, it seems clear that the poet was not merely mythmaking, but genuinely thought of the feminine side of humanity as a separate, complementary version of human being.

Milton's depiction of the birth of Eve would therefore seem to call into question the standard Aristotelian tenet that the birth of any female represents a botched job, a deviation from the implanted masculine ideal, or, as Adam says at his most misogynist moment, "This noveltie on Earth, this fair defect / Of Nature" (10, 891–92). On the contrary, the "daughter of God and Man," as Eve is regularly called, represents not an anomaly but an ontologically and formally discrete version of human being (4, 660; 9, 291). The narrative of her beginning indicates that her attachment and subordination to Adam derive from what would today be considered the cultural construction of her gender, rather than from the imperatives of her biological sex. She *learns* to appreciate Adam and yield to him (4, 489–91). She does not do so automatically or instinctually. This learning process, too, has no scriptural precedent. Milton is thus atypical at least to this extent: he consistently presents Eve as representative of a distinct version of humanity in her own right. She is not a failed copy of the masculine ideal, lacking in heat sufficient to attain the perfection of the male form.[50]

Quite the contrary, the generation of Eve presents a problem not because she is defective or deficient in some way but because she is too perfect, though the poem comes down with its highest authorities on the side of male superiority. According to the narrator – not Adam – an angel could almost be excused for falling in love with her:

> If ever, then,
> Then had the Sons of God excuse to have bin
> Enamourd at that sight. (5, 446–48)

How are we supposed to take this? Does Eve's appearance give the impression that she would make an appropriate mate for an angel and that she may therefore be hierarchically superior to Adam? Certainly this is too large a claim to make on the basis of such slender evidence. In the next section, I want to look more closely at the generation of Eve for a more solidly based and articulate sense of the problematical inconsistencies, and thus the challenge to a rational theodicy, that she embodies. Also, placing the creation of Eve in the context of generation should allow us a more detailed understanding of her position, and Adam's, too, in the cosmic order of *Paradise Lost*.

"ACCOMPLISHT EVE"

> Would it not grieve a woman to be overmastered with a piece of valiant dust, to make an account of her life to a clod of wayward marl?[51]

Let us consider the lines immediately preceding the narrator's exclamation that Eve's innocent beauty is so potent that it makes the prospect of unfallen angels loving Adam's unfallen wife seem nearly excusable – emphatically so, with the repetition of "then." Oddly, the narrator leads up to this observation first by noting that Raphael really eats his lunch and then by justifying this marvel scientifically:

> nor wonder; if by fire
> Of sooty coal th' Empiric Alchemist
> Can turn, or holds it possible to turn
> Metals of drossiest Ore to perfet Gold
> As from the Mine. Mean while at Table *Eve*
> Ministerd naked, and thir flowing cups
> With pleasant liquors crownd: O innocence
> Deserving Paradise! if ever, then,
> Then had the Sons of God excuse ...   (5, 439–47)

The movement from Raphael's wonderful digestion, to alchemical metamorphosis, to the all but irresistible desirability of Eve, may not be so random or casual as at first it seems. These disparate topics all involve the subject of generation and help to place Eve organically within the web of relations that her world comprises. We observed a similar linkage of nutrition, generation, alchemical transformation, and feminine beauty in Comus's appeal to the Lady to obey the implications of her beauty and participate in the wild fertility of the world around her. The Lady abhors such vile participation. Eve, on the other hand, already embodies the enormous generative power of her own world. She is in perfect innocence what the Lady of *Comus* fears to become, perhaps understandably so, given a fallen world in which the facts of generation have been drastically altered for the worse.

Harvey's follower Walter Charleton was particularly emphatic in identifying nutrition with generation.[52] After all, how does one generate a complex living organism from almost nothing if not by feeding it? And alchemists commonly appealed to nutrition as a natural model for the substantial changes they hoped to produce in metals.[53] Raphael's digestive miracle may therefore be described as a kind of generation, or alchemical transubstantiation, of relatively crude matter into angelic substance. What then allows for the easy transition from Raphael's alchemical digestion to Eve's desirability? My tentative reply is that Milton associates Eve, as he does Raphael, with gold.

In Renaissance metallurgy and alchemy gold figures as the culmination of all metals; in Renaissance medicine as the ultimate pharmaceutical. Aside from its value as a commodity, gold thus held almost universal symbolic currency and Milton readily traded with it, whether writing of Ovid's golden age, Cupid's golden arrow, Aristotle's golden mean, or the Pythagorean and theological golden rule. In *Paradise Lost* gold appears consistently as the chief accouterment of earthly and heavenly paradises and either metonymically conveys or substantially constitutes phenomena as diverse as sand, edible vegetables, potable rivers, and angel wings of "downie Gold" (4, 220, 238, 249; 3, 607–08; 5, 282).[54] That Eve, too, is in some sense golden owes to more than simply the color of her hair. God brings her forth from Adam, "earths hallowd mould," via a process reminiscent of the generative metallurgical intercourse between sun and earth (5, 321):

> Th' Arch-chimic Sun so farr from us remote
> Produces with Terrestrial Humor mixt
> Here in the dark so many precious things
> Of colour glorious and effect so rare.   (3, 609–12)

The same sort of natural, subterranean operation occurs in heaven, whose "bright surface," adorned with "Gemms and Gold," is generated out of "materials dark and crude, / ... toucht / With Heavens ray" (6, 472, 475, 478–80). If we were to hold *strictly* to the analogy with natural processes, Adam, "this Man of Clay" would have to be considered mere terrestrial humor in comparison with "fair angelic Eve" (9, 176; 5, 74).

Yet we cannot hold strictly to this analogy or, rather, it tells only part of Eve's story, for the production of gold is not the only generative process with which Eve's nativity invites comparison. She is, for example, made out of a rib extracted from the "wide ... wound" in Adam's left side (8, 467). The usual association is with the birth of Sin, who is born from the left side of her father's head "op'ning wide" (2, 755). Yet Eve's birth hearkens back with more extensive verbal resonance to the fabrication of Pandemonium from "ribs of Gold" taken out of the "womb" of a masculine hill after "a spacious wound" has been opened in it (1, 690, 673, 689). What seems a far-fetched comparison to us would have come easily to Milton, who knew that scripture, literally translated, represents God as "building" Eve out of Adam's rib.[55] Given this linguistic background and led by these verbal echoes, we may also construe Satan's palace as a bitter allegorical foreshadowing of her fated role as mother of mankind. The mortal danger to Eve's numberless children begins with the resolution reached by numberless fallen spirits within "her [Pandemonium's] ample spaces" (1, 725).[56] The exterior of Satan's palace, however, like Eve, presents a magnificently ornamented "outside," moving the narrator, who anticipates Raphael admonishing Adam, to question the value of such grand edifices (1, 692–99).

The story of Eve's birth thus aligns her with evil phenomena as well as good. "Riches grow in Hell," too, as the Narrator explains of the "precious bane" dug up by the devils (1, 691–92). Milton was certainly familiar with the topos of the hypocritical gift – the Trojan horse, for example – a desired object, often involving a hollow enclosure loaded with evil, so endowed as to entice acceptance and bring woe. If indeed, "too much" is "bestowed" on Eve, as Adam complains (8, 537–38), Pandora, to whom Eve is explicitly compared, would compete with Pygmalion's sculptured bride as the Ovidian referent for her creation (4, 714–15). The implications of this competing mythological reference, to the extent that it applies, would disable the theodicy. For, like the Greeks erecting a hollow horse of "ample space" to hold their warriors, the gods deliberately made Pandora to ensnare humanity. These distressing implications seem to have at least a circumstantial rightness about them.

For example, when Raphael reprimands Adam for his weakness concerning Eve, Adam defends himself before the censorious angel with a lecture on human psychology:

> I to thee disclose
> What inward thence I feel, not therefore foild,

> Who meet with various objects, from the sense
> Variously representing; yet still free
> Approve the best.   (8, 607–11)

As an analysis of human psychology, this assertion recalls Adam's comforting words after Eve's dream:

> Evil into the mind of God or Man
> May come and go, so unapprov'd, and leave
> No spot or blame behind.   (5, 117–19)

The broad similarity suggests a ratio: Adam's weakness before Eve is as threatening to his innocence – or, from the ethical standpoint of *Areopagitica*, as potentially constructive of his virtue – as the dream vision of eating the fruit is to Eve's. We recall that, unknown to the human couple, Satan attempts to manipulate "the Organs of her Fancie" to "forge / Illusions as he list" during the dream he inspires in Eve (4, 802–03). Adam's narrative of Eve's creation does not encourage us to suppose that God similarly manipulated the womb of Adam's imagination as he shaped Eve. Yet the parallel is troubling, as the Creator bends over an unconscious but imaginatively active Adam, like Satan squat by sleeping Eve's ear.

On closer examination, however, this parallel may be tentatively explained as a function of aligned moments in a spiraling narrative pattern established during the war in heaven. When Satan is apprehended endeavoring to load the womb of Eve's mind with vanity and presumption, he is compared to a heap of gunpowder set off before it can be stored in its hollow "Tun" (4, 814–18). As has been frequently recognized, this comparison continues the insistent and sometimes ironic association of Satan with his explosive invention, but it also suggests that Eve is in some sense akin to the devil's artillery or can be so transformed. Anticipating the circumstances of Eve's nativity, Satan's followers delve into the heavenly terrain to find materials out of which to concoct explosives: "up they turnd / Wide the Celestial soile" (6, 509–10). As we have seen, God similarly delves into Adam in order to obtain "in thir dark Nativitie" materials for shaping Eve (6, 482). And though the rib extracted from Adam's side is quite distinct from the raw materials for gunpowder, the effect of Eve on Adam and others is roughly comparable to that of Satan's arsenal on the good angels:

> transported I behold,
> Transported touch; here passion first I felt,
> Commotion strange.   (8, 529–31)

Though the resemblance between Eve and artillery is barely percep-
tible in this instance, it is persistently reinforced by the narrative. Thus
Adam reports that he requested Eve from God, who had already
conceived her, so to speak. Similarly, Raphael reports that Nisroch
requested a tactical innovation from Satan, who also had already
invented it (8, 444–45; 6, 470–71).

The link between the generation of Eve and the invention of
explosive weaponry is perhaps the most variously significant one in the
extensive chain of symbolic thought that has Eve, and particularly her
maternal sexuality, as its focus. The unusual emphasis that Milton
placed on rational companionship in marriage can be misleading if it
causes us to ignore Eve's most consequential historical role. Raphael's
scripturally familiar first words to Eve identify the anatomical site of
that consequentiality, only hours after Satan has mounted his first
assault on her:

> Haile Mother of Mankind, whose fruitful Womb
> Shall fill the World more numerous with thy Sons
> Then with these various fruits the Trees of God
> Have heapt this Table. (5, 388–91)

Raphael compares the produce of Eve's womb to fruit, not explosive
charges, of course. But then Satan has yet to accomplish the transformation of her children into "food for powder," to borrow Falstaff's
ruthless phrasing.

The strange symbolic connection between devilish artillery and Eve's
womb is compelling especially for what it tells us about Satan's habitual
mode of proceeding. Eve makes a likely target for Satanic intervention
not because she exhibits a native propensity for wickedness, but
because the lethal potential of her womb as a weapon against God
allures him, just as he was drawn to the womb lying beneath the
surface of heaven for its destructive potency. According to the narrator,
Satan's bad eminence as the author of evil manifests itself in precisely
this tendency to foul things at their generative seat:

> for whence,
> But from the Author of all ill could Spring
> So deep a malice, to confound the race
> Of mankind in one root, and Earth with Hell
> To mingle and involve. (2, 380–84)

Milton would have agreed with Robert Baillie, though on different
grounds, that the devil is particularly interested in corrupting midwives.

Suborning the power of generation at the most basic level possible is
Satan's characteristic method of proceeding against God.

Satan's various interventions in generation, moreover, are particularly noteworthy in the context of Harvey's "univocal" theory of
conception. In discussing Harvey's conflation of mind and womb, I
noted that while he attributed artistic status to women's wombs, the
attribution works also in reverse, affording the artist's figurative claim
on feminine procreative power a scientific rationale. Harvey's theorizing may thus dimly reflect a certain cultural anxiety over male
superfluity in sexual reproduction. If so, Satan's monstrous exemplifica-
tion of Harvey's theories strips the cloak of science from the anxiety.
While still in heaven, Satan gives birth with his mind and then
impregnates his mental progeny. When he invents gunpowder, as we
have seen, he mines the "originals of Nature in thir crude / Conception," first intruding on the womb of heaven, and then perverting
"with suttle Art" the natural process by which these "originals" would
have been transformed into gems and gold (6, 511–13). The paradigmatic weapons program requires trespass into the generative depths,
extraction of raw materials, and construction of hollow engines to store
and shoot the explosive.

If we agree with Freud that in the realm of symbols hollowness
generally signifies the womb, it seems significant that after they concoct
gunpowder, Satan has his troops place it in manufactured "hollow
Engins," which are themselves concealed "in hollow Cube" (6, 484,
552). The rebels then impudently expose these "hollowd bodies" that
"with hideous orifice gap't ... wide, / Portending hollow truce"
(6, 574, 577–78). The actual discharge "from those deep-throated
Engins" into the air, which "all her entrails / Tore," recalls the birth of
Death, who "breaking violent way / Tore through [Sin's] entrails" (6,
586, 588; 2, 782–83). The firing of Satan's guns, in other words, may be
described as an untimely birth of embryonic matter from artificially
constructed womblike spaces, "as violently as hasty powder fir'd /
Doth hurry from the fatal cannon's womb."[57] Sin's entry into being
follows the same pattern; she explodes with flame from the original
womb of evil – Satan's imagination. The construction of Pandemonium modulates the theme, suggesting that Milton, as Freud would
later, discerned in the arts of civilization an indirect working out of the
death instinct. Whether perched on the tree of life, or enthroned within
Pandemonium's "ample" spaces, Satan devises death by enlisting the
power of creation in the cause of destruction. Hence, God establishes

hell as the place where "all life dies, death lives, and Nature breeds, / Perverse, all monstrous, all prodigious things," and among the vanity-filled occupants of the paradise of fools are "all th' unaccomplisht works of Natures hand, / Abortive, monstrous, or unkindly mixt" – "Embryo's and Idiots" (2, 624–25; 3, 455–56, 474).

The possibility of associating Eve with Satanic phenomena – and not least with the strategic hypocrisy used in its deployment – is evident. From a postlapsarian perspective, furthermore, the original distinctions between Eve and Satanic phenomena, not to mention Eve's potential for even greater goodness, are not as easily grasped. I am in any case not concerned to deny or affirm the implications concerning Eve that the generation of gold, invention of gunpowder, erection of Pandemonium, or birth of Sin allow. The nativity of Eve is, as I have suggested, a sticking-place for diverse symbolic associations in the epic. Her creation is a mythopoetic axis upon which the epic, and the encyclopedic knowledge it deploys, turns – not without trepidation. Roughly speaking, we could compare her making to the episode of the forging of the shield of Achilles in *The Iliad*. More precisely, as both daughter and mother, rebellious child and matrix of salvation, she is the human site for a world of sometimes irreconcilable symbolic associations signifying the *poesis* of creation. That is, the creation of Eve can be placed in relation to various generative processes spoken of in the poem, processes that constitute the fabric of Milton's epic cosmos. So much meaning therefore accrues to the making of the first mother that she defies confident or consistent assessment, particularly with respect to her ethical significance.[58]

CHAPTER 6

Culture and anarchy

There were to be five great proofs of the existence of chaos, of which the first was the absence of God. The other four could surely be located. The work of definition and explication could, if done nicely enough, occupy the angels forever, as the contrary work has occupied human theologians. But there is not much enthusiasm for chaos among the angels.

Donald Barthelme[1]

In light of Milton scholars' penchant for the angelic perspective, it should not surprise us that we share the lack of enthusiasm for chaos that Barthelme attributes to the angels. When we look closely enough into *Paradise Lost*, however, whether the subject be Eve, gold, gender, astronomy, alchemy, or medicine, we find instability and excess; we find incoherence and undecidability. We find chaos. Little has been written on the subject, however, even though the epic, as Robert Adams has observed, "*does* make it necessary for us to look at Chaos, or think of Chaos, again and again."[2] In the last chapter, we saw that an uncertain Adam worries that there is something excessive about Eve, or lacking within him. His confusion and the association of Eve with various kinds of generation, both natural and artificial, can be construed as the basis for discomforting questions about the theodicy. Despite suspicions raised by the analogy between Eve and Pandora, I will argue that the problematic of incoherence and excess derives from the influence of chaos and applies not only to Eve but is pervasive in Milton's cosmos, an expression of the nature of things – and therefore of God himself – rather than evidence of a divine plot to ensnare humanity.

Milton scholars have argued that the allegorical character of Chaos in *Paradise Lost* represents either a neutral, passive condition or an ominous and evil state of being. (In what follows, I will write "Chaos"

when referring to the allegorical character and "chaos" when referring to the state of being.) A. B. Chambers, for example, insisted in a
classic essay that "Chaos and Night are the enemies of God,"
"opposed to him only less than hell itself."[3] Given Milton's narrative
in book 2, during which Chaos gives Satan directions to our world
and expresses his interest in destruction of created order, the charge
seems indisputable.

Yet, puzzling consequences follow from the claim that Chaos is
belligerent. Milton's metaphysics are monistic and materialist, and no
one disputes that in *Paradise Lost* chaos is "the Womb of Nature,"
containing the "dark materials" necessary for divine creation (2, 911,
916). How could Milton, in an explicit theodicy, depict this first matter
as hostile to God and his creations? If a disposition toward destruction
were latent in the very substance of existence, the attempt to justify the
Creator's ways toward his creatures would be absurd. Still Miltonists
persist in describing chaos as either passively ominous or actively evil.
In so doing, they not only acquiesce in a narrative impression left by an
allegory that occurs early in the epic; they also reproduce – as Milton
himself does not – traditional, Western, philosophical and religious
attitudes concerning matter.

The qualified bias against matter in the Christian West reflects the
political environment and theological structure of early Christianity. In
establishing the limits of orthodoxy, the Church fathers dammed up
certain of Christianity's deepest Hellenistic tributaries by declaring
matter – like all being in Augustine's metaphysics – good. If, alterna-
tively, Christianity had designated matter evil, the consequence would
have been a dualist religion. It is just such dualism, in the form of
Manichaeism, that Augustine battled. A dualistic exemption of matter
from God's dominion would have contradicted the Augustinian conviction that a single, omnipotent deity governs everything, and thereby
undermined order – at the cosmic or imperial level.

Matter was thus deemed acceptable, but only if kept in its place, that
of passive stuff created from nothing and ordered into shape by God.
So, although the church acknowledged this Neoplatonic thing of
darkness its own, it also reckoned matter and the virtues associated
with it to be marginal and inferior, the Sancho Panzas or Spenserian
dwarfs among possible goods. Furthermore, matter in the form of
human flesh was thought to require discipline and direction before it
could achieve these lowly virtues. Christianity in effect sponsored a
practical dualism, which, as with Augustinian theology generally, suited

patriarchal government of church and state: its ready resort to coercive force, and suppression of the lower classes generally.[4] Like unruly matter, which had long been identified as a feminine and maternal metaphysical principle, the lower orders were thought naturally to require correction and direction before they could aspire to the appropriate minor virtues.[5] Such doctrine and discipline remained a commonplace of political theory throughout the English Renaissance.

Materialism has historically been regarded by orthodoxy as a philosophy meriting shame and indignation as much as punishment because it involves the assignment of bodies – or some sort of material nature – to angels and to God himself. In his epic, the unabashed Milton responds most obviously to the prospect of such cultural embarrassment by insisting that angels really eat – and digest – and by having Raphael describe the physical delights of angelic sexuality. Materially based pleasures and processes occur at the most exalted levels of Milton's epic cosmos. Similarly, in *Christian Doctrine* Milton describes matter as the necessary basis of *all* good. For him, the idea that God contains the potency of unrestricted matter is no insult:[6]

It is, I say, a demonstration of God's supreme power and goodness that he should not shut up this heterogeneous and substantial virtue within himself, but should disperse, propagate and extend it as far as, and in whatever way, he wills. For this original matter was not an evil thing, nor to be thought of as worthless: it was good, and it contained the seeds of all subsequent good. It was a substance, and could only have been derived from the source of all substance. It was in a confused and disordered state at first, but afterwards God made it ordered and beautiful. (6, 308)

The original matter lacks order but, like a nursery garden (*seminarium* [*CW* 15, 22]), breeds "all subsequent good."[7] By comparison, Plato's widely influential apology for material creations characterizes the original matter as ugly and stubborn: "God made them as far as possible the fairest and best, out of things which were not fair and good."[8]

I stress Milton's deviation from orthodox theology not because I think that we should use his materialist theology to *explain* the meaning of chaos in his epic. Matter is an ontological and metaphysical principle; chaos a poetic realm and allegorical personage. They are not commensurate. But accurate knowledge of Milton's theological peculiarities can help us to gauge the plausibility of readings of his poetry through *other* traditions. As we have seen, such readings are vulnerable to ideological or religious bias. The interpretation of chaos is especially subject to such corruption, for although Milton scholars generally admit that Milton's metaphysics were monistic and that he considered matter the basis of all good, most of us are still suspicious of chaos as presented in *Paradise Lost*.

In the case of chaos, as in the case of Milton's Arianism, the scholarly record testifies to the power of orthodox cultural traditions to bias judgment. A different explanation has recently been offered for the apparent confusion over chaos, however. Also intrigued by the "lack of critical interest" in the subject, Regina Schwartz uncovers "something like a critical conspiracy to detoxify chaos," a strategy for slipping the mythopoetic punch of Milton's poetry and tying up the threat of unformed matter on the ropes of philosophical precedent.[9] Even Chambers's explicit indictment of the anarch exemplifies this methodological tactic; he transforms "the fierce enemy of God into a problem of scientific history" (p. 24). I find it difficult to register Chambers's description of the anarch – "opposed to [God] only less than hell itself" – as part of "a conspiracy to detoxify chaos," however.

If Milton's theology of matter informs his epic at all, Chaos should not appear in it as God's enemy. In an attempt to negotiate this impasse, Schwartz questions the relevance of such logic to "the realm of symbols" (p. 33).[10] For her, the symbolic precedent of ancient Mesopotamian traditions informs *Paradise Lost* at a more basic and poetically meaningful level than Milton's theological principles (pp. 24, 26). These ancient creation myths stand behind rigorous biblical prohibitions against transgression of created order. The boundlessness and confusion of chaos thus render it the principal enemy of God's creative will, at least symbolically: "a greater threat in Milton's moral universe than the Satanic one of a definite willed disobedience" (p. 18). The anarchic impulses of matter, which paternalistic Augustinian theology attempted merely to discipline and direct, are in this moral frame charged with an incorrigibly transgressive malevolence.

Yet it is precisely at the level of the epic's symbolic fabric – as opposed to the overtly allegorical narrative of book 2 – that the boundary-breaking energy of chaos does *not* appear threatening or at odds with God. Quite the contrary. Legalistic emphasis on limits is in *Paradise Lost* linked *not* to the sanctity of unfallen creation, but to loss, reduced status, and makeshift safeguards against further encroachment by sin. The categories of sacred and profane color discourse concerning the forbidden fruit only when the nearly fallen Adam advances a pharisaic justification for his projected sin:

> perhaps the Fact
> Is not so hainous now, foretasted Fruit,
> Profan'd first by the Serpent, by him first
> Made common and unhallowd ere our taste.   (9, 928–31)

The holiness of the garden, destined "haunt of Seales and Orcs," has little bearing on the decision to evict Adam and Eve (11, 835). As Michael insists, "God attributes to place / No sanctitie," at least not to place in and of itself (11, 836–37). Similarly, in the case of shame and recognition of nakedness, Milton traces the dichotomy of clean and unclean to a *post*lapsarian point of origin (9, 1091–98).

In the unfallen order, remembrance of creation and praise of the Creator never evoke what Michael calls the "servil fear" of trespass fostered by "strict Laws" (12, 304–05). Adam and Eve celebrate "choice / Unlimited of manifold delights," "abundance [that] wants / Partakers," and elements that "mix / And nourish all things," whose "ceasless change / Varie to [the] great Maker still new praise" (4, 434–35, 730–31; 5, 183–84). In Milton's heaven, bounds and limits seem meant to be overcome with ease. On Earth, Raphael crosses species-specific boundaries as soon as he enters the Garden. Adam wonders in morally charged gustatory language if earthly food will be "unsavourie" for spiritual natures even though "one Celestial Father gives to all" (5, 401–03). The angel replies by describing a cosmos of nutritional communion, not separation. He then hungrily partakes of human food, relying on his alimentary alchemy to transubstantiate grosser into more refined matter. A similar digestive process promises eventually to transform the unfallen Adam and Eve into spiritual beings capable of visiting and dining with angels (5, 493–500), a prospect implying that God's establishment of "bounds / Proportiond to each kind" was never meant to be inviolable (5, 478–79).

Oddly, we Milton scholars do not look to the angels for illustrative example when it comes to understanding the ethical function of limits and boundaries. The narrator says that spirits can "either Sex assume, or both" (1, 424); "all heart they live, all Head, all Eye, all Eare, / All Intellect, all Sense," with no anatomical restriction of function (6, 350–01). Synesthetic confusion abounds in heaven, so that angels literally smell good news coming (3, 135–37). Bounds and boundlessness coincide where "full measure onely bounds / Excess" and celebrations are most regular "when most irregular they seem" (5, 639–40, 624). Those angels who venture past the gates of heaven to investigate creation and glorify God thus indulge in

                    no excess
That reaches blame, but rather merits praise
The more it seems excess.   (3, 696–98)

Boundaries provide points of connection and synergy rather than demarcations of trespass. They are thresholds meant to be crossed, often for the sake of mere pleasure. Small wonder that Gabriel glows with anger when Satan calls him a "limitarie Cherube" (4, 971). Even amorous pleasure among the angels subsists in the total crossing of boundaries between otherwise distinct partners.

Except in defiance of God's express command, the desire to cross boundaries consistently appears in Milton's epic as noble and godlike. It is the desire that from the beginning characterizes the epic's inspired authorial voice. The character of the Son is exemplary as, according to his Father's wishes, he bridges the holiest of distinctions – that between creature and Creator – first by appearing as the head of the angels, then as the divine Word, and finally as a real, individual man who nonetheless remains divine. Already a *theangelos*, he will become a *theanthropos*, a god-man as the heretical Milton entitles him, thereby diverging from the orthodox representation of Christ's humanity as a generic cloak for a singularly divine subsistence (*CP* 6, 421–25). The boundary-crossing Son is the instrument through whom God intends to allow all creation to share in the divine – "God shall be All in All" (3, 341). As a comparison between human and angelic sex suggests, the more refined the creature the more obviously the impulse to join hearkens back to the primal elemental mix. At the most exalted level of all, the apocalyptic love between creature and Creator resonates with the wild energy of chaos. Ultimate heavenly bliss is in Milton's imagination chaotic, its profusion of pleasure and joy endlessly "luxurious" by consciousness of what was once formal "restraint" (9, 209). Even its chronology recalls descriptions of chaos: "beyond is all abyss, / Eternitie, whose end no eye can reach" (12, 555–56).[11]

The textually based argument above, though not in itself decisive or complete, nevertheless offers sufficient reason to speculate that the hostility that critics find in chaos owes to something beyond the extra-logical power of Milton's poetry. Often, the degree of hostility attributed to Milton's chaos seems a function of the context invoked. Chambers's Hellenistic contextualizing distinguished the proper skein of thought to tie Milton to a philosophical prejudice against matter. In

Plato's *Timaeus* persuasive force is required to overcome, insofar as possible, the reluctance of "the receptacle," or "mother substance," to accept form (51a-b; see 48a). Schwartz in turn cites ancient creation myths as the point of origin for Milton's chaos symbolism, specifically the *Enuma elish*, a Babylonian epic behind the Genesis account.

Rather than deploy persuasive reason to achieve his ends, Marduk, the heroic creator in the *Enuma elish*, kills and butchers the maternal chaos deity, Tiamat, and builds creation out of the pieces. Paul Ricoeur in writing on this moment observes that "the creative act, which distinguishes, separates, measures, and puts in order, is inseparable from the criminal act that puts an end to the life of the oldest gods."[12] There is a "deicide inherent in the divine."[13] Schwartz mitigates this violence, however, by calling Tiamat the "rebel leader" (p. 28) and avoids mention of Tiamat's divinity and gender, although she definitively is, according to the *Enuma elish*, "mother of them all" – including those younger gods who rebel against her.[14] The Hebrew word for *Tiamat* is the grammatically feminine *tehom*, rendered in English translations of Genesis as "the deep."[15]

This mythology, like Augustinian theology, has political implications. The tale of heroic Marduk, like that of Perseus among the Greeks, took shape during the period when an order of kingship took control of politics and religion throughout the Near East. Ricoeur notes that the evolution of a kingship order, with its supporting castes of priests and elite warriors, parallels developments in the depiction of evil in Mesopotamian mythology.[16] Citing the *Enuma elish* and the relatively late addition of the Marduk narrative, feminist critics have suggested that the rough, revisionist treatment of once honored maternal deities like Tiamat reflects the attitudes of the victors in "phallocratic wars" that established patriarchal government and overthrew the cult of the goddess.[17]

The difference between the *Enuma elish* and Milton's account of creation is evident when one attempts to correlate the matricidal violence of the Babylonian myth with the anticlimactic nonviolence of the Miltonic Marduk. This discrepancy Schwartz takes as evidence of the Son's irresistible military prowess, which reduces all of his battles "to so much shadow boxing" (p. 31). Is it not more likely, however, that "the stately ease" with which the peace-wishing Son achieves victory in *Paradise Lost* indicates that Milton did not register creation as the beginning of a continuing battle against "the chaos monster" (p. 31)?

Except when his narrative tracks Satan or his children, Milton never describes chaos in terms of war, though in book 7 it does appear "outrageous" and "wilde," with "furious winds / And surging waves" that move the divine Word to describe it as "troubl'd" (7, 212–16). The peace he bids it is such peace as might quiet stormy waters, not foes at war. The arms he wields against this sea of troubles are not the holy terror and overpowering thunder that blast the enemy angels, but his ministering word and "gold'n Compasses," meant to circumscribe, not dismember, the "dark materials" of a new world (7, 225; 2, 916).

The entry on chaos in Mircea Eliade's *Encyclopedia of Religion* notes that theologians often draw a "dualistic distinction" between "the absolutely sacred and creative being of a transcendent 'kindlier' God, on the one hand, and the utterly profane nothingness and nonbeing of a passively neutral or actively belligerent chaos."[18] Milton scholarship obviously conforms to this tendency. But the entry goes on to register an alternative to dualistic condemnations of chaos:

The apparently fundamental contrast between chaos and cosmos may reveal more of a dialectical relationship ... In the broadest sense, chaos stands for the root "otherness" and "strangeness" of existence and the ironic indeterminacy of all human constructs.[19]

Which paradigm is more appropriate to Milton's depiction of chaos: that which polarizes creator and chaos or that which locates in chaos a principle of ironic indeterminacy and the implicit basis of all subsequent order?

Those myths that feature the violent defeat of a hostile chaos often function to celebrate "the heroic finality of some authoritarian order." The emphasis in such cases is on "the permanent suppression of chaos."[20] As we have seen, the evolution of the myths comprising the *Enuma elish* betrays an impulse to ground the order of kingship in cosmic hierarchy, thus affording monarchical prerogative a divine right. The same impulse had influential exponents in Milton's century. Hobbes in *Leviathan* invokes "the first Chaos of Violence, and Civill Warre" to deplore the consequences of rebellion against the divinely sanctioned monarch.[21] More generally, the *Enuma elish* magnifies the political bent of Augustinian, practical dualism, which, as we have already seen, seems to justify subjection of women and of the social classes associated with undisciplined matter. Admittedly, the Creator in *Paradise Lost* also suppresses chaos, and circumscribes part of it. But his suppression is temporary, and once creation has occurred, chaos is left as boundless and wild as the Creator found it, available to substantiate alternatives to the established order.

Chaos is far from being the enemy of God or creation, although like Uriel he is tricked into helping Satan. If anyone in the poem desires the establishment of "some authoritarian order" and the lasting suppression of chaos it is Satan. Suiting their fixed opposition to God, their lock on despair, Milton's fallen angels could never champion indeterminacy but incline instead to rigidity and parodic orderliness. Hardened, their bodies are no longer supple enough to allow them to cross physical boundaries and make love (4, 509–11). They occupy themselves instead with niceties of place and status, with boundary and limit, and observe the externals of distinction with punctilious grandiosity or servility. The images of hell we remember from the first two books are those of parading military precision, monumental edifice, and overwrought gestures of obeisance or grandeur. It should not surprise us to find that the success of Satan's mission on earth actually impairs chaos.

The damage done to chaos because of the Fall appears allegorically in the description of Sin and Death working to connect the postlapsarian world to hell. Death employs "his Mace petrific" to fix the once indeterminate matter, now "bound with Gorgonian rigor not to move," and secures the structure "with Pinns of Adamant / And Chains" making "all fast, too fast" (10, 294, 297, 318–19). The comparison of Death striking chaos to the tyrant Xerxes whipping "th' indignant waves" of the Hellespont establishes the absolutist aspect of this massive construction (10, 306–10). The response of the double-crossed Chaos to Death's violence against his realm generally goes unrecognized in Milton scholarship:

> on either side
> Disparted Chaos over built exclaimd,
> And with rebounding surge the barrs assaild,
> That scornd his indignation.   (10, 415–18)

Though the mortised rigor of Death's pontiface arouses his ire, Chaos, his realm now "*dis*parted" – with Satan's son playing a role much closer to Marduk's than that played by God's son – cannot undo the division. The Fall has imposed a created order on his realm: the tyrannically oppressive, ontologically shriveled structure of evil.[22] It seems appropriate that the allegory has Death consolidate this structure of oppression. The imposition of death has always had strategic appeal to those who wish to establish order and require a solution to the threat of indeterminacy. The Marduk-like Hobbes, for example, maintains that the "natural punishment" for rebellion is "slaughter."[23]

If indeed a natural symbolism of moral evil operates in *Paradise Lost*, the Fall and the consequent suppression of chaos – not the "triumph" over chaos at creation – is the original moment to which that symbolism hearkens. The Satanic suppression of chaos, in which Death appears as the ultimate silencing of ironic otherness, echoes in Milton's version of biblical history when Nimrod erects a great tower. Bent on transcendent construction, Nimrod wars on "such as refuse / Subjection to his Empire tyrannous" (12, 31–32). God responds derisively to Nimrod's presumption by reaffirming the power of chaos and so disabling his tyranny:

> great laughter was in Heav'n
> And looking down, to see the hubbub strange
> And hear the din; thus was the building left
> Ridiculous, and the work Confusion nam'd. (12, 59–62)

The connection with chaos sounds distinctly in "the din," "the hubbub strange" and "confusion" enforced by God on those who would ignore the "ironic indeterminacy underlying all human constructs" (cf. 2, 1040, 951, 897). Raphael imagines a similar divine response to the theoretical shifts of Ptolemaic astronomers contriving "to save appearances" (8, 81). To act as a tyrant is to leave oneself vulnerable to God's derision – and the vengeance of chaos.[24] It is a vengeance that Milton believed "temporal Death" himself will suffer at the resurrection (12, 433).

ALLEGORY AND THE EXCESSIVENESS OF EVE

As opposed to ancient Babylonian accounts of creation, *Paradise Lost* does not represent the Creator's intentions toward chaos as matricidal or tyrannical. Yet, symbolic associations and mythological antecedents aside, brute narrative evidence of the malignancy of Chaos remains. The anarch supports Satan's mission and menacingly proclaims: "Havock and spoil and ruin are my gain" (2, 1009). William Empson consequently rejected the identification of preexistent matter with God as a bit of doctrine irrelevant to *Paradise Lost*: "it makes nonsense of most of its narrative."[25]

The allegorical anarch undeniably supports Satan's mission of destruction. His encouraging words make this scene one in a series of theodically challenging moments during Satan's odyssey. The arch-fiend survives to stir up trouble in the first place because "his doom" reserves him to more suffering (1, 53). Satan then escapes from hell because God has entrusted Sin with the key (2, 850–53). In view of the fact that Sin *means* disobedience, God's forbidding her to open the gates would seem virtually to guarantee the reverse outcome. Then, after Satan survives the journey through chaos, the unwitting Uriel – a prime interpreter of God's "great authentic will" (3, 656) – points the tempter on his way to Paradise. And when the angelic guard apprehends the intruder there, God himself, in one of the epic's most complex and ambiguous scenes, decides that the prisoner should again be let go (4, 990–1005). In comparison with these occasions, the incoherent intelligence offered by a faltering figure like Chaos seems relatively insignificant.

Nevertheless, against the background of seventeenth-century epistemology and aesthetics, the use of allegory to present chaos seems formally to confirm Empson's opinion of his malignancy. In an increasingly nominalist and anti-scholastic intellectual climate, allegory had become, in the words of Stephen M. Fallon, "an ideal vehicle for presenting deficient ontology."[26] Milton accepted the Augustinian tenet that evil registers itself in creatures as ontological decay – a progressive condition of ever-increasing loss. Hence, Sin and Death – reflecting aspects of Satan's degradation – are allegorical characters.[27] The conclusion seems inevitable that in choosing allegory to represent chaos, Milton bolstered formally what the narrative makes plain anyway: Chaos is evil and an enemy of divine creation.

Small wonder that so many Milton scholars have remained silent on the subject of chaos: logically it should not be evil, yet the narrative and aesthetic evidence against it looks damning. The alternatives for criticism seem to be either selective dismissal of Milton's heretical materialism in interpretation of his orthodox poetry, or construction of the contradiction as a culturally revealing instance of aporia. There is another solution, however, one that both admits the formal meaning of allegory in *Paradise Lost* and accounts for the narrative facts – without resorting to the claim that Milton's poetry denies basic principles of his theology.

In *Paradise Lost* the aesthetic choice of allegory does indicate "deficient ontology." Such deficiency need not imply a loss of being resulting from evil, however. I would argue that in the case of chaos, the choice of allegory instead indicates an as yet unrealized potential for being, the precondition of creation. Augustine, because he believed in creation *ex nihilo*, had no equivalent of chaos in his philosophy, no ontological well from which creation proceeds. For the materialist Milton, on the other hand, the realm of potential creation preceding actual creation possesses a shadowy existence of its own. In a realm that exists *before* creation, any ontological deficiency conveyed by Miltonic allegory signifies only – to indulge in an instructive tautology – that the matter has not yet undergone creation.

When the allegorical anarch acts eager to regain a world restored to its original material confusion, therefore, he speaks as the factitious representative of a kingdom that, relative to creation, is unorganized and deficient in being. The realm or state of being that Chaos speaks for *would* in some sense profit from the uncreation – not the perversion – of our world. Empson's narratological objection to chaos ignores a fundamental principle of allegory, not to mention its etymology, that "allegorical agents reveal by their actions not internal psychologies but the abstractions ... that lie behind them."[28] The formal capacity of allegory to convey ontological and epistemological assumptions exemplifies its characteristic polysemy, "leaning away at various oblique angles from soldierly directness."[29] If a too rigorous distinction between agent and abstraction oversimplifies the complex knotting of such polysemy, we can at least agree that Chaos's attitude toward creation does not *necessarily* make him God's enemy.

On the other hand, allegorical refraction of the narrative does not entirely exonerate Chaos. Robert Adams precedes me in reading Chaos as a morally and ideologically significant principle of indeterminacy. Yet, like Schwartz, he regards it as a principle of evil more dangerous than Satan's, an insidious, irremediable entropy that infects the fallen world:

It is built into the very structure of the cosmos, of society, of the mind ... It is not an empire to be fought by ranked battalions; it is discord, passivity, weakness – Chaos, in other words, seen not from the outside as a stuttering, moping old man with a facial tic, but from the inside, as a constant ingredient of the Christian life, an intimate, and ultimately invincible enemy. (p. 85)

The influence of chaos is not only a *post*lapsarian phenomenon however. What Adams calls passivity, weakness, and discord pervade the unfallen world as well, at least as represented by Milton.

Angels, for example, can be and regularly are tricked, mistaken, or befuddled so that at critical moments they stand passively not knowing what to do. God's announcements often leave them nonplussed. In the realm of dreams, unfallen fancy sometimes produces, *without* Satanic influence, "wilde work," a phrase redolent both of chaos and of warfare (5, 112). In one of the most crucial moments in the narrative, a touchy and less than efficacious Gabriel misreads or only partially understands the significance of a sign that God displays in the heavens (4, 990–1013). God himself before displaying this ambiguous sign is compared to "the careful plowman doubting" what action to take (4, 983). The consequence of this most unfathomable moment is that nothing happens; Satan goes free, his apprehension neutralized. This pervasive sense of confusing indeterminacy, of things being constitutionally unpredictable and resistant to easy explanation, is richly conveyed by the excessiveness of unfallen Eve.

Once a portion of chaos undergoes creation, the same quality of unshaped potency that makes Chaos an allegory of deficiency appears as unpredictable plenitude of being – as excess. Creatures possess the potential for becoming more than they are. As an allegorical figure, Chaos represents a state of being – mere potency – that by definition cannot become more than it is. Milton uses allegory to express qualities or states of being that are not subject to development in time, that are estranged from diachrony. (The chronology of eternity, as we have already seen, is described in terms that evoke chaos). For Milton, the quality of life that I am describing as *excessive* – indicating unformed potency – typically elicits symbolic expression. It is a characteristic condition of being in time. In his epic, Milton consistently associates this quality with phenomena erotic and perplexing. I want to pursue an investigation of excess in just these terms.

According to Eliade's *Encyclopedia*, one category of symbolism that allows for a less censorious conception of chaos concerns "imagery of an embryonic condition or womblike form."[30] Yet, despite the erotic pulse of the creation that it substantiates and despite Milton's plain identification of it as a womb or a pregnant deep, Milton scholars have ignored the link between chaos and sexual fruition. Like Chambers before her, Schwartz describes the ongoing threat of Chaos entirely in military terms: "the war in heaven is only the beginning, not the end, of the battle against Chaos. It is fought again at creation, at the Fall, with Cain and Abel, at Babel and the flood; all of human history is played out on this battlefield" (p. 38). This is a very selective synopsis, however. The embrace of Sin precedes the war in heaven; Adam and Eve's fallen lust produces Cain; his daughters seduce the sons of God; their union brings forth the warlike giants – and so on and so on: "lust hard by hate," as Milton's bawdy pun has it (1, 417).

That chaos is first described in terms of warfare hardly invalidates these associations with sex. Like battle, sex requires its participants to mix it up, so to speak. A Homeric Raphael acknowledges this chiastic intersection when, in a single line he uses the same verb – "meet" – for both loving and fighting (6, 93).[31] The sexual charge of Milton's descriptions of creation has long been felt. Margaret Drabble, for example, notes references "to the womb of waters, to genial moisture, to heaving mountains, laps and entrails and bosoms, to shaggy hills and bushes with frizzled hair and hills with 'hairie sides.'" Milton, she concludes, "sees the world as a living being, conceived, gestated, born, passing through unadorned childhood to the springing tender grass of puberty."[32] Where do the conception, gestation, and birth of that living being occur, if not in chaos?

After birth, furthermore, the enclosed spaces of creation surge with the procreative energy of unbounded, illimitable chaos, "the Womb of Nature and perhaps her Grave" (2, 911). Had Milton neglected to call chaos a womb, its generative capacity still would appear in the pattern that Satan follows in subverting it, a pattern that we have seen to be intensely recursive. First, he persuades his daughter to take "from her side the fatal Key" and open gates that should remain closed (2, 871). (In Milton's usage, "side" often means womb or site of generation, as it does in the case of Psyche in *Comus* and of Adam in *Paradise Lost*.) Immediately thereafter, the "impetuous recoile and jarring sound" of the opening gates, the accompanying noise of "Harsh Thunder," and the "redounding smoak and ruddy flame" that spew into the abyss recall again the firing of Satan's artillery during the war in heaven (2, 880, 882, 889). It is a moment also anticipated early in book 1 when

> the universal Host upsent
> A shout that tore Hells Concave, and beyond
> Frighted the Reign of *Chaos* and old Night.   (541–43)

As we have seen, the rulers of chaos have good reason to fear the enthusiasm that tears out of hell.

With the cooperation of his children, then, Satan fires himself out of "the hollow Abyss" of hell and into chaos, the first locale he is said to "tempt" (2, 518, 404). He intrudes on "the secrets of the hoarie deep," until, propelled by yet another fiery blast, he arrives at the vicinity of the allegorical rulers of chaos (2, 891). We could continue to trace out the by now familiar pattern of uterine intrusion and abortive, explosive birth, as Satan reloads to depart from chaos "like a Pyramid of fire" and proceeds to violate a series of enclosed spaces until at last he reaches "the sweet recess of *Eve*" (2, 1013; 9, 456). By now, Satan's *modus operandi* is familiar enough. What I want to consider instead are the chaos-based commonalties among the underground of heaven, Eve's imagination, hell – indeed, any generative place.

First, all of these places take their material substance from chaos. The imbecilic anarch thus considers the creation of Satan's "dungeon" and "Now lately Heav'n and Earth" encroachments on his realm (2, 1003–04). The purest expression of chaos, however, is not a place but the procreative energy that flows through these various created structures and locales without being reducible to or bound by them. "Eldest *Night* / And *Chaos*" are "Ancestors of Nature" not only on Earth as in Heaven but also in hell, where

> Nature breeds,
> Perverse, all monstrous, all prodigious things,
> Abominable, inutterable, and worse
> Then Fables yet have feignd, or fear conceiv'd
> *Gorgons* and *Hydra's*, and *Chimera's* dire.   (2, 894–95, 624–28)

Chaos can provide the matter for a landscape of horrors or of bliss, but either way, the place burgeons with life.

To the extent that any part of creation manifests its chaotic origins, therefore, it is wildly procreative and excessive. The irrational extravagance of creation, often erotic in character, afflicts Adam on a daily basis, if in small ways:

> now the mounted Sun
> Shot down direct his fervid Raies, to warme
> Earths inmost womb, more warmth than *Adam* needs.
>
> (5, 300–02)

Coping with the erotic excessiveness of life in the garden represents one of the main challenges of paradise:

> Nature here
> Wantond as in her prime, and plaid at will
> Her Virgin Fancies, pouring forth more sweet,
> Wilde above Rule or Art; enormous bliss.   (5, 294–97)

Milton does not use a word with the etymological force of "enormous" (out of rule, beyond the norm or limit) unadvisedly. The "enclosure wild" (9, 543) of the garden expresses in finite space the original and infinite wildness that Milton persistently attributes to chaos (e.g. 2, 588,

910, 917, 951, 1014). The passage above also characterizes nature's outpourings of new life as "virgin fancies" – the prodigious yield of an innocent imagination. In hell, the imaginative tenor of chaos-based procreative power might be described as nightmarish, or violently psychotic. Working backwards, we may propose that prior to creation chaos is like an imagination based in matter and ungoverned by reason – wild, in its case, *before* rule or art.

The distinction between the unlimited wildness of chaos and the harnessed wildness of the garden is easy enough to grasp. But the quality of innocent wildness is not so easily distinguished from the wildness of rebellion against God, a difficulty that I think helps account for scholars' ill opinion of chaos. Adam describes even the normal psychology of human dreamwork as wild, for example, and, as in Milton's portrayal of chaos, uses allegory to do so:

> Oft in [reason's] absence mimic Fansie wakes
> To imitate her; but misjoining shapes,
> Wilde work produces oft. (5, 110–12)

Oddly, God chooses the same telltale phrase – "wild work" – to describe the havoc wrought during the war in heaven, though, unlike Adam, he knows that this "wild work" is the consequence of evil (6, 698). It is almost as if the war were a dream of evil come into the mind of a sleeping God, a notion that suits Milton's tendency, reminiscent of Harvey, to express natural generation in psychological terms – whether he speaks of the fear-conceived horrors of hell or the virgin fancies of Eden. The dream ends, though, when the Son as representative of divine reason returns and forcibly defeats those "who reason for thir Law refuse" (6, 41).

The moral ambiguity of wildness poses problems for judgment. The garden's relentless fecundity, "tending to wilde," frustrates Adam and Eve's labors to control their environment, provides a rationale for their separation, and establishes a material cause for the Fall (9, 212). Does this mean that we should blame the influence of chaos for the first disobedience? How can we reconcile the view of chaos as the copious material basis of life with evidence that suggests that the wild presence of chaos in creation threatens rational order? The problem is both cosmically general and humanly specific. Descriptions of nature's wanton profusion and the Garden's "enormous bliss" often and rightly remind readers of Eve. As the source of human life, her "fruitful Womb" represents chaos on the human level, and among men and angels, especially angels, is unprecedented (5, 388). Her "wanton" appearance famously challenges the reader, Raphael, and Adam to see her as a danger to moral order. Her beauty exceeds rational expectations. Attitudes toward Eve thus have a tendency to echo attitudes toward chaos.

Raphael, for example, explains Eve's beauty as mere surface ornamentation, a function of her "outside" (8, 568), and as Satan demonstrates with the beautiful surface of heaven, the potency beneath can easily be perverted to evil ends. Eve herself undermines the impression of perfection left by her appearance when she espouses the hierarchical position that "beauty is excelld by manly grace / And wisdom, which alone is truly fair" (4, 490–91). Although these words do not limit wisdom – later personified as Urania's sister (7, 10) – to men, they exalt wisdom over beauty as being more authentic. Raphael says that Eve's "shows" pale next to the more substantial "realities" possessed by her husband, as if Adam's "own compleat / Perfections" rendered Eve a gaudy novelty, not much better than a groom "besmeard with Gold" (8, 575; 5, 352–53, 356). The angel's attitude anticipates that of Swift's reason-mongering madman in *A Tale of a Tub*, when he blandly submits horrifying evidence of deceptive appearances: "Last week I saw a woman *flayed*, and you will hardly believe how much it altered her person for the worse."[33]

The most external and chaotically "wanton" aspect of Eve is her much-remarked golden hair, which falls in wild ringlets that partially obscure her nakedness. They may imply "subjection" but subjection of an insistently complementary sort – "as the Vine curles her tendrils" (4, 308, 307). The comparison of a wife to a vine is a favorite of Renaissance authors, but as J. Martin Evans has observed, Milton in developing the topos extends unusual attention to its tenor of reproductive sexuality.[34] Adam and Eve as they garden, for example, lead "the Vine / To wed her Elm" so that it might bring "her dowr th' adopted Clusters, to adorn / His barren leaves" (5, 215–19). If the problematic that attaches to Eve concerns the reliability of appearances, therefore, that which attaches to Adam is one of reproductive deficiency. Adam defines himself as deficient in his barren solitude – and immediately receives divine congratulations on his self-knowledge; Eve, on the other hand, seems "absolute ... / And in her self compleat" (8, 547–48).

I bring up the unfruitfulness of the elm's masculine leaves because it leads to another subject of Raphael's teachings, on the seemingly unrelated topic of solar astronomy:

> the Earth
> Though, in comparison of Heav'n, so small,
> Nor glistering, may of solid good containe
> More plenty then the Sun that barren shines,
> Whose vertue on it self works no effect,
> But in the fruitful Earth; there first receavd
> His beams, unactive else, thir vigor find. (8, 91–97)

Raphael allows that the substantial fecundity of the Earth may actually be preferable to the "barren" light of the sun. Moreover, he concedes "the fruitful Earth" a "solid" goodness that clashes with the classical depiction of wombs as empty, passive receptacles, and indeed with Raphael's depiction of Eve as merely a show, lacking Adam's inner perfections.

Although the subjects that open and close book 8 – celestial dynamics and love – seem unrelated, therefore, their topical incoherence belies a consistent concern with problems of value and rational expectation.[35] Adam's misgivings over the prospect of a geocentric universe, for example, resonate with his misgivings over the excessive appearance of Eve, or his excessive susceptibility to her erotic charms:

> reasoning I oft admire,
> How Nature wise and frugal could commit
> Such disproportions, with superfluous hand. (8, 25–27)

> Or Nature faild in mee, and left some part
> Not proof anough such Object to sustain,
> Or from my side subducting, took perhaps
> More then anough. (8, 534–37)

The same dichotomy that in chapter 4 we saw expressed in the debate between Comus and the Lady comes into play here. Adam would prefer it if, rather than work lavishly – "with superfluous hand" – in establishing the cosmos or Eve, Nature behaved as the Lady of *Comus* insists she does, like a modest and rational cateress whose dispensations exemplify "unsuperfluous eeven proportion" (line 773).

At the cosmic level, the Ptolemaic model is most clearly linked with chaotic excess and confusion. The divine laughter that Raphael predicts will follow human attempts "to model Heav'n" comes at the particular expense of those geocentric Nimrods who attempt to "weild / The mightie frame," and whose efforts end in the babble of "Cycle and Epicycle, Orb in Orb" (8, 79–81, 84). "Heav'n is for [them] too high" (8, 172). For Adam, however, the problem is not simply one of astronomy. If the way things appear indicates the way things really are, then not only would the Earth sit at the center of the cosmos, but Eve would be superior to her mate. Adam is ignorant of the astronomical truth – Raphael as we have seen problematizes the relative value of earth and sun – but he has been assured of his superiority to the earth-identified Eve. In her case at least, he is told that appearances *are* deceiving. If they were not, then it would be appropriate for "Author-itie and Reason" to wait on Eve, as Adam says they do, just as in a geocentric cosmos the Earth appears to be "serv'd by more noble then her self" (8, 554, 34). Indeed, if appearances held true on the cosmic level, scribbling astronomers' epicyclical contrivances "to save appeer-ances" and leave the Earth "sitting still" would despite their extra-vagance accurately reflect reality, rather than a tyrannical imposition of the human perspective on the heavens (8, 82, 89).

The Copernican model better suits Adam's desire for a nature that does not exceed rational expectations. At odds, though, with the "unsuperfluous eeven proportion" of a Copernican cosmos is Ra-phael's digressive and unbalanced approval of the earth's comportment in such a system:

> Whether the Sun predominant in Heav'n
> Rise on the Earth, or Earth rise on the Sun,
> Hee from the East his flaming rode begin,
> Or She from West her silent course advance
> With inoffensive pace that spinning sleeps
> On her soft Axle, while she paces Eev'n,
> And bears thee soft with the smooth Air along,
> Sollicit not thy thoughts with matters hid.   (8, 160–67)

Although this speech tilts toward approval of the decorous rationality of Copernicanism, it does so, oddly, by virtue of an extravagant rhetorical turn. The prolonged description of Eve's celestial counter-part attributes maternal care and a graceful inevitability to her "inoffensive pace" as she "beares thee soft ... along" – like a mother carrying her baby.

In short, Adam's complaints over Eve's excessive appearance link her with the Ptolemaic cosmos, but Raphael's lyrical description of a maternal Earth's smooth motions ties her to the Copernican. The narrative order also encourages this superimposition of images. Silent Eve's decorous and graceful departure from Adam and Raphael, occurring when it does, mimics the transition from a geocentric to a heliocentric cosmos. Yet how can she support these opposed associations? Adam in discussing Eve's excessive appearance says that she seems "so well to know / Her own," a compliment that recalls Raphael's description of a moving Earth as being "industrious of her self" (8, 548–49, 137). Paradoxically, this aura of entirely doing what is proper to oneself – so that the weight of cosmic order seems to amplify the least action – sets off the finite and deficient as a representation of completeness and perfection. Eve's profound absorption in what is proper to her thus gives off an air of completeness and majestic centrality inconsistent with her relatively humble position.

One might conclude that Milton leans toward Copernicanism and agrees with Raphael's reflections on Eve's misleading shows. Copernicanism in *Paradise Lost* seems to be aligned with rational stripping of misleading appearances so as to arrive at the orderly truth of creation. That Satan before tempting Eve soliloquizes within a Ptolemaic framework and exaggerates the value of the Earth – as he will the value of Eve – adds to this impression:

> Terrestrial Heav'n, danc't round by other Heav'ns
> That shine, yet bear thir bright officious Lamps,
> Light above Light, for thee alone, as seems,
> In the concentring all thir precious beams
> Of sacred influence. (9, 103–07)

Even the movement of the serpent, "a surging Maze" that "swiftly rowld / In tangles," recalls the velocity and intricacy associated with a geocentric cosmos (9, 499, 631–32). If indeed we see the epic as covertly heliocentric and as aligning Eve with the errors of geocentricism, the clichéd critique of Milton as the epic prophet of a phallologocentrism so totalizing that it stretches from human relations to celestial motions might be validated.

Despite the plentiful evidence supporting such a conclusion, endorsing it would require us to ignore too much. Even the simple correspondence between the Earth and Eve, on the one hand, and the Sun and Adam, on the other, cannot go unqualified. We tend automatically to identify Eve as "Mother of Mankind" with the fertile Earth, "all-bearing Mother" (5, 388, 338). We correlate Adam with the Sun, whose traditionally masculine rays Raphael describes as "barren," as we have already noted, like the "barren leaves" of the masculine elm (8, 93; 5, 219). Yet the Apollonian Adam is the Earth from which Eve is taken, and the Dionysian Eve shooting darts of desire is the more brilliantly sunlike in beauty. Light itself, in isolation from the Sun, despite its masculine-sounding abilities to "pierce" and "plant," is represented as female in Raphael's report of its pre-solar existence: "*shee* in a cloudie Tabernacle / Sojournd the while" (7, 248–49; my italics). In *Christian Doctrine* Milton insists that, though "we cannot imagine light without some source of light, ... we do not therefore think that a source of light is the same thing as light, or equal in excellence" (*CP* 6, 312). We may suppose, then, that the radiant light informing the masculine Sun is not essentially a masculine force, and that its creative energy, though lodged in a masculine orb, may be considered feminine and more excellent than the body in which it lodges. On the other hand, a masculine body such as that possessed by Milton, may contain the "solid" but feminine virtue that enables him to be fruitful in response to light.

Gender is a center of perplexity in the epic, and the depiction of Eve in particular works as a site for the coincidence of opposites. I am again struck by the import of Milton's description of her rising from her seat and moving away from Adam and Raphael:

> on her as Queen
> A pomp of Winning Graces waited still,
> And from about her shot Darts of desire
> Into all Eyes.   (8, 61–63)

I have suggested that in *Paradise Lost* excessive appearance reflects the capacity to be more than is present, a capacity well suited to the mother of humanity. The suspicion associated with the Copernican hypothesis is that such symbolic manifestations not only defy reason in their excessiveness; they are also misleading.[36] Hence, for Raphael, despite appearances, rational order and the male sex reign supreme in creation, or they should. Yet, if we define creation as the adornment or ornamentation of chaos, then Eve, daughter of both God and man, surely represents the most created human. The last ironic turn comes with the realization that it is her very richness of adornment – her cosmetic excess – that ties Eve to the irrational wildness of chaos, another coincidence of opposites pushing us to the edge of paradox. As with Raphael's unbalanced rhetoric in the service of a rationally pleasing Copernicanism, the capacity of Eve's beauty to intimate cosmic perfection is all out of proportion to the frailties that reason detects beneath her brilliant surface.

At least from Raphael's point of view, then, Adam faces a dilemma similar to the one developed by Swift's mad narrator: either be a fool content with the deceptive sight and intoxicating touch of beautiful surfaces, or cut through with reason and undo the misleading appearance. It is a dilemma that underlines a question crucial to Milton's theodicy: why *should* a rationally good creation present an excessive aspect? Why *does* the universe give the appearance of being out of proportion? If this eccentric tendency supports a capacity to symbolize, then perhaps it is the power of symbols that Milton must justify.

Despite Raphael's wrinkled brow, it seems unjustifiable to explain the perplexing excessiveness of Eve's beauty as if it were merely a function of Adam's subjective bias. The narrator's own exclamations over her attractiveness note her desirability before the sons of God and are occasioned by the proximity of Raphael himself. When she withdraws from Raphael and Adam, the darts of desire strike *all* Eyes. The newborn Eve, too, as she gazes unwittingly at her reflection, experiences the power of her own beauty. Nor is Satan immune:

> her Heav'nly forme
> Angelic, but more soft, and Feminine,
> Her graceful Innocence, her every Aire
> Of gesture or lest action overawd
> His Malice. (9, 457–61)

The specifics of Satan's amazement distinctly echo Adam's stirring insistence that neither the vision of Eve's "out side" nor the tactile pleasures of sex move him so much as

> those graceful acts,
> Those thousand decencies that daily flow
> From all her words and actions (8, 600–02)

One comparison Adam uses to describe Eve's loveliness – "as a guard Angelic plac't" – juxtaposes her beauty and the garden's supernatural defenders (8, 559). The only time that the "guard Angelic plac't" does act to protect the garden, moreover, its efforts amount to a defense of Eve in particular. We recall that it is Eve's beauty that renders Satan "stupidly good" and thus momentarily incapable of attack (9, 465). Accordingly, Milton's narration of Satan's encounter with the guardian angels prepares us for Adam's later suggestion that beauty can inspire awe and feelings of inadequacy. The "severe … beautie" of Zephon's words adds to them "grace / Invincible" – remember Eve's *winning* graces – and wrings from his captive pained recognition of "how awful goodness is, … / Vertue in her shape how lovly" (4, 845–48). Although the response described is Satan's, the narrator validates it. Zephon validates the same principle, if in reverse, when he points out that Satan's loss of sanctity has ruined his looks – an observation that seems to shame Satan more than any other of the indignities he suffers.

The exchange between Satan and Zephon at least seems to fit the ordinary Platonic paradigm – that beauty is the good registered according to its aesthetic appeal. Roughly speaking, the good is for Plato a condition in which things, or people, do what is proper to them – as is eminently characteristic of Eve, "so well to know / Her own." A disproportionate beauty such as that which attends Eve – one that seems to exceed her actual worth – poses a challenge for such a definition, however. She should only be as beautiful as she is good. Would Plato allow her in the Republic?

One escape that Christian theology offered Milton from this classic and pervasive problematic of Western philosophy was the concept of grace: undeniably good, undeniably excessive, and undeniably irrational. The theodically minded Milton may reject a conspicuously irrational scheme of grace such as Calvin's, yet he concedes that ultimately grace is beyond reason. The salvation plan announced in book 3 thus nods lightly in the direction of Geneva. The theological implications of the consistent association of Eve's beauty with grace should not be ignored, moreover, or chalked up to a quirk of the language: "whether waking or asleep," she shoots forth, says Milton, "peculiar Graces" (5, 14–15). These last two words appear together in only one other place in the epic:

> Some I have chosen of peculiar grace
> Elect above the rest; so is my will.   (3, 183–84)

Like Eve's graces, God's "peculiar" grace is out of the ordinary, excessive, and, as in Calvin's scheme, irresistible. It is grace out of proportion to merit, without relevance to a rationalist conception of the good. It stands out as the least reasonable moment of God's plan for salvation, beyond explanation. If indeed Eve is "too much," at least in this she accurately reflects her maker: "so is [his] will."

CHAOS AND GOD

The allegorical presentation of chaos does not necessarily signify the realm's hostility to God and creation. The neglected erotic influence of chaos and the perplexity brought about by the excessiveness of creation further suggests the pervasive influence of chaos in divine creation. I want now to enlarge on the implications of the link between Eve's graces and divine grace, an aspect of the deity synonymous with irrationality, irresistible power and inevitable victory. Chaos represents a principle of indeterminacy and randomness essential to divine power, a principle symbolized on the human level by Eve.

W. B. C. Watkins in 1965 entertained the possibility that "matter is to all intents and purposes the feminine aspect of God."[37] "All intents and purposes" appears to be a disclaimer, perhaps tacitly acknowledging the equivocal gendering of chaos in *Paradise Lost*. In his theology Milton clearly follows Plato's lead in representing the realm of the first matter as feminine: "in a manner the nurse of all generation."[38] Yet in *Paradise Lost* the state of chaos is spoken for by a masculine anarch. As his name implies, however, his rule is no rule. He represents an absence. It is the "Scepter of old *Night*," his consort, that the allegorical figurehead describes as "weakning," and *her* standard that Satan promises to erect in reducing the new creation "to her original darkness" (2, 1002, 984). Although "Eldest *Night*" never utters a word, like Eve in the presence of Raphael, chaos is her realm. Her relatively voluble masculine companion, for all his rant, figures forth only a lack of efficacy and significance.

From the excerpts cited above, it seems that the consort of Chaos, "*Eternal Night*" is not just "old," she is "unessential," "uncreated" and "unoriginal" – that is, without beginning (3, 18; 2, 1002, 439, 150; 10, 477). She is also without end; the "Anarchie" of chaos is repeatedly described as "eternal" (2, 896). The terms "anarchy" and "anarch," the latter which seems to have been Milton's own coinage, can themselves be taken to mean that the eternal night of chaos lacks a beginning as well as governance (etymologically, both are possible translations of "an-arch"). Milton has God himself call the abyss infinite and boundless, and not only chronologically: "Boundless the Deep, because I am who fill / Infinitude" (7, 168–69). Here, God uses the scripturally authoritative "I am," as he does when he introduces himself to Adam ("Whom thou soughtst I am" – 8, 316), which suggests that, aside from describing chaos, God is also describing himself by insisting "I am who fill / Infinitude." It is God who fills the deep; hence it is infinite and boundless.

What does it imply to say that the wild abyss of chaos – "the Womb of Nature and perhaps its Grave" – is filled with God? Logically, the answer seems inevitable: chaos functions as God's womb and is essential to his deity. God is the confused and dark matter of chaos even as he is the creative virtue of light. Schwartz is right to stress the "unstable visage" of Chaos as the crucial image conveying his kingdom's lack of definition (p. 18). Yet she fails to notice that Chaos's face is not represented as *dis*figured or *dis*composed – as Satan's is on Niphates' top, or as Adam's and Eve's are after the Fall. His visage instead is "*in*compos'd," even as God's essence is "*in*create" (2, 989; 3, 6; italics mine). The anarch represents the infinite material dimension of God, which has not yet been ordained for creation. Without such matter in God, how could there be creation *ex deo*?

Unfortunately, the part of this argument that deals with Milton scholarship now depends on what scholars have *not* said, or have been unable to say because of contrary assumptions, and an argument from silence is inherently weak. The only evidence available to demonstrate that a certain conclusion has not been drawn is to show critics not drawing it – a difficult task to accomplish convincingly. Still, the unspeakability of the idea that God is chaos (after the model of "God is light") has in at least some instances been painfully apparent. In some cases, critics have been on the verge of speaking the unspeakable, only to stop short.

Denis Saurat, for example, long ago recognized that in Milton's poetry and theology, preexistent matter is "part of the substance of God," but he did not link this matter to chaos, though he then had difficulty explaining chaos's preexistence:

Since in [Milton's] philosophy everything comes from God by his "retraction," which produced first that divine matter from which the universe is evolved it is difficult to explain the anterior existence of chaos.[39]

Chaos cannot be the first matter in Saurat's view because *before* creation, matter is part of God. The unspoken assumption is that chaos cannot be identified with God. Saurat thus ignores repeated descriptions of chaos as a womb and concentrates instead on the singular and tentative description of it as a "grave" (2, 911), a reference that he then glosses from the *Zohar*:

God, before creating this world, had created several others and, not being pleased with them, had destroyed them. ... It seems evident that, in Milton's mind, unless the Earth fulfil the aims for which God created it, it will be destroyed also and become part of this chaos of lost worlds.[40]

The *Zohar* may well partly "explain" Milton's chaos as a grave for botched worlds preceding the existence of our own, but Saurat's failure to recognize chaos as a primordial womb is more significant for the present argument than his claims for the relevance of *kabbalah* to Milton studies.

Empson did recognize chaos as the first matter and so was able to follow Saurat's theological analysis to its conclusion. But he in turn rejected the identification of God and the first matter in *Paradise Lost* so as to preserve the logic of Milton's narrative. Perhaps his recognition that the identification of God with chaos would tend to rehabilitate Milton's deity hardened his sense of narrative logic.[41]

Isabel MacCaffrey allowed that the potency of chaos participates in "the brilliant actuality of Heaven," but she would not go so far as to accept chaos as a part of God, whom she identified, with words that have a distinctly Aristotelian ring, as "pure actuality."[42] MacCaffrey's appreciation of the potency of chaos stretched all the way to heaven, but she denied it to God himself, despite the fact that the failure to include him required direct contradiction of Milton's own writings in favor of standard, Thomist doctrine. Milton the heretic explicitly refutes the orthodoxy MacCaffrey assumes must apply: "God cannot rightly be called Actus Purus, or pure actuality ... for thus he could do nothing except what he does do, and he would do that of necessity, although in fact he is omnipotent and utterly free in his actions" (*CP* 6, 145–46). If we are accurate in identifying unformed matter as God's potential, chaos should be recognized as the realm that substantiates his sovereignty. In light of his monist materialism, Milton's God must be identified with both the active, formative principle behind creation and the passive material one.[43]

The only scholar I know of, other than Empson, who actually registers the possibility that chaos might represent an essential dimension of God is Walter Clyde Curry, who in the 1950s asked a hitherto (and thereafter) unexpressed question and answered it in revealing fashion:

could ... matter, the substrate of all created things, [be] a 'part' or a diversification of God's essence? If so, Milton cannot escape the charge of being a rank materialist and a pantheist.[44]

The adjective "rank" neatly sums up the derisive contempt that materialism historically has elicited within orthodox Christianity and suggests the pressure to preserve the poet from such reproach. The question-begging impulse to assume what Milton by definition cannot be – and to judge evidence correspondingly – is apparent.

Yet Curry at least recognized that Milton termed chaos infinite, limitless, boundless, and eternal. Curry also acknowledged that the antitrinitarian Milton was insistent, as we saw in chapter 2, in assigning the traits repeatedly attributed to chaos solely to the true God. Nevertheless, Curry strove to preserve the sanctity of Milton's God by claiming that these attributions are hyperbolic:

> For purposes of epic grandeur, however, the poet expands in concept the total spatial reality to whatever hyperbolical infinitude may be desired or imaginable – short of the Infinity of God. Accordingly, in some sense, he may represent certain aspects of the space-continuum as "vast infinitude" (3, 711), as "immeasurable abyss" (7, 211) or "boundless deep" (1, 177), a suggestion of extension so illimitable and vast as to be incalculable or inconceivable. But such are epic phrases and must not be taken literally.[45]

Chaos cannot be infinite, except in a figurative sense and for the purpose of setting a stage of epic proportions because only God is infinite.

To understand this denial fully – denial of a proposition, to give Curry credit, that the rest of Milton scholarship has not made conscious enough to deny – we must remember the cultural role played by orthodox Christian theology in justifying the subservience of matter and women. The allegorical character of Chaos speaks for that part of God over which he does *not* exercise control, from which he is absent as an active, governing agent. Consider the rest of God's self-revelation prior to creation:

> Boundless the Deep, because I am who fill
> Infinitude, nor vacuous the space
> Though I uncircumscrib'd my self retire,
> And put not forth my goodness, which is free
> To act or not, Necessitie and Chance
> Approach not mee, and what I will is Fate. (7, 168–73)

Chaos is boundless and infinite because God fills it. Chaos also is "not vacuous" – continues to be filled, that is – even though God in some respect refrains from being there. How can God both fill the space and not be there? The terms "my self" and "my goodness" do not necessarily refer to all of God, even as "I am who fill infinitude" does not refer to all of God. Though God's *self* – which we might gloss as his actualized, volitional persona – is absent from chaos, his material potency still remains behind, filling the infinite.[46]

Implicit in Milton's materialist understanding of God is a certain paradox, one glimpsed at in the beginning of this chapter: God cannot take complete control of chaos without sacrificing his freedom and sovereignty – without ceasing to be God. At bottom, divine substance is the as yet unrealized capacity for otherness. Hence, in the frame of *pre*lapsarian allegorical narrative, Chaos appears as Satan's material accomplice, hostile to God's actual creation. Without the capacity that Chaos represents, Satan could not succeed, or conceive of success. Indeed, the psychological correlative of this substantial, divine capacity for otherness is freedom of will, the foundation of Milton's ethical beliefs at least since the composition of *Areopagitica*. Milton's deity, for the sake of his sovereignty and omnipotence, must always have access to the realm of possibility, to the well of new life. And this condition means that God must also remain essentially passive and dark in one aspect of his being.

Milton's allegorical personification of chaos signifies an absence of the deity that really is always already there – the vital core of his omnipotence, his "consort," as Eve is authoritatively described in relation to Adam (7, 529), with all that word's fateful etymological associations. If God cannot live with eternal Night, except in the shadowy allegorical guise of the unruling anarch, he also cannot live without her. In certain respects, chaos is to God as Eve is to Adam. If God has no separate, female other *external* to him, he neverthless acquiesces in his own feminine otherness – a gender-specific negative capability – and can only exercise sovereignty and creative power by virtue of her. There could be nothing without indeterminacy, certainly not a sovereign deity who creates beings with free will. The symbolic deep structure of Milton's epic, if anything, goes even further than his theology in its commitment to the absolutely vital necessity of a good first matter in the constitution of the cosmos, indeed in the constitution of a hermaphroditic deity.

It may only be now that the reading of chaos this chapter offers has become possible. N. Katherine Hayles has suggested as much in noting that for contemporary science, chaos is now seen as "order's precursor and partner rather than its opposite."[47] Modern communication theory has similarly placed a positive value on entropy and fuzziness, finding in disorder and equivocation the condition of informational complexity and richness. Perhaps, as Hayles claims, "a major fault line has developed in the episteme," now that the opposition between order and disorder has been "destabilized."[48] It is not an unprecedented destabilization, however. According to Eliade and Girardot, the concept of chaos has made this ironic perspective available in various cultures throughout human history. And if, as Hayles claims, some contemporary literary theorists value the attributes of chaos because they wish to expose the ideologies underlying traditional political orders, I would argue that their critical practice was anticipated by Milton's more than three centuries ago.[49]

When faced with the complexity of a work like *Paradise Lost* and a syncretic yet stunningly idiosyncratic mind like Milton's, scholars too often assign him to a more readily assimilable tradition, usually a reconstruction of the Christian mainstream, whether conceived of generically (Lewis) or with a Neoplatonic (Chambers) or Neohebraic (Saurat, Schwartz) spin. Dividing Milton the thinker from Milton the poet, however, is a serious mistake and one that eventually leads to absurdities as interpreters discount certain portions of his stated thought in an attempt to establish his poetic allegiance with whatever tradition it is that they themselves favor or to which they have responded. Furthermore, such a division lends credence to one of the more obnoxious canards of Milton criticism, T. S. Eliot's accusation that Milton is responsible for modern poetry's "dissociation of sensibility." I propose that rather than see Milton's poetry as distinct from or opposed to his thought, we practice a hermeneutics that finds in the union of his poetry and thought more than the sum of its parts. For it is in the symbolic realm of Milton's poetry that his thought may be appreciated most fully, living and breathing before us in astounding images that convey the emotional, even sensuous force of his considered beliefs. Readers of Milton's poetry should attempt to come to terms with him, not as a standard-bearer of traditional Western culture – the Protestants' Dante – but as perhaps the West's most challenging, uniquely integrated, philosophical poet.

Notes

I INTRODUCTION: THE INVENTED MILTON

1 *Milton's God* (1961; Cambridge, 1981), p. 287.
2 Empson, *Milton's God*, p. 11.
3 C. S. Lewis, *A Preface to Paradise Lost* (London, 1942), p. 91.
4 Christopher Hill, *Milton and the English Revolution* (London, 1977), p. 3.
5 Hill, *Milton and the English Revolution*, p. 3.
6 Thomas Kuhn, *The Structure of Scientific Revolutions* (Chicago, 1970), p. 23.
7 Kuhn, *The Structure of Scientific Revolutions*, p. 23.
8 Stanley Fish, *Surprised by Sin* (1967; Berkeley, 1971).
9 Kuhn, *The Structure of Scientific Revolutions*, p. 10, 23–25.
10 Mary Nyquist and Margaret Ferguson, eds., *Re-membering Milton* (New York, 1987).
11 Kuhn, *The Structure of Scientific Revolutions*, pp. 25.
12 See, for example, John T. Shawcross, *John Milton: The Self and The World* (Lexington, 1993); Stephen M. Fallon, *Milton Among the Philosophers* (Ithaca, 1991); David Loewenstein, *Milton and the Drama of History* (Cambridge, 1990); Joan S. Bennett, *Reviving Liberty* (Cambridge, MA, 1989); Joseph A. Wittreich, *Interpreting* Samson Agonistes (Princeton, 1986). I single out these works because each, like most of the works that will be cited in my critique of the invented Milton, won the annual Hanford Award for distinguished book, as selected by the Milton Society of America. The fact that over the last decade as many works either opposed or oblivious to the invented Milton have received such institutional approval may suggest that the paradigm is losing its hold, or that it represents only one, albeit relatively dominant, strain of contemporary Milton scholarship. I should admit that the article from which this chapter derives, "Uninventing Milton," *Modern Philology* 87 (1990), pp. 249–65, won a Hanford Award for distinguished article. The point of focusing on recent works publicly honored by the Milton Society is to indicate the extent to which the invented Milton is institutionally sanctioned. There are other recent, admirable works of Milton scholarship. I cite these award-winning studies as representative examples.
13 William Kerrigan, *The Sacred Complex* (Cambridge, MA, 1983).

14 Philip Gallagher, "Beyond the Oedipus Complex," *Milton Quarterly* 18 (1984), p. 87.

15 Bennett, *Reviving Liberty*, is particularly forceful in criticizing the reductionism and inattentiveness of those who use Milton to build theoretical systems: "no system involving Milton – however internally interesting – will have the value it might have if it were to read the poetry closely and in context" (p. 32).

16 I do not deny the role of such communities in shaping meaning or of the role played by the material form in which that meaning is expressed. In his *Critique of Modern Textual Criticism* (Chicago, 1983), Jerome McGann points persuasively to the "essential fact" that "literary works are not produced without arrangements of some sort" (p. 48) and that they "do not even acquire an artistic form of being until their engagement with an audience has been determined" (p. 44). See also Stephen B. Dobranski, "Letter and Spirit in Milton's *Areopagitica*," forthcoming in *Milton Studies* 32 (1995).

17 Stanley Fish, *Is There a Text in this Class?* (Cambridge, MA, 1980), pp. 16.

18 Lance Bertelsen, "Journalism, Carnival, and *Jubilate Agno*," *ELH* 59 (1992), p. 458.

19 Roland Barthes, "The Death of the Author," in *Image, Music, Text*, trans. Stephen Heath (London, 1984), pp. 142–48, argues that a text is a pastiche or "tissue" of multiple allusions and quotations "drawn from many cultures and entering into mutual relations of dialogue, parody, contestation," which only the anonymous and ever-changing reader can collect into a single whole (p. 148). Michel Foucault, "What is an Author?", in *Language, Counter-memory, Practice*, trans. Donald F. Bouchard and Sherry Simon (Ithaca, 1977), pp. 113–38, observes that indifference to the author stands out as "one of the fundamental ethical principles of contemporary writing" (p. 116).

20 Dan Sperber and Deirdre Wilson, *Relevance* (Oxford, 1986), p. 24.

21 Salvaging meaning from a deliberate wreck of language always involves, as a prerequisite and check, reconstruction of a context. The British at Bletchley Park, for example, who broke the German code during World War II, at first found messages they had unscrambled to be useless simply because they lacked context. Once they assembled one – this more than cryptography was the work of Intelligence – testing the validity of the interpretation of unscrambled messages became satisfyingly direct and empirical. Submarines would surface at the predicted coordinates; troops advance at the cryptographically recovered time. On the process of reconstructing the Germans' intentions from their coded messages, see Andrew Hodges, *Alan Turing: The Enigma* (New York, 1983), pp. 160–241.

22 Sperber and Wilson, *Relevance*, pp. 173–74.

23 Sperber and Wilson, *Relevance*, pp. 172–73. The place of intention is fundamental to a theory of communication that abandons the code model: "human interaction is largely determined by the conceptualization

of behavior in intentional rather than physical terms"; "as long as there is some way of recognizing the communicator's intentions, then communication is possible" (pp. 24–25). Although I rely on Sperber and Wilson, their emphasis on intention has precedent in communication and in linguistic interpretive theory, especially speech-act theory. See, for example, H. P. Grice, "Meaning," *Philosophical Review* 66 (1957), pp. 377–88, and "Utterer's Meaning and Intentions," *Philosophical Review* 78 (1969), pp. 147–77. The origins of speech-act theory lie in J. L. Austin's *How to do Things With Words*, ed. J. O. Urmson (Oxford, 1962). See also John R. Searle, *Speech Acts* (Cambridge, 1969). Quentin Skinner has related Grice's theory of meaning to Austin's arguments in "Intention and Convention in Speech-Acts," *Philosophical Quarterly* 20 (1970), pp. 118–38.

24 Georgia B. Christopher, *Milton and the Science of the Saints* (Princeton, 1982), p. 144. The honor mentioned is the annual Hanford Award for distinguished book. See note 12.

25 James Grantham Turner, *One Flesh: Paradisal Marriage and Sexual Relations in the Age of Milton* (Oxford, 1987), p. 183.

26 Turner, *One Flesh*, p. 260.

27 Marshall Grossman, *Authors to Themselves* (Cambridge, 1987), p. 50. Grossman shared the 1987 Hanford Award with Turner.

28 The most familiar exposition of subversion and containment is Stephen Greenblatt's "Invisible Bullets," most recently published in *Shakespearean Negotiations* (Berkeley, 1988), pp. 21–65. In carrying psychoanalysis beyond the pleasure principle, Freud established a structurally similar false dualism in opposing eros to thanatos and then revealing that the former is only a strategic working out of the latter. In light of their shared structure, the psychoanalytic and New Historicist visions seem to invite further comparison. Both models can be described as pessimistic and determinist. Yet in Greenblatt's model, the organizing, ideology-producing power always, ultimately, wins. For Freud, the subversive, anarchic forces of randomness and disorder always, ultimately, win.

29 Kathleen Swaim, *Before and After the Fall* (Amherst, MA, 1986), uses this phrase to describe the lessons that Milton wants his readers to "effectively interiorize" (p. 32).

30 Christopher Kendrick, *Milton: A Study in Ideology and Form* (London, 1986), p. 139.

31 Kendrick, *Milton: Ideology and Form*, p. 231.

32 Fish, "Driving from the Letter: Truth and Indeterminacy in Milton's *Areopagitica*," in Nyquist and Ferguson, *Re-membering Milton*, p. 248.

33 Christopher Kendrick, *Milton: Ideology and Form*, pp. 35–42. Dobranski, "Letter and Spirit," offers a detailed analysis of Fish's, Kendrick's, and others' dialectical impositions on the meaning of *Areopagitica*.

34 Fish, "Driving from the Letter," *Re-membering Milton*, p. 249.

35 William Kerrigan, *Sacred Complex*, pp. 98–99.

36 William Kerrigan, *Sacred Complex*, pp. 6, 67, 243.

37 Frank Kermode, "Milton's Crises," *The Listener* 80 (1968), p. 829.
38 In his preface to the second edition of *Surprised by Sin*, Fish admitted that it is a " 'thesis' book" and thus reductive (p. x). This frank admission anticipated most of the reservations that have been expressed over the years about his version of Milton.
39 Fish, *Surprised by Sin*, p. 289.
40 The view of theodicy as presumption rests on premises more properly associated with Puritanism or reformed Christianity in general than with Christian humanism. Miltonists of an earlier generation, led by Douglas Bush and James H. Hanford, were inclined to categorize Milton as a Christian humanist, whereas more recently scholars have tended to emphasize instead the poet's Puritanism. Neither group of Miltonists adequately defines the distinction between Puritans and humanists, who in many respects overlap. Margo Todd details the inadequacy of customary assumptions regarding Puritanism and assesses the Puritans' debt to Erasmian Christian humanism, especially in the realm of social reform, in *Christian Humanism and the Puritan Social Order* (Cambridge, MA, 1987). A distinction between Puritanism and humanism does hold, however, in relation to the theodicy, and here we properly identify Milton with the humanists. Dennis Danielson has convincingly argued that Milton's identification with the Arminian dissent from orthodox Puritan determinism recapitulates Erasmus's humanist aversion to Lutheran bondage of the will. See *Milton's Good God* (Cambridge, 1982), pp. 66–69, 75–82.
41 This brief discussion of belief in free will and its consequences for theodicy recapitulates a somewhat fuller presentation in my *Matter of Glory: A New Preface to Paradise Lost* (Pittsburgh, 1987), pp. 9–11.
42 Desiderius Erasmus and Martin Luther, *Free Will and Salvation*, ed. E. Gordon Rupp and Philip Watson (Philadelphia, 1979), p. 244.
43 Fish, *Surprised by Sin*, p. 346.
44 Philip J. Gallagher, *Milton, the Bible, and Misogyny*, ed. Eugene R. Cunnar and Gail L. Mortimer (Columbia, MO, 1990), offers an insightful account of Adam's state of knowledge at the moment of his Fall (pp. 96–123). For Gallagher, Adam's sin is worse than Eve's because Adam is not deceived. I would dissent from Gallagher's analysis only to the extent that Adam's thoughts do reveal him to be deceived about the irresistibility of his connection with Eve and in his assessment of the situation as "remediless" (*PL* 9, 919).
45 Fish, *Surprised by Sin*, pp. 254, 250.
46 So closely does Milton identify reason and choice in *Areopagitica* that he famously misremembers Spenser by having the Palmer Reason accompany Guyon into the Cave of Mammon (*CP* 2, 516). Much has been written on the applicability to *Paradise Lost* of Milton's arguments in *Areopagitica*. The scene in the epic basic to this controversy is not primarily that of Eve's decision to eat the apple, however, but that of her separation

from Adam, where Milton draws heavily on reasoning from the prose tract. For a partial summary of the relevant critical opinions, see Diane Kelsey McColley, *Milton's Eve* (Urbana, 1983), pp. 141–45.

47 Fish, *Surprised by Sin*, p. 183.
48 Fish, *Surprised by Sin*, p. 188.
49 Fish, *Surprised by Sin*, p. 187.
50 Fish, *Surprised by Sin*, p. 187.
51 On the devils' loss of free will, see *Matter of Glory*, pp. 135–40; Fallon, *Milton Among the Philosophers*, pp. 216–22, persuasively relates Milton's representation of the devils' fate to Calvinism and Hobbesian determinism.
52 On the subject of specifically human modes of ethical knowledge in Milton, see Edward W. Tayler, "Milton's Grim Laughter and Second Choices," in *Poetry and Epistemology*, ed. Roland Hagenbüchle and Laura Skandera (Regensburg, 1986), pp. 72–93. For differences between humans and angels, see *Matter of Glory*, pp. 117–21.
53 Patricia A. Parker, *Inescapable Romance* (Princeton, 1979), p. 156. For Parker, humanity as depicted by Milton occupies the moment of suspension that, according to Aquinas, angels occupied only at the first moment of their existence (pp. 114–20).
54 In a paper presented at the International Milton Symposium in Vancouver, British Columbia (1991), J. Martin Evans argued that the narrative detail of *Paradise Lost* pointedly questions British imperialism and colonialism at the moment of its historical origins.
55 Fish, *Surprised by Sin*, p. 12.
56 Samuel Johnson, *Life of Milton*, in John T. Shawcross, ed., *Milton 1732–1801: The Critical Heritage* (London, 1972), p. 301.
57 On the confusion of hell and its implications, see *Matter of Glory*, pp. 86–93.
58 J. Martin Evans, in private correspondence, reminded me of this allusion.
59 Fish, *Surprised by Sin*, p. 9.
60 As Shawcross, *Milton: Self and World*, observes, the "great purpose of instruction ... was the goal of his life" (p. 98).
61 Fish, *Surprised by Sin*, p. 9.
62 John Keats, *Selected Poems and Letters*, ed. Douglas Bush (Boston, 1959), p. 261.

2 THE QUESTION OF CONTEXT

1 *Middlemarch*, ed. David Carroll (Oxford, 1988), p. 483.
2 *Milton's God* (1961; Cambridge, 1981), p. 253.
3 Dan Sperber and Deirdre Wilson, *Relevance* (Oxford, 1986), p. 45. Kent Bach and Robert M. Harnish, *Linguistic Communication and Speech Acts* (Cambridge, MA, 1979), anticipate Sperber and Wilson's emphasis on recognition of communicative intention. Like them, I view the discovery

of meaning as a process that begins with this recognition. Hence, I grant the premise often associated with deconstruction that there is no "infallible way of knowing" (Jacques Derrida, *Spurs: Nietzsche's Styles*, trans. Barbara Harlow [Chicago, 1979], p. 123.) Unlike proponents of deconstruction, however, I find intentionality to be the basis of meaning, rather than irrelevant to it. Denial of intention's place in interpretation is inevitable given deconstruction's resort to the linguistic code. With only the code to guide us, we are inevitably left with the endless "iterability" and significance of linguistic forms. See Derrida, "Signature Event Context," *Glyph* 1 (1977), pp. 172–97. See also note 23 of chapter 1.

4　Sperber and Wilson, *Relevance*, p. 18.

5　Sperber and Wilson, *Relevance*, p. 39. The question of context has been much studied, of course. For a good, recent guide with extensive reference to related studies and particular bearing on the history discussed in this chapter, see James Tully, ed., *Meaning and Context: Quentin Skinner and His Critics* (Cambridge, 1988). For a lively debate of theoretical issues related to context and interpretation, see Umberto Eco, Richard Rorty, Jonathan Culler, and Christine Brooke-Rose, *Interpretation and Overinterpretation*, ed. Stefan Collini (Cambridge, 1992).

6　E. D. Hirsch, *Validity in Interpretation* (New Haven, 1967), pp. 1–67, 209–44, argues for a rigorous distinction between meaning and significance. His argument depends on Husserl's specialized concept of intention as conscious representation. Sperber and Wilson's concept of intention is consistent with Husserl's, but, as they insist, "the fiction that there is a clear-cut distinction between wholly determinate, specifically intended inferences and indeterminate, wholly unintended inferences cannot be maintained" (*Relevance*, p. 199). On these issues, with particular reference to Hirsch, see P. D. Juhl, *Interpretation* (Princeton, 1980), pp. 16–44.

7　Henry James, *The Ambassadors* (New York, 1948), p. 191.

8　There is an unfortunate likelihood of confusion in Sperber and Wilson's category of "*manifest* assumptions" inasmuch as in their usage it overlaps with the psychological category of *latent* knowledge. I also accept the notion of *latent* unconscious meaning in the Freudian sense of the word.

9　Sperber and Wilson, *Relevance*, p. 200.

10　David Aers, *Community, Gender, and Individual Identity* (London, 1988), p. 3, quoting the words of V. N. Volosinov (M. Bakhtin?), *Marxism and the Philosophy of Language* (Cambridge, MA, 1986), p. 86.

11　Sperber and Wilson, *Relevance*, p. 43.

12　See Claude E. Shannon, "The Mathematical Theory of Communication" in Claude E. Shannon and Warren Weaver, *The Mathematical Theory of Communication* (1949; Urbana, IL, 1963), pp. 3–91. For an explanation of the mathematics behind Shannon's revolutionary claim, see John R. Pierce, *Signals* (San Francisco, 1981), pp. 46–57.

13　N. Katherine Hayles, *Chaos Bound* (Ithaca, 1990), p. 8.

14　For Sperber and Wilson, poetic utterances are those that "marginally increase the manifestness of a great many weakly manifest assumptions" (*Relevance*, p. 224).

15 Sperber and Wilson, *Relevance*, p. 118–23.

16 *A Preface to Paradise Lost* (London, 1942), p. 91; Stanley Fish, *Is There a Text in this Class?* (Cambridge, MA, 1980), p. 160.

17 Fish in appealing to *Protestant* doctrine is more specific than Lewis, who was content to make the poet a self-censored celebrator of "mere" Christianity. Yet Lewis admits the possible import of Milton's heresies while Fish avoids the subject altogether.

18 C. A. Patrides, *Milton and the Christian Tradition* (Oxford, 1966), pp. 5–6.

19 Patrides, *Milton and the Christian Tradition*, p. 209.

20 Patrides, *Milton and the Christian Tradition*, p. 58.

21 Patrides, *Milton and the Christian Tradition*, p. 195.

22 Patrides, *Milton and the Christian Tradition*, p. 154.

23 Stanley Fish, *There is No Such Thing as Free Speech, and It's a Good Thing, Too* (Oxford, 1994), p. 103.

24 H. J. McLachlan, *Socinianism in Seventeenth-Century England* (Oxford, 1951), p. 82, notes Locke's response. The book that Cheynell threw into Chillingsworth's grave, *The Religion of Protestants a Safe Way of Salvation*, maintains the right of free inquiry into the truth and locates the basis for faith primarily in the individual's intellectual assent. Although both Chillingsworth and Milton may be described as rationalist and tolerationist, Chillingsworth was a royalist, the godson of Laud, and the spy who reported to Laud the young Alexander Gill's insults of Charles and Buckingham after the latter's assassination (Masson 1, 208–12).

25 *The Dictionary of National Biography*, ed. Leslie Stephen and Sidney Lee, 63 vols. (London, 1885–1900), 10, 222. Henceforth, I will refer to this source as *DNB*.

26 Fish, *Surprised by Sin*, p. 12. Fish cites the "c. 1650" edition of *The Saints Everlasting Rest*, which was licensed in January 1649, old style, and printed in London. The quotation appears on p. 652. Though Fish here accurately represents what Baxter says (in other places he does not), he still misquotes him, substituting words and deleting phrases.

27 Baxter, *Saints Everlasting Rest*, pp. 650–51 and *Dedication*.

28 Masson details Baxter's transition from conservative Presbyterianism to moderate Episcopalianism (6, 99–105).

29 Masson describes Baxter's uneasiness over Cromwell's inclination to religious toleration (3, 385–87, 525). Joan Bennett, *Reviving Liberty* (Cambridge, MA, 1989), as she sketches the evolving concept of *recta ratio* crucial to Milton's radicalism, notes that Baxter thought Richard Hooker's standard, Anglican beliefs concerning liberty to be "inexcusably radical" (p. 15).

30 Christopher Hill, *The Experience of Defeat* (London, 1984), p. 73, quotes Baxter's remark.

31 Baxter is cited, for example, by Dennis Danielson, *Milton's Good God* (Cambridge, 1982), pp. 79–80. For Patrides's citation of Baxter, see n. 20.

Marshall Grossman, *Authors to Themselves* (Cambridge, 1987), p. 218, equates Raphael's teachings on obedience with Baxter's, though without developing or substantiating the identification.

32 As Bennett, *Reviving Liberty*, observes, "we cannot remind ourselves too often that a seventeenth-century author's basic views cannot be predicted with certainty from his terminology" (p. 15). In his *Dedication* to *The Saints Everlasting Rest* Baxter describes the expressly anti-Armenian views of the Synod of Dort as moderate and closest to the truth concerning the bondage of the will.

33 William Lamont, *Richard Baxter and the Millennium* (London, 1979), pp. 187-92.

34 Richard Baxter, *Reliquiae Baxterianae* (London, 1696), p. 53.

35 Fish, *Surprised by Sin*, p. 48. Fish cites *Pilgrim's Progress* as didactically equivalent to *Paradise Lost* eight times. Besides the many citations of Bunyan and Baxter, Fish cites Daniel Dyke's *The Mystery of Selfe-Deceiving* (five times), John Preston's *Sins Overthrow or a Godly and Learned Treatise of Mortification* (four times), John Corbet's *Self-Imployment in Secret* (twice). Along with Bunyan, these authors and works largely provide the historical context for the didactic Milton of *Surprised by Sin*.

36 Lewis, *Preface*, p. 91.

37 C.A. Patrides, "Milton and the Arian Controversy," *Proceedings of the American Philosophical Society* 120 (1976), pp. 245-52.

38 Regina Schwartz, *Remembering and Repeating: Biblical Creation in "Paradise Lost"* (Cambridge, 1988), p. 10. This argument is considered in detail in chapter 6. The opinion of B. Rajan in *Milton and the Seventeenth Century Reader* (1947, 1962; London, 1966), pp. 23-31, seems to me more plausible as an account of the undeniable differences between Milton's presentation of theological doctrines and poetic fictions. Neither whimsies put aside nor inept theology forsaken, Milton's heretical doctrines, though not omitted or falsified, are for Rajan mixed in with the narrative fiction tactfully enough not to upset the orthodox.

39 See William B. Hunter, "The Provenance of the *Christian Doctrine*," *Studies in English Literature* 32 (1992), pp. 129-42. This essay was given the Hanford Award for distinguished article. For devastating rebuttal see Christopher Hill, "Professor William B. Hunter, Bishop Burgess, and John Milton," *Studies in English Literature* 34 (1994), pp. 165-93. On the textual history of *de doctrina*, including its transcription by Milton's amanuenses Jeremy Picard and Daniel Skinner and the latter's failure to have it published according to Milton's wishes, see Parker, pp. 496, 610-12, 1056-57. On the steps taken in 1676-77 to intimidate Daniel Skinner and prevent the publication in Amsterdam of Milton's heretical views, see Maurice Kelley's account (*CP* 6, 37).

40 Barbara K. Lewalski, *Protestant Poetics and the Seventeenth-Century Religious Lyric* (Princeton, 1979), p. 14. Lewalski, *Protestant Poetics*, asserts that a "broad Protestant consensus" marked attitudes toward "doctrine and the spiritual

life" (p. ix). On the basis of this proposed consensus, she challenges the usual division between Anglican and Puritan poets according to ecclesiastical allegiance. Instead she insists on a shared "biblical poetics" underlying the work of poets as diverse as Donne, Herbert, Vaughan, Traherne, Milton, and Edward Taylor. There is much to recommend this claim inasmuch as the areas of agreement among these poets are extensive. Georgia B. Christopher in *Milton and the Science of the Saints* (Princeton, 1982), locates a basis for Protestant artistic unity in the writings of Calvin and Luther and a reformation theology of the word. This is a more troubled basis for argument. Disagreements over the theological (and essential) significance of words like "this is my body" were definitive of the distinction between Calvinists and Lutherans.

41 On Laud's Arminianism and that of the Tew circle generally, see Hugh Trevor-Roper, *Catholics, Anglicans, and Puritans* (London, 1987), pp. 40–119, 166–230. One point that Trevor-Roper does not stress is that Laud's tolerationist ideas stretched only to private intellectual life and did not conflict with a brutally repressive absolutism. The basis of Laud's dissent from Roman Catholicism was nonetheless significant and characteristic of the rationalism associated with Arminianism. Like Chillingsworth, Laud could not accept the notion of the Catholic Church's inerrancy. Both believed that the individual conscience had to remain the final authority. In this respect, the Oxford rationalists and Independents like Milton can be said to agree. The key difference is that for Milton rational conviction in theological matters was not simply a matter of gentlemanly discussion in a library but had political consequences. The "outward" conformity prescribed by the Laudians rested on a quasi-Cartesian dualism and practical trivialization of belief that Milton never accepted.

42 Max Weber, *The Protestant Ethic and the Spirit of Capitalism*, trans. Talcott Parsons (New York, 1958). Hill, *Milton and the English Revolution* (London, 1977), does invoke the "Protestant ethic" of Bread Street in Milton's childhood as if it were a prudential code for businessmen (pp. 22–23). He may be alluding to Weber only in the loosest way, however, or has since changed his mind. In "Daniel Defoe and *Robinson Crusoe*," *The Collected Essays of Christopher Hill* (Brighton, Sussex, 1985), Hill argues convincingly that the Protestant ethic is primarily an eighteenth-century phenomenon and agrees with critics of Weber who claim that he drew too much of his evidence "from late seventeenth- and even eighteenth-century Puritanism" (p. 110). Defoe's Puritanism, like that of most of his generation, Hill contends, is less intensely spiritual, more secular, than the embattled Puritanism of mid-century. Further, its developments had occurred according to the determinative needs of "England's commercial greatness" (p. 126).

43 This basis of the Puritans' social activism in sixteenth-century humanism is set forth in detail by Margo Todd, *Christian Humanism and the Puritan Social Order* (Cambridge, MA, 1987).

44 On the religious geography of the Civil War, see Trevor-Roper, *Religion, the Reformation and Social Change* (London, 1967). Andrew Milner, *John Milton and the English Revolution* (London, 1981), criticizes Weber's thesis also for its theoretical emphasis on Calvinist predestination as central to the Protestant ethic (pp. 91–93).

45 There are exceptions, of course, notably Hill's *Milton and the English Revolution*. See especially pp. 69–116. Milner in *John Milton and the English Revolution*, though he admits the relevance, specificity, and comprehensiveness of Christopher Hill's knowledge, criticizes him for his "insistence on 'cultural,' as opposed to 'political' explanations." Hill's "cultural" analysis depicts Milton as an author of unpredictable complexity, open to various traditions and class influences, whose attitudes are subject to inconsistency, and whose works can be troubled and uncertain in significance. For Milner, once Milton is properly understood in terms of "class conflict" the difficulties Hill describes evaporate and Milton's "precise social and political location becomes much easier to situate" (p. 199). In my opinion, Hill's detailed factual understanding of Milton's complexity carries more weight than Milner's theoretical sophistication. But I would follow Milner in stressing Milton's distinctive and fairly consistent *political* allegiance to the Independents.

46 Pierre Bourdieu has argued that the aesthetic distinction between spiritual and natural satisfaction correlates with the class distinction between the bourgeoisie and the lower orders. See *Distinction*, trans. Richard Nice (Cambridge, MA, 1984), p. 490. His arguments, like Weber's, apply better to late- and post-seventeenth-century conditions where, again, attitudes we ascribe to the bourgeoisie are less spiritually intense, reflect the complacence of social dominance, and may, perhaps legitimately, be interpreted as appurtenances of economic life. Contrary to the thesis advanced by Bourdieu, it would in Milton's case be more accurate to speak of an attempt to *collapse* the distinction between spiritual and natural satisfaction, and to construe the latter as a material dimension of the former. At the very least the order of precedence between natural and spiritual satisfaction is in Milton's philosophy blurred – a metaphysical distinction without an ontological difference.

47 Bennett, *Reviving Liberty*, p. 32, notes the perplexity, confusion, and sloppiness of certain Marxian critics (namely Jameson and Kendrick) in dealing with the assumption of free will behind Milton's theodicy.

48 Richard S. Westfall, *Never At Rest* (Cambridge, 1980), p. 581.

49 The quotation of Newton appears in Frank E. Manuel, *The Religion of Isaac Newton* (Oxford, 1974), p. 114.

50 On Mead's profound influence on Newton, see Manuel, *Religion of Isaac Newton*, pp. 90–92, 114. On relations between Mead and Milton, see my "Mead and Milton," in *Milton Quarterly* 20 (1986), pp. 136–41, and *Matter of Glory*, pp. 14, 72–73, 108, 113. For the extent of Mead's influence on scriptural interpretation throughout the seventeenth century and beyond,

see James W. Davidson, *The Logic of Millennial Thought* (New Haven, 1977), pp. 45–47.

51 J. G. A. Pocock, *The Machiavellian Moment* (Princeton, 1975), comments on the movement away from an anti-historical, Augustinian eschatology and the revolutionary effect of the new apocalyptic sensibility in mid-seventeenth-century England (pp. 31–48, 343–47).

52 See my "Mead and Milton," pp. 138–41.

53 McLachlan, *Socinianism*, p. 9.

54 Parker, p. 395; Masson, 4, 423, 438–39. The account of Milton's response to his questioners derives from the report of the Dutch diplomat and intelligence broker, Lieuwe Van Aitzema in March, 1652: "There was recently printed here the Socinian Racovian Catechism. This was frowned upon by Parliament; the printer says that Mr. Milton had licensed it; Milton, when asked, said yes, that he had published a tract on the matter, that men should refrain from forbidding books – and in approving of that book he had done no more than follow his conviction." Van Aitzema wrote Milton in 1655 to ask permission to print a Dutch translation of *Doctrine and Discipline of Divorce* (*CP* 4, ii, 870–72). Though it was long thought that this translation was never carried out, Professor Paul Sellin of UCLA has informed me in private correspondence that a Dutch translation has now been found. For a summary of Van Aitzema's relations with Milton, see Sellin's entry in *A Milton Encyclopedia*, ed. William B. Hunter, Jr., 9 vols., (London, 1978–83), 1, 34–35.

55 Thus Regina M. Schwartz's "Citation, Authority, and *De Doctrina Christiana*" in *Politics, Poetics, and Hermeneutics in Milton's Prose* (Cambridge, 1990) describes Milton's theological treatise as "a curious relic of dated controversies," potentially interesting by virtue of "its contribution to theoretical issues in literary studies" (p. 228).

56 Thomas Fuller, *The Church History of Britain*, x, iv, as cited by McLachlan, *Socinianism*, p. 33.

57 Fuller, *Church History*, x, iv, cited by McLachlan, *Socinianism*, p. 33. Although Legate's and Wightman's in 1612 were the last such executions in England, in Edinburgh, Thomas Aikenhead, 18, was executed in 1697 for insulting the supreme being. See McLachlan, *The Religious Opinions of Milton, Locke and Newton* (Manchester, 1941), pp. 103–04.

58 The relation of Milton's beliefs to Nicene orthodoxy is the subject of Michael Bauman's theological study, *Milton's Arianism* (Frankfurt, 1987). My analysis depends on his trenchant arguments.

59 *A Milton Encyclopedia*, 8, 14, 90.

60 Patrides, *Milton and the Christian Tradition*, p. 16.

61 John Fry is quoted by McLachlan, *Socinianism*, p. 241.

62 Against Hunter, Barbara K. Lewalski observes that though for Milton the Son shares in divine substance, this does not fundamentally distinguish him from the rest of creation. See *Milton's Brief Epic* (London, 1966), pp. 138–46.

63 Richard S. Westfall, *Never at Rest* (Cambridge, 1980), p. 748. Although Newton's metaphysics are not precisely the same as Milton's, he nevertheless believed God "to be omnipresent in the literal sense," according to his contemporary, fellow Arian, and confidant, David Gregory: "he supposes that ... God is present in space where there is no body [and] he is present in space where a body is also present" (p. 647). Newton believed all space to be the "sensorium of God," which accounted for his omniscience. He accounted gravity, too, a function of this substantial omnipresence (p. 647–48).

64 Manuel, *Religion of Isaac Newton*, p. 60, cites this passage from the *Yahuda Manuscript*, 15.5,fol.98^v.

65 Newton, *Yahuda Manuscript*, 15.7,fol.108^v; cited by Manuel, *Religion of Isaac Newton*, p. 69. For Hunter's proposal of the two-stage logos theory see "Milton's Arianism Reconsidered," in William B. Hunter, Jr., C. A. Patrides, and J. H. Adamson, *Bright Essence* (Salt Lake City, 1971), pp. 38–41.

66 If for Milton consciousness of a phenomenon constituted its existence, what would become of the distinction he so carefully draws between foreknowledge and free will? See *Matter of Glory*, p. 165.

67 Manuel, *Religion of Isaac Newton*, pp. 42–43.

68 Manuel, *Religion of Isaac Newton*, p. 60.

69 For Milton's insistence on the Son's strictly voluntary obedience, see *Matter of Glory*, p. 165.

70 Newton corresponded with Locke about the trinity and at his behest nearly allowed material from the letters to be published concerning the lack of scriptural evidence for the trinity. Westfall observes that a fairly wide circle of Arians was "connected with Newton" (*Never at Rest*, p. 650). Manuel, *Religion of Isaac Newton*, lists Edmund Halley, David Gregory, Fatio de Duillier, Hopton Haynes, and Samuel Clarke (p. 7). Newton's successor at Cambridge, William Whiston, was ejected from his chair when his Arian opinions became known (Westfall, *Never at Rest*, p. 332).

71 Newton, *Keynes Manuscript*, 5,f.5v, cited by Westfall, *Never at Rest*, p. 354.

72 Newton's knowledge of scripture and church history may have surpassed even Milton's and his writings on the subject run to volumes. Manuel, in *Religion of Newton*, observes that Newton "could string out citations like a concordance" (p. 83). After his death, the truth of Newton's religious beliefs was suppressed, and his voluminous, unpublished, religious writings were, as Manuel again puts it, "bowdlerized, neglected, or sequestered" (p. 10). It is a history that should not seem altogether strange to Milton scholars.

73 Westfall, *Never at Rest*, p. 318.

74 Westfall, *Never at Rest*, p. 315.

75 Westfall, *Never at Rest*, pp. 321, 331, 315.

76 Lamont, *Richard Baxter and the Millennium*, p. 13, observes that Baxter's position hearkens back to that of John Foxe, *Acts and Monuments*, 8 vols.

(rpt., New York, 1965), who portrayed Elizabeth as following Constantine's example (1, xvi–xxiv, 4–5, 248–50, 285).

77 Robert Baillie, in *A Dissuasive from the Errors of the Time* (London, 1645), expressed the common Presbyterian opinion that the notion of a literal reign of Christ was a heretical misreading of mystical and allegorical apocalyptic scriptures (pp. 80–85, 224–27). For the opposed, Independent position, see, for example, the sermon *A Glimpse of Sion's Glory* (published in London, 1641) usually attributed to Thomas Goodwin, in *The Works of Thomas Goodwin*, ed. Thomas Smith, 12 vols. (Edinburgh, 1861–66), 12, 66. Hugh Peters preached on the same, implicitly anti-monarchical theme before Parliament in April of 1645, *Gods Doings and Mans Duty* (London, 1646), pp. 9–25. John Cooke, Charles's prosecutor in 1649, wrote to similar effect and explicitly counter to the Presbyterian position in *Reintegration Amoris* (London, 1647), pp. 80–84. Or refer to various works of John Goodwin, including *Theomachia* (London, 1644), p. 48, *Innocency and Truth* (London, 1646), p. 10, and, with particular relevance to the Independents' disagreement with the Presbyterians, *The Obstructours of Justice* (London, 1649), p. 85.

3 RESPONSES AND THEIR VICISSITUDES

1 *On the Genealogy of Morals*, trans. Walter Kaufmann and R. J. Hollingdale (New York, 1967), p. 93.

2 Frank Kermode, "Milton's Crises," *The Listener* 80 (1968), p. 829.

3 Andrew Milner, *John Milton and the English Revolution* (London, 1981), p. 200, uses the term "ruthless" to describe the senior Milton's business practices.

4 On Weber, see chapter 2, note 42. For a recent, highly theoretical account of the economic nexus linking Milton and his father, see John Guillory, "The Father's House: *Samson Agonistes* in its Historical Moment," *Remembering Milton*, ed. Mary Nyquist and Margaret Ferguson (New York, 1987), pp. 148–76. Guillory combines Weber with Freud to read *Samson Agonistes* in the context of Miltonic autobiography.

5 William Kerrigan, *The Sacred Complex* (Cambridge, MA, 1983), pp. 49–50.

6 The notion of Milton's vow of virginity was first proposed by James Holly Hanford, "The Youth of Milton" in *Studies in Shakespeare, Milton, and Donne* (New York, 1925), pp. 89–163. See also E. M. W. Tillyard, *Milton* (1930; New York, 1967), pp. 318–26 and Ernest Sirluck, "Milton's Idle Right Hand" *Journal of English and Germanic Philology* 60 (1961), pp. 749–85, who build off Hanford's suggestion. This hypothesis has achieved something like factual status among many Milton scholars, though it is based on flimsier evidence than is widely supposed, specifically the illegitimate conflation of two distinct passages from the book of Revelation. This conflation and its role in the arguments for Milton's celibacy were

brought to my attention by John Leonard in a paper read at the International Milton Symposium, Vancouver, Canada, 1991.

7 Kerrigan, *Sacred Complex*, p. 53.

8 *All's Well That Ends Well* (1.1.144, 136–37), in G. Blakemore Evans, ed., *The Riverside Shakespeare* (Boston, 1974). Traditions celebrating virginity also were common in the Renaissance and Milton would surely have been aware of them too. Much depended on the rhetorical circumstances, obviously.

9 *Lycurgus and Numa, Plutarch's Lives*, trans. Bernadette Perrin, 11 vols. (London, 1914) 1, 249.

10 *All's Well*, 1.2.126.

11 Kerrigan (*Sacred Complex*, p. 44) quotes this phrase from Erik Erikson's *Young Man Luther* (New York, 1958), p. 83.

12 Hugh Trevor-Roper, "Milton in Politics," *Catholics, Anglicans, and Puritans* (London, 1987), pp. 231–82, diagnoses Milton's tendency to merge public and private utterances as a kind of solipsistic megalomania. At one point he equates Milton's "hysterical hatred" of bishops with Hitler's hatred of Jews (p. 254). The account of Milton in Trevor-Roper's essay recalls Cavalier slanders of the poet during the Restoration. For a comparatively disinterested study of the intersection of the public and private Milton, see Annabel Patterson's "No meer amatorious novel?" in *Politics, Poetics, and Hermeneutics in Milton's Prose*, ed. David Loewenstein and James Grantham Turner (Cambridge, 1990), pp. 85–101.

13 Regarding Puritanism and family relations, see Lawrence Stone, *The Crisis of the Aristocracy 1558–1641* (Oxford, 1965). Puritanism has been seen as an ideological engine driving society toward reliance on the patriarchal, nuclear family as the fundamental social organization. Despite the evidence for this thesis presented in *Crisis of the Aristocracy*, Stone's subsequent study of the early modern family, *The Family, Sex and Marriage in England, 1500–1800* (Oxford, 1977), portrays the close-knit family of post-1800 as something radically new. His claims are exaggerated. Alan Macfarlane persuasively argues that there are many more cultural continuities in English history from the thirteenth century onward than contemporary historians have typically found it convenient to recognize. See his *The Origins of English Individualism* (Oxford, 1978), and *The Culture of Capitalism* (Oxford, 1987).

14 Michel Foucault, *The History of Sexuality, Volume I: An Introduction,* trans. Robert Hurley (New York, 1978) accounts for Freudian analysis as an instance of the sexual repression of its own historical moment. Yet Freudian psychology, even with its overdetermined emphasis on and expression of repression, need not be considered valueless as an explanatory tool of the past. If we grant that Foucault's works go beyond mere reflexive expression of the epistemological despair and suspicion to which our own time is given, we may grant Freud, too, his moments of transcendence. Nevertheless, without denying the relevance of Oedipal tensions to seventeenth-century

psychology, it seems likely that they had greater impact in the centuries following Milton's. Bruno Bettelheim also notes the historical limitations of the Oedipal model in *Symbolic Wounds* (New York, 1954), pp. 46–51. His observations concern a much greater historical difference than Foucault's, however. Freud attributed more rigor to primal fathers than he did to modern and suggested that the strength of castration anxiety among modern children owed to the amplifying effect of racial memory. Anthropological studies paint a less frightening picture of primitive fathers, however, and Bettelheim suggests that Freud's theory "is the result of a projection of relatively recent events into the distant past" (p. 51).

15 Kerrigan, *Sacred Complex*, pp. 48–49.

16 Helen Darbishire, ed., *The Early Lives of Milton* (Oxford, 1932), p. 5.

17 On Milton's father, see Parker, pp. 4–5.

18 Darbishire, *Early Lives*, comments that "Milton must have been proud of this tale, and fond of relating it" (p. lix).

19 Darbishire, *Early Lives*, pp. 255–56.

20 For a summary of the scrivener's business activities, see Parker, pp. 689–93, 735–37, 772, 797. He draws heavily on J. Milton French, *Milton in Chancery* (New York, 1939).

21 Darbishire, *Early Lives*, p. 1.

22 Darbishire, *Early Lives*, p. 18.

23 Ernest Brennecke, Jr. directed a choir that performed the senior Milton's compositions. See *John Milton the Elder and His Music* (New York, 1938), pp. xiii, 56–7.

24 Brennecke, *John Milton the Elder and His Music*, p. 87.

25 The passage from *ad Patrem* corresponds to lines 86–92. Translations of Milton's Latin poetry are my own. Where necessary for the argument, I supply the original. I wish to thank my colleague Elizabeth Richmond-Garza for checking my explication of the passage from *ad Patrem*.

26 Unlike most translators, Merritt Hughes, *John Milton: Complete Poems and Major Prose* (New York, 1957), p. 84, rendered *genuisse* (line 61) in the passive, thereby completely isolating Milton's begetting as a poet from the agency of his father: "it is my lot to have been born a poet." Although I do not follow his example, Hughes's rendering does no violence to the spirit of the passage and, given Greek precedent and the established theological usage, may be preferable. The same cannot be said for a translation that transforms Milton's passive father into an active mother: "you have happened to bear a poet." *The Complete Poems*, ed. Gordon Campbell (London, 1980), p. 535.

27 Darbishire, *Early Lives*, pp. 6–7.

28 In the seventeenth century at least, extraordinary and habitual intensity of effort need not imply a father's threats or expectations. Two children could hardly have found themselves in more opposite emotional situations than Newton and Milton, to return to the main comparison of the last chapter, yet remarkable resemblances of attitude, belief, and, more to the point,

work habits appear in their lives. Newton was a posthumous child. In an early history reminiscent of yet another contemporary, Jonathan Swift, Newton's mother deserted her 3-year-old child for a new husband, and left her baby with one of his grandmothers. By his teens and early twenties Newton begrudged time spent sleeping and forgot to eat while engaged with his studies. Optical experiments he carried out on himself endangered his eyesight. These experiments included sticking a needle between his own eye and orbital lobe (to see what visual sensations might occur) and staring at the sun so long that the image of it would not leave his vision even after days spent in utter darkness. See Richard S. Westfall, *Never at Rest* (Cambridge, 1980), p. 94. Newton's legendary absorption in contemplation and experiment was not encouraged by anyone in his family and gained him only the mistrust of his peers. Milton's studious behavior appears to have earned him ridicule in some quarters, not to mention hints from his beloved Diodati that he should relax. Frank Manuel, *A Portrait of Isaac Newton* (Cambridge, 1968), like Kerrigan relies on the Oedipal triangle as the basis for his psychohistory, but he construes the strenuousnous of Newton's efforts as a search for his missing father (p. 118).

29 Darbishire, *Early Lives*, pp. 18, 54, 86.
30 Proud James characteristically took up the argument on behalf of the insensible opponent and after enduring the rest of Chappell's unmitigated assault, remarked, in effect, that he was glad that in ecclesiastical debates the Laudian Chappell was on his side (Masson 1, 128).
31 See Kerrigan, *Sacred Complex*, p. 44.
32 *Surprised by Sin* (1967; Berkeley, 1971), p.44.
33 Kerrigan, *Sacred Complex*, pp. 98–99. See chapter 1, note 35.
34 John H. Walter, ed., *The Arden Edition of "Henry V"* (London, 1954), 1.2.243.
35 Christopher Kendrick, "Milton and Sexuality," *Re-membering Milton*, ed. Mary Nyquist and Margaret Ferguson (New York, 1987), pp. 43–73.
36 John Guillory, "The Father's House: *Samson Agonistes* in its Historical Moment," *Re-membering Milton*, pp. 148–76
37 Stanley Fish, "Wanting a Supplement," in *Politics, Poetics, and Hermeneutics in Milton's Prose*, ed. David Loewenstein and James Grantham Turner (Cambridge, 1990), pp. 66–67.
38 Fish, "Wanting a Supplement," *Politics, Poetics, and Hermeneutics*, p. 66.
39 Fish, *Surprised by Sin*, p.44.
40 Fish, "Driving from the Letter," *Re-membering Milton*, p. 249. See chapter 1, note 34.
41 Michael Lieb, *Poetics of the Holy* (Chapel Hill, 1981), p. 174.
42 Fish, *Surprised by Sin*, p. 192. Empson, *Milton's God*, p. 113.
43 On the traditional victory of the good angels following Michael's decisive duel with Satan, see Stella Purce Revard, *The War in Heaven* (Ithaca, 1980), pp. 182–86.
44 Alastair Fowler, in his edition of *Paradise Lost* (London, 1971) accounts for Gabriel's remarks as a hypothetical adoption of Satan's perspective for the

sake of argument. Empson saw the confrontation between Gabriel and Satan as one of the most ambiguous and complex moments in the poem. See *Milton's God*, pp. 110–14.

45 See Roy F. Baumeister, *Masochism and the Self* (Hillsdale, NJ, 1989), pp. 56-8.

46 Female masochists do not generally enter fantasies involving escape from superior status, a fact that may be attributable to the rarity of women in high places in society. Recent studies indicate that those women who do occupy positions of high status and authority are increasingly prone to the typically "male" version of masochism. In this case at least, sexual preferences seem to derive from social and not biological constructions. See Baumeister, *Masochism*, pp. 167–69.

47 Some argue that gender is flexible in Milton's heaven because Milton insists that spirits can assume either sex. But the angels are consistently depicted as masculine. There is hardly any hint, for example, that Raphael could desire Adam as a sexual partner, but Milton explicitly allows that possibility with Eve so that he might discount it.

48 Baumeister notes that manuals for sadomasochistic sexual practices are mainly instructions on how to inflict pain without causing injury (*Masochism*, p. 14)

49 Pain makes the masochist aware of the "self as a body"; it has the effect of emptying the self of higher significance while strengthening and focusing a version of the self as a mentally and physically unified site of sensation: "the self is denied as a thinking, choosing, deciding entity, but it is emphasized as an active mouth or functioning set of hands and feet" (Baumeister, *Masochism*, pp. 86, 81). See also Elaine Scarry, *The Body in Pain* (New York, 1985), who argues that pain in effect deconstructs the self and the world, emptying both of meaningful contents and replacing those contents with the brutal idiocy of mere anguish.

50 Sigmund Freud, "Instincts and Their Vicissitudes," in James Strachey, trans., *Standard Edition* of *The Complete Psychological Works of Sigmund Freud*, 24 vols. (London, 1953–64), 14, 127–129. Subsequent references are to this edition *(SE)*.

51 Freud, "Instincts and Their Vicissitudes," *SE* 14, 127.

52 See, for example, Esther Menaker, *Masochism and the Emergent Ego*, ed. Leila Lerner (New York, 1979); Maria Carmen Gear, Melvyn A. Hill, Ernesto Cesar Liendo, *Working Through Narcissism: Treating its Sadomasochistic Structure* (New York, 1981); Carolyn Dean, *The Self and Its Pleasures: Bataille, Lacan, and the History of the Decentered Subject* (Ithaca, 1992).

53 Narcissism, like sadomasochism, may be described as bipolar in structure. Indeed, the "bipolar organization of the psychic apparatus" in narcissism, according to Gear, Hill, and Liendo, *Working Through Narcissism*, "always alternates between a sadistic and a masochistic position, each being the necessary complement and mirror of the other" (p. 3). If this is so, the sadomasochistic dialectic is not just similar to but definitive of narcissism

as a psychological and, if Christopher Lasch, *The Culture of Narcissism* (New York, 1979), is correct, cultural formation. It echoes from individual to institutional behavior, including the academic, such that what clinically might be diagnosed as a tendency toward sadistic narcissism would seem to be a prescription for success. This would be true regardless of whether we conceive of that prescription as oblivious immunity to the mitigating influence of others in the pursuit of dominance, or as skill in negotiating others into a submissive posture.

54 Peter Berger, in *The Sacred Canopy* (New York, 1967), has described Protestant Christianity in particular as religious masochism because of the emphasis on the worshipper's worthlessness and utter dependence on God for any sense of value or worth.

55 Charles A. Huttar, "The Passion of Christ in *Paradise Regained*," *English Language Notes* 19 (1982), pp. 236–60.

56 Empson, *Milton's God*, p. 269.

57 Robert M. Adams, "A Little Look into Chaos," *Illustrious Evidence: Approaches to English Literature of the Early Seventeenth Century*, ed. Earl Miner (Berkeley, 1975), p. 71.

58 Wilhelm Reich, *Character Analysis* (New York, 1949).

59 Menaker, *Masochism and the Emergent Ego*, pp. 65–83.

4 *COMUS*: A FIT OF THE MOTHER

1 *The Language of the Goddess* (London, 1989), p. 208.

2 See Kerrigan's chapter on *Comus* in *The Sacred Complex* (Cambridge, MA, 1983), pp. 22–72.

3 Obviously, I am unpersuaded by John Leonard's insistence that *Comus* "lends no support to [psychoanalytic] readings," or at least no "hard evidence," or by his observation that critics who take such an approach produce only "a gooey mess." See "Saying 'No' to Freud: Milton's *A Mask* and Sexual Assault," *Milton Quarterly* 25 (1991), p. 130.

4 Freud, *Totem and Taboo*, in James Strachey, trans., *Standard Edition of the Complete Psychological Works of Sigmund Freud*, 24 vols. (London, 1953–64), 13, ix. Subsequent citations are to this edition (*SE*). See also Bruno Bettelheim, *Symbolic Wounds* (New York, 1954), p. 86, and note 27.

5 Kerrigan, *Sacred Complex*, p. 51.

6 In translating *matre probatissima* as "a mother of approved character," I adapt H. Grose Hodge's translation of Cicero's "*probatissimam feminam*," in *Pro Caecina*, 4, 10. See *Cicero in Twenty-Eight Volumes*, The Loeb Classical Library, (London, 1927), 9, 106–7.

7 See 1 Cor. 13, Milton's main authority for *caritas* in *Christian Doctrine*, *CP* 6, 717.

8 On the cultural force and persistence of classical metaphors comparing earth to a mother, see Carolyn Merchant, *The Death of Nature* (San Francisco, 1980). Renaissance metallurgy was of the opinion that light from the sun and stars penetrated the earth and acted on vaporous

substance (or dew) to produce metal and gems. See, for example, Joseph Duchesne, *A breefe answere of Josephus Quercetanus Armeniacus ... concerning the original, and Causes of Mettalles* (London, 1591), pp. 8–15. E. H. Duncan, *Osiris* 11 (1954), p. 388, finds classical precedent in Aristotle's *Meteorologica* 1, 4 (341b) and 3, 6 (348a). On the relevance of the theory to *Comus*, see Harry F. Robins, "The Key to a Problem in Milton's *Comus*," *Modern Language Quarterly* 12 (1951), pp. 422–28.

9 See George Sandys, *Ovid's Metamorphosis Englished* (Nebraska, 1970), p. 480. Quotations of Ovid follow this translation and will be cited in the text, parenthetically.

10 Legends of subterranean creatures surface in *Comus* – the "swart Faery of the mine" (line 436) – and in *Il Penseroso* – "Daemons that are found / ... underground" (lines 93–94).

11 Leah S. Marcus, *The Politics of Mirth* (Chicago, 1986), pp. 187–200.

12 Philip Slater, *The Glory of Hera* (Boston, 1968).

13 See my "The Milton-Diodati Correspondence," *Hellas* 3 (1992), pp. 76–85.

14 Karl Kerényi, *Athene: Virgin and Mother in Greek Religion*, trans. Murray Stein (Zurich, 1978), pp. 17–18. At Ephesus, Diana was worshipped in what Robert Graves calls her "second person": "an orgiastic Aphrodite with a male consort." See *The Greek Myths*, 2 vols. (Baltimore, 1955), 1, 83–85.

15 See note 1.

16 On the myth of Perseus and its record of the seizure by Hellenic invaders of powers associated with the cult of the moon goddess, see Graves, *The Greek Myths*, 1, 237–45. On Diana's bow and Minerva's aegis, see Graves, 1, 85, 99. Archeological evidence supporting Graves's claims and particularly the association of the Medusa's head with pre-classical, old European culture is presented by Gimbutas in *The Language of the Goddess*, pp. 205–09. She comments that "the early Gorgon was a potent Goddess dealing with life and death, not the later Indo-European monster to be slain by heroes such as Perseus" (p. 208). Medusa appears to have been an aspect of the figure we know as Artemis: "the Erinys side of Artemis, the dangerous one" (p. 208). On Medusa, see also Slater, *Glory of Hera*, pp. 16–23, and Catherine Keller, *From a Broken Web* (Boston, 1986), pp. 50–73. Graves notes that the myth of Perseus, during whose adventures Pegasus is born, is closely related to that of Bellerophon, another hero with whom Milton associates himself (1, 17, 244).

17 On the Medusa myth as it figures in the patriarchal discourse of early modern science, see Dolora A. Wojciehowski, "A Gendered Cosmos: Galileo, Mother Earth, and the 'Sink of Uncleanliness,'" forthcoming in Laura Benedetti, Julia Hairston, and Silvia Ross, eds., *Gendered Contexts: New Directions in Italian Cultural Studies* (New York, 1995). For a more politically oriented discussion, see Neil Hertz, "Medusa's Head: Male Hysteria under Political Pressure," *Representations* 4 (1983), pp. 27–54.

18 Leah Marcus, "The Earl of Bridgewater's Legal Life: Notes toward a

Political Reading of *Comus*," *Milton Quarterly* 21:4 (1987), pp. 13–23. (This was a special number of *MQ*; its pagination is not consistent with the rest of vol. 21.) See also Barbara Breasted, "Comus and the Castlehaven Scandal," *Milton Studies* 3 (1971), pp. 201–24.

19 *Ovid's Metamorphosis Englished*, p. 221.

20 "Scylla represents a Virgin; who as long as chast in thought, and in body unspotted, appears of an excellent beauty, attracting all eyes upon her, and wounding the Gods themselves with affection. But once polluted with the sorceries of *Circe*; that is, having rendred her maiden honour to bee deflowred by bewitching pleasure, she is transformed to an horrid monster" (*Ovid's Metamorphosis Englished*, p. 645).

21 The association of Sin's Skylla-like girdle of yelling monsters with hideous maternity is continued as Milton's simile links her with "the Night-hag" (i.e. Hecate), "Lur'd with the smell of infant blood" (*PL* 2, 662, 664). The witches' rites Milton alludes to are similar to those begun by Comus (lines 128–44). The allegorical conception and birth of Death is echoed in the "pangs" of mother Earth trembling "from her entrails" at the completion of original sin (9, 1000–01).

22 Freud, "The Medusa's Head," *SE*, 18, 273–74. In discussing Spenser's attribution to Elizabeth I of a Medusan power to petrify, Lowell Gallagher notes that the paralysis inflicted is a function of the fact that her actual exercise of power cannot be seen: "There was only a gaze, only a continuous emanation of power." See *Medusa's Gaze* (Stanford, 1991), pp. 24–25. The paralyzing absolute power emanated by Elizabeth can be considered analogous to that of a mother over her child. It too is experienced as a condition of being, especially for an infant utterly dependent on maternal care and unable to move of its own volition.

23 Slater, *Glory of Hera*, p. 126.

24 Otto Weininger, *Sex and Character* (New York, 1906), p. 297. In "The Uncanny," Freud describes fear of engulfment as a version of the castration complex, "a transformation of ... the phantasy ... of intra-uterine existence" (*SE* 17, 244).

25 See Karen Horney, "The Dread of Women," *International Journal of Psychoanalysis* 13 (1932), pp. 348–60. Slater cites Horney in *Glory of Hera*, p. 17, as he addresses the significance of the Medusa myth within classical Greek patriarchy (pp. 12–20).

26 Bettelheim, *Symbolic Wounds*, pp. 27–37. Bettelheim further notes, against Freud's interpretation of such rituals, that "if ... the purpose of initiation rites is to enforce the incest taboo, they occur much too late in the child's life" (p. 75).

27 Bettelheim, *Symbolic Wounds*, p. 155.

28 Christopher Hill, *Milton and the English Revolution* (New York, 1977), p. 119.

29 Slater, *Glory of Hera*, notes that for the Greeks, "the child's world before the age of 6 or 7 was an almost entirely feminine one," though the father was theoretically in charge (p. 10).

30 Freud, "On Narcissism," *SE*, 14, 91.
31 Richard D. Chessick, *Psychology of the Self and the Treatment of Narcissism* (Northvale, NJ, 1985), p. 9.
32 Freud, "On Narcissism," *SE* 14, 86.
33 Nancy Chodorow, "Gender, Relation, and Difference in Psychoanalytic Perspective," *The Future of Difference*, ed. Hester Eisenstein and Alice Jardine (New Brunswick, NJ, 1980), pp. 3–20.
34 Although he insists on the centrality of the Oedipal paradigm, Kerrigan recognizes the relevance of narcissistic desire to *Comus*, attributing it to Milton's defensive regression in response to paternal intimidation (*Sacred Complex* p. 111). On the fundamental psychological significance of pre-Oedipal experience, see Nancy Chodorow, *The Reproduction of Mothering* (Berkeley, 1978). Chodorow acknowledges substantial indebtedness to Slater.
35 Freud, "An Outline of Psychoanalysis," *SE*, 23, 188–89. See also note 4.
36 On the near exclusive responsibility of seventeenth-century mothers for the early upbringing of their children, see Alan Macfarlane, *The Family Life of Ralph Josselin, a Seventeenth-Century Clergyman* (Cambridge, 1970), pp. 89–91. I do not deny that John Milton, Sr. would also have felt narcissistic involvement in his son's development. But the child's early years would almost certainly have been under maternal control.
37 Slater, *Glory of Hera*, p. 33.
38 In discussing the crucial role of the story of Orestes in Greek culture, Slater notes its continual retellings, reshapings, and elaborations as a story of sex-antagonism generally and mother–son conflict in particular (*Glory of Hera*, pp. 161–92).
39 Parker guesses that Milton wrote *Death of a Fair Infant* in English because it was for his sister Anne and "also a poem to be shown to his mother, and by her, perhaps, to admiring neighbours and relatives" (p. 40). Again, though there is no historical basis for his guess, Parker I think shows acute insight into what Milton supposed his mother wanted from him. Certainly the young poet identified closely enough with the woman's point of view to attribute the fair infant's death to the "cold-kind embrace" of an insecure and inept god of winter and his punctilious concern for his masculine reputation (line 20).
40 The mother–daughter relation seems for the Greeks to have been the least problematic of family relations and, as Agamemnon learned, one to be reckoned with when contemplating sacrifices for the success of heroic male enterprises. Milton has little to say about Iphigenia, but one of the mythological moments most powerfully lodged in his memory is the sorrowful search of Ceres for her lost daughter, a search impelled solely by pure parental *affection* (see, e.g. *PL* 4, 268–72). Slater also notes the importance of the Demeter-Kore myth, though he perhaps exaggerates its emotional uniqueness (*Glory of Hera*, pp. 23–33).
41 Comus's strategy is reminiscent of an apologetic tack standard in

seventeenth-century defenses of learning, in which the indulgence of intellectual appetite is construed as testimony to the all-giver's bounty. The apology for scientific investigation as praise of the Creator appears in the writings of Thomas Browne, Robert Boyle, Henry More, Robert Hooke, Isaac Newton, and Richard Bentley, among others. For detailed citations, see Frank E. Manuel, *The Religion of Isaac Newton* (Oxford, 1974). Among Miltonists, the defense is generally associated with Francis Bacon, and its appearances in Milton's writings are cited as evidence of his advocacy of the new knowledge (see *The Advancement of Learning* (London, 1951), first book, 1, 3; 6, 16). Certainly, it underlies the argument of Prolusion 7, and Uriel makes a similar case in pointing the disguised Satan to God's latest creations. In *Areopagitica*, however, Milton construes "profuseness" as God's provision of limitless opportunities for the exercise of temperance (*CP* 2, 527–28).

42 E. M. W. Tillyard recognizes the flexibility of this deductive strategy, familiar from Milton's prose, in his famous observation that if Milton had been in the garden, he would himself have eaten the apple and "immediately justified the act in a polemical pamphlet." See *Milton* (London, 1930), p. 282.

43 On the first audience for Milton's masque, see Cedric Brown, *John Milton's Aristocratic Entertainments* (New York, 1985).

44 A key word for Milton, "vehemence" derives from the Latin for "mindless." Neither Comus's speech criticizing virginity nor the Lady's abstention from defense of "the sage / And serious doctrine" were delivered in the 1634 performance (lines 786–87). The Lady's ominous restraint occasions the only reference in the masque to a threatening paternal power, that of Jove's thunder and the "chains of *Erebus*" (line 804).

45 Slater, *Glory of Hera*, p. 88.

46 Marcus, *Politics of Mirth*, pp. 186–206.

47 Kerrigan, *Sacred Complex*, p. 63.

48 The correct date for the letter is probably 1633 (Parker pp. 786–87).

49 The scorn that Milton later directs at the story of Origen's literal interpretation of such a sacrifice (*CP* 2, 334) might be construed as support for a connection between the threat of castration and Milton's alleged vow of virginity.

50 Slater, *Glory of Hera*, notes that the classic oral-narcissistic dilemma concerns boundaries, the conflict, as Slater tells us, "between the desire to merge and the desire to be free and separate" (p. 88).

51 Slater, *Glory of Hera*, pp. 17–23, 77.

52 Helen Darbishire, ed., *The Early Lives of Milton* (Oxford, 1932), p. 205.

53 The argument I make works best if the sonnet refers to Milton's second wife, Katherine Woodcock, and was composed not long after her death in 1658. Although the reference to "purification in the old law" is arguably inconclusive, the description "late espous'd Saint" certainly seems more aptly applied to a veiled Katherine Woodcock than to Mary Powell.

54 Gerald Hammond, *Fleeting Things* (Cambridge, MA, 1990) p. 216. Hammond also notes that as compensation for this heroic resistance, Milton will also soon become a mother – of his greatest poetry. And this will come about through Milton's identification with his "Celestial Patroness," who, like his dead wife, comes to him in his sleep.

55 *Iliad* 23, 99–107; *Odyssey* 11, 204–09; *Aeneid* 6, 700–02.

56 The other reason Dalila gives for betraying him is the benefit his downfall has brought to her nation. It is her strongest defense and one that Samson has difficulty refuting convincingly. A woman of approved character among the Philistines, she delights in "the public marks of honour and reward" (line 992).

57 Spenser in book 2 of the *Faerie Queene* tells the story of Sabrina in more detail (10, 17–19). The prime source is Geoffrey of Monmouth's *Historia Regum Britanniæ*. Milton relates the story himself in his *History of England*.

58 Bettelheim, *Symbolic Wounds*, p. 17.

59 With characteristic philological precision Milton in *Paradise Lost* names Adonis "*Thammuz*" and geographically associates his cult with Syria – hence the title "th' *Assyrian* Queen" in lieu of Venus' name (1, 446–52; *Comus* line 1002). The Syrian cult of Adonis was widely known in Milton's time, and described by John Selden, in *De Dis Syris* (London, 1617), as a nature cult (II, x). Milton could have known from a variety of sources that the monument to Adonis and Aphrodite in Ghineh, Syria, presents the goddess "seated in an attitude of sorrow."

60 See book 3, canto 6 of the *Faerie Queene* (30, 4–5).

5 THE ART OF GENERATION

1 William Shakespeare, *The Third Part of Henry VI*, Andrew S. Cairncross, ed. (London, 1989), 3.2.161–62.

2 William Kerrigan, *The Sacred Complex* (Cambridge, MA, 1983). Kerrigan addresses Milton's gender attitudes in "Gender and Confusion in Milton and Everyone Else," *Hellas* 2 (1991), pp. 195–220. John T. Shawcross, in "Milton and Diodati: An Essay in Psychoanalytic Meaning," *Milton Studies* 7 (1975), pp. 127–63, was the first to discuss this aspect of Milton's psychology. See also Michael Lieb, *Milton and the Culture of Violence* (Ithaca, 1994), pp. 84–86, 92–94, 97–99.

3 Feminist attacks on and defenses of Milton are too numerous to list. Of the attacks, Sandra M. Gilbert, "Patriarchal Poetry and Women Readers: Reflections on Milton's Bogey" *PMLA* 93 (1978), pp. 368–82, reprinted in *The Madwoman in the Attic* (New Haven, 1979), pp. 187–212, is both representative and widely known. Barbara Lewalski, "Milton on Women – Yet Once More" *Milton Studies* 6 (1974), pp. 3–20, anticipated and preemptively answered most of Gilbert's charges. Later, Joan Malory Webber replied explicitly (and not always fairly) to Gilbert in "The Politics of Poetry: Feminism and *Paradise Lost*," *Milton Studies* 14 (1980),

pp. 3–24. These and various other attacks and defenses published in the 1970s and early 1980s reflect the tendency of liberal feminism to ignore history (in making accusations) or to assume an evolutionary model of progress toward equality (in defending against them). More recently, various feminist scholars have questioned the notion of equality, its uses, and what it presumes. See Mary Nyquist, "The Genesis of Gendered Subjectivity in the Divorce Tracts and in *Paradise Lost*," in *Re-membering Milton* (New York, 1987). Other recent writings on Milton and feminism include Joseph A. Wittreich, *Feminist Milton* (Ithaca, 1987) and Philip J. Gallagher, *Milton, the Bible, and Misogyny*, ed. Eugene R. Cunnar and Gail Mortimer (Columbia, 1990), as well as the essays collected in *Milton and the Idea of Woman*, ed. Julia M. Walker (Urbana, 1988).

4 Wittreich offers a similar assessment of feminist criticism in relation to the invented Milton: "Milton's male readership fostered the notion to which today's feminists typically, but not unilaterally, subscribe" (*Feminist Milton*, p. 8). I would add only that there were women, too, among the "readership" that fostered the notion of Milton lambasted by contemporary feminists.

5 Harold Bloom, *The Anxiety of Influence* (Oxford, 1973), p. 11.

6 James Turner, *One Flesh: Paradisal Marriage and Sexual Relations in the Age of Milton* (Oxford, 1987), p. 155, suggests that Milton's presentation of Sin parodies Jakob Boehme's Gnostic interpretation of Genesis. For Boehme, the Fall is a descent from spiritual sexuality (parodied in Satan's cephalogenesis of Sin, according to Turner) into physical sexuality (Death's rape of Sin). In brief, says Turner, we witness a descent from "magical birth" to birth via "wormes-*Carkasse*" (p. 155). "Wormes-*Carkasse*" translates Boehme's graphic term for male genitalia, *Madensack*, which Turner tells us would be better rendered "*maggot-bag*" (p. 145). What is the relevance of "maggot bags" to the birth of Sin? The farfetched comparison with Boehme exemplifies Turner's concern with Milton's relation to and representation of a largely misogynist tradition of scriptural interpretation. With its focus on masculine attitudes toward the act of sex and the origins of masculine sexual desire, Turner's work betrays the limitations of much New Historicist criticism. His stress on coition and body parts excludes a great part of human sexuality, including pregnancy and childbirth. Justifying his focus on male sexual excitement or its absence, Turner observes that "imaginative readers can in any case participate in the experience of the opposite gender vicariously" (p. 270). Heterosexual male readers are apparently spared the imaginative effort.

7 Robert Baillie, *A Dissuasive from the Errours of the Time* (London, 1646), reports that during a birth in New England involving a midwife notorious for her sympathy with the devil, all of the neighborhood women who should have been in attendance were either driven or kept away by sudden accidents or illness. The child of course did not survive. On the tendency to place midwives in the same category as witches, see Barbara

Ehrenreich and Deirdre English, *Witches, Midwives, and Nurses* (New York, 1973). Baillie was a Scottish Presbyterian who found the views of Independents like Milton – or like Anne Hutchinson and Mary Dyer – abhorrent.

8 See R. V. Schnucker, "The English Puritans and Pregnancy, Delivery and Breast Feeding," *History of Childhood Quarterly* 1 (1974). Schnucker calls childbirth in the Renaissance "a mystery reserved for the observation of women only," though as the seventeenth century progressed this rule increasingly admitted exception (p. 640).

9 Christopher Hill, "Sex, Marriage and Parish Registers," *The Collected Essays*, vol. 3 (Amherst, MA, 1986), p. 213. Hill also notes that in 1655 "the Lord Mayor of London ordered a precept to be read against the murder of bastard children by their mothers – so frequent was the practice thought to have become" (p. 213). Hill's evidence is indirect, but his conclusions concerning infanticide seem plausible. See Keith Wrightson, "Infanticide in Earlier Seventeenth-Century England," *Local Population Studies* 15 (1975), pp. 17–19, as cited by Hill, and Arthur Rackham Cleveland, *Women Under the English Law* (London, 1896), pp. 177–78. *The Diary of Lady Margaret Hoby 1599–1605*, ed. Dorothy M. Meads (London, 1930), records various instances when Lady Margaret was summoned to a childbearing neighbor's or relative's side (pp. 63, 191–92, 195).

10 Lucy Hutchinson, *Memoirs of the Life of Colonel Hutchinson*, ed. James Sutherland (London, 1973), p. 19.

11 Lawrence Stone, *The Crisis of the Aristocracy 1558–1641* (Oxford, 1965), p. 619. Stone's statistics, based on parish registers, are somewhat unreliable, as Christopher Hill demonstrates in "Sex, Marriage and Parish Registers," pp. 188–225. My point – that a large number of seventeenth-century women died in childbirth – does not depend on the precise accuracy of Stone's calculations.

12 Although Milton attributes the death to childbirth, the Marchioness seems actually to have died of an infection soon after delivering her stillborn child. An abscess on her cheek was lanced and "the humour fell down into her throat and quickly dispatched her" (see Masson 1, 244; Parker pp. 766–68). Milton's sorrow over the Marchioness's death, if at a distance, could well have been genuine. Masson notes that "she was spoken of as one of the most beautiful and accomplished of the ladies of her time" (1, 244).

13 Ralph A. Houlbrooke, *The English Family, 1450–1700* (London, 1984), p. 133.

14 Jacob Rueff, *De Conceptu et Generatione Hominis* (Frankfurt, 1587), pp. 24–26. The work was translated into English as *The Expert Midwife, Or An Excellent and most necessary Treatise of the generation and birth of Man* (London, 1637).

15 The first effective obstetric forceps were developed by members of the Chamberlen family and probably perfected by Peter Chamberlen the Elder, the first of two sons named Peter by William Chamberlen, a

French Huguenot who came to England in 1569. Compared to that of
their European neighbors, early modern England's skill in obstetrics
appears to have been relatively primitive and until the seventeenth
century preserved only in the oral tradition. Both of William Chamberlen's sons became members of the Barber Surgeons Company and
specialized in difficult deliveries of children. The third generation of
Chamberlens, in the person of Peter III, proposed to incorporate English
midwives under his control. This would have meant greater power and
prestige for Chamberlen, of course, but it also would have allowed for
more widespread use of the forceps and secured a professional niche for
the midwives. Chamberlen's initiative was blocked, primarily by the
College of Physicians. The motive for the College's actions does not
require a great stretch of historical imagination. In the words of Nicholas
Culpeper, from his "Epistle Dedicatorie" to *A Directory for Midwives*
(London, 1651), "*if any want Wisdom, let him ask it of God* (not of the *Colledg of
Physitians*, for if they do, they may hap to go without their Errand, unless
they bring Money with them)." For the Chamberlens' family history,
which reflects the conflicts between midwives and doctors in the seventeenth century and reveals how, gradually, female midwives were pushed
out of obstetrics, see Herbert R. Spencer, *The History of British Midwifery
from 1650 to 1800* (London, 1927), pp. ii–v, 1. For a feminist perspective on
this history, see Hilda Smith, "Gynecology and Ideology in Seventeenth
Century England," *Liberating Women's History*, ed. Berenice A. Carroll
(Champaign, IL, 1976), pp. 97–114. Elizabeth Gasking, *Investigations into
Generation 1651–1828* (Baltimore, 1967), is a reliable guide to the history of
this branch of science.

16 Peter Boaystuau, *The Theatre or Rule of the World*, trans. John Alday
(London, 1574), p. 49. Boaystuau (or Boaistuau) notes that childbirths
requiring such extreme measures cannot be apprehended "with out
horror" (p. 49).

17 Charles Stuart, *Eikon Basilike* (London, 1648), pp. 18–19. Milton's para-
phrase and response to this particular passage, part of which serves as
epigraph to the present section, appears in *Eikonoklastes* (*CP* 3, 391).

18 In a letter written in 1654 Milton describes for Leonard Philaris the
symptoms that accompanied the failure of his eyesight, which included
generally reluctant bowels, vexed with gas ("*visceraque omnia gravari,
flatibusque vexari*") (*CW* 12, 66).

19 For anecdotal evidence of Milton's fear of assassination after the Restoration, see John Richardson's biography, in Helen Darbishire, ed., *The Early
Lives of Milton* (London, 1932), p. 276.

20 Darbishire, *Early Lives*, p. 276.

21 Manoa's false hope is described in terms of what was known as a "wind
egg," that is, an unfertilized egg, defined by Aristotle as one that lacks
"the principle of soul ... so that it does not develop into a living creature,
for this is introduced by the semen of the male" (*De Generatione Animalium*,

trans. Arthur Platt, *The Works of Aristotle*, ed. J. A. Smith and W. D. Ross [Oxford, 1912], 737a30–34). Milton uses precisely this term in satirizing Charles's belief that legislation proposed by Parliament requires the monarch's assent to be enacted: "Parliament, it seems is but a Female, and without his procreative reason, the Laws which they can produce are but wind-eggs." Milton goes on to claim that if Parliament is female, it should be understood as Charles's mother, "which, to civil being, created both him, and the Royalty he wore." Charles's desire for "Masculine coition" with Parliament would thus be incestuous and a classic sign of a tyrant (*Eikonoklastes CP* 3, 467).

22 William Kerrigan, *The Sacred Complex* (Cambridge, MA, 1983), argues that "the rupture of enjambment between 'men' and 'cut off' in the invocation to light reduces to one the strokes of a paternal vengeance that, beginning with the headaches of a young student, smote and smote until, light denied, it smote no more" (p. 184). Kerrigan proceeds to argue that Milton consequently imagines himself as female and capable of being impregnated by God. I follow Kerrigan in supposing that Milton, wounded by blindness, imagines himself as poetically fruitful after a feminine model. I do not accept the Oedipal etiology of the wound.

23 Kerrigan, *Sacred Complex*, p. 179.

24 Charles W. Bodemer, "Materialistic and Neoplatonic Influences in Embryology," *Medicine in Seventeenth-Century England*, ed. Allen G. Debus (Berkeley, 1974), p. 183. Accounting for the orderly development of a fetus – from almost nothing to a complex living organism – involved seventeenth-century embryology with heated and consequential disputes among dualistic and monistic philosophies, some mechanistic and others vitalist. For a lucid exposition of Milton's place in this larger philosophical context, see Stephen M. Fallon, *Milton among the Philosophers* (Ithaca, 1991).

25 William Harvey, *Anatomical Exercitations, Concerning the Generation of Living Creatures* (London, 1653), p. 549. I am indebted to Stephen Dobranski for recommending Harvey's treatise. Further citations of this edition appear parenthetically in the text and have been checked against Harvey's original Latin, *Exercitationes de Generatione Animalium* (London, 1651). Where the seventeenth-century translation seems misleadingly antiquated, or potentially so, and especially in cases where the point seems to me critical, I have included a more modern substitute in brackets.

26 See Walter Charleton's *Natural History of Nutrition, Life, and Voluntary Motion* (London, 1659), p. 40. Harvey's singular stature in the history of physiology is generally acknowledged and was recognized in the seventeenth century. John Smith, *King Solomons Portraiture of Old Age* (London, 1666), pp. 233–34, credits the "for ever to be renouned Dr. *William Harvey*, the greatest honour of our Nation" with recovering knowledge forgotten since the time of Solomon. Kenelm Digby, *Two Treatises* (London, 1658), asked "what secret of nature can be hidden from so sharp a wit?" (p. 291).

The Dictionary of National Biography, ed. Leslie Stephen and Sidney Lee, 63 vols. (London, 1885–1900) calls Harvey's work on circulation "the greatest of the discoveries of physiology" (25, 97).

27 Aristotle, *De Generatione Animalium*, 747a17–18.

28 See, for example, the subsection "Parents a Cause [of melancholy] by Propagation" in Robert Burton, *The Anatomy of Melancholy*, ed. Thomas C. Faulkner, Nicolas K. Kiessling, and Rhonda L. Blair 2 vols. (Oxford, 1989), pp. 205–10 (Part 1, Sect. 2, Memb. 1, Subs. 6). Burton cites various authorities, such as Roger Bacon, Paracelsus, and Bede among many others, and records fascinating anecdotes, e.g. he writes of a man who saw "a Cittizen that looked like a karkasse," the cause of the appearance being that his mother while pregnant "saw a carcasse [*sic*] by chance" and "from a ghastly impression the child was like it" (p. 209).

29 Robert Baillie, *Dissuasive from Errours*, p. 63. Neither the currency nor the credibility of this story had lessened more than sixty years after the actual controversy in New England during the late 1630s; hence Masson reports the same story from Cotton Mather's *Magnalia* of 1702 (3, 150–51).

30 Aristotle, *De Generatione Animalium*, 738b20–22.

31 Aeschylus, *The Oresteian Trilogy*, trans. Philip Vellacott (Baltimore, 1956), pp. 171–72.

32 Nathaniel Highmore, *The History of Generation* (London, 1651), pp. 88–89.

33 Harvey was hardly unique in connecting mental phenomena with procreation, though for Paracelsus and Van Helmont the link is not one of resemblance but one of instigation, with the imagination effecting the activation of the semen. See Walter Pagel, *William Harvey's Biological Ideas* (New York, 1967), p. 270.

34 Bodemer, "Materialistic and Neoplatonic Influences," notes that few seventeenth-century embryological theorists "had been able or willing to dispense with them" – that is, with positing a formative faculty (p. 195). Harvey's insistence on a plastic faculty found enthusiastic approval in the work of Cambridge Neoplatonists like Henry More and particularly Ralph Cudworth, whose notion of "plastic" nature may be taken as evidence of the macrocosmic salience of Harvey's account of embryogenesis (Bodemer, p. 205). Digby, however, in *Two Treatises*, rejects the notion of "a forming virtue," attributing the development of the fetus to various causes acting together toward a single end (p. 289). In this analysis, Digby sounds almost Darwinian.

35 See, for example, Aristotle, *De Generatione Animalium*, 729b15–18 and 730b10–32, where nature is described as using semen as a tool that possesses "the motion of the art."

36 Aristotle, *De Generatione Animalium*, 729a35. Highmore begins his *History of Generation* with a metaphysical discussion of the four elements, the dualism of matter and form, and the creation out of chaos as the prototype for all generation (pp. 42–46).

37 On masculine anxiety over gender identity and the male's apparently

tangential role in reproduction, see Bruno Bettelheim, *Symbolic Wounds* (New York, 1954).

38 Aristotle, *De Generatione Animalium*, 741a5–9.

39 Aristotle claims that the male is necessary because the female is not fully human, or rather, a defective example of the human form. The male's ability to concoct semen from blood particularly distinguishes him from the female, whose inferior generative matter is only fit to be shaped by the semen. See *De Generatione Animalium*, 766b8–15 and notes 50 and 52 below.

40 See Pagel, *Harvey's Biological Ideas*, p. 273. The specific political allegiances involved with the science informing *Paradise Lost* are notoriously difficult to pin down. Milton and Harvey (Charles I's physician) were on opposite sides: Harvey protected Charles II during the Civil War, and some of Harvey's work was destroyed by Republican mobs. Harvey's critic Nathaniel Highmore dedicated his *History of Generation* to Lady Ranelagh's brother Robert Boyle and would have been politically more amenable to Milton, as the less ideological and more practical Culpeper also would have been. Yet I can trace no consistent correlation between specific theories of generation and political allegiance. Highmore aside, Harvey's genius seems to have had few detractors of any political persuasion. That Milton would have been acquainted with the latest theories concerning generation seems likely, given his acquaintance with Dr. Nathan Paget.

41 Harvey's comparison of human generation to that of plants marks yet another significant departure from the hierarchically minded Aristotle, for whom the hermaphroditic nature of plants signals their ontological inferiority. The philosopher claims that plants do not require a distinction between male and female because they do not possess a sensitive soul in addition to a nutritive soul (*De Generatione Animalium*, 741a10–15).

42 Pagel, *Harvey's Biological Ideas*, p. 44.

43 Culpeper, *Directory for Midwives*, p. 72. The admirable Culpeper ignores these points of disputation and actually concentrates on spreading useful information.

44 Highmore, *History of Generation*, p. 100. Highmore's work concludes with an extensive rebuttal of the claim that semen never enters the womb (pp. 96–112).

45 Highmore, *History of Generation*, p. 102.

46 The voice in Eve's dream, however, identifies the "night-warbling Bird" as masculine (5, 41). Whether or not this is an instance of gender confusion seems debatable. The myth clashes with natural observation. Milton presumably would have known that it is the male nightingale that sings.

47 On Adam's giving birth to Eve in relation to seventeenth-century obstetrics, see Louis Schwartz, "'Spot of Child-Bed Taint,'" *Milton Quarterly* 27 (1993), pp. 94–106. Schwartz also discusses Sonnet 23 in this context.

48 Aristotle, *De Generatione Animalium*, 737a28, 767b8–9, 766a31–32, 766a27. For a critique of Western philosophy's characteristic rendition of the

female as inferior or defective and of the male as superior and relatively perfect, see Luce Irigaray, *Speculum of the Other Woman*, trans. Gillian C. Gill (Ithaca, 1985).

49 Some later interpretations of the biblical story do allow Adam to dream while Eve is being created, most notably Henry More in *Conjectura Cabbalistica* (London, 1653), cited by J. M. Evans, *"Paradise Lost" and the Genesis Tradition* (Oxford, 1968), pp. 263–64.

50 For Aristotle's emphasis on the relative coldness of females, see *De Generatione Animalium*, 765b8–766a5. Stephen Greenblatt appeals to temperature as the distinguishing cause of gender and consequently of Renaissance gender anxieties in "Fiction and Friction," *Shakespearean Negotiations* (Berkeley, 1988), pp. 66–93. Lorna Hutson challenges his claim in her illuminating essay "On Not Being Deceived: Rhetoric and the Body in *Twelfth Night*," forthcoming in *Texas Studies in Literature and Language* 38 (1996).

51 William Shakespeare, *Much Ado about Nothing*, ed. A. R. Humphreys (London, 1987), 2.1.56–58.

52 Bodemer, "Materialistic and Neoplatonic Influences," notes that as a natural philosopher Charleton combined Epicurean atomism with the mechanistic rationalism of Descartes, but in embryology he followed Harvey (pp. 192–96). Like Charleton, Digby also placed great emphasis on the relation between generation and nutrition (see *Two Treatises*, p. 268). The emphasis on nutrition in connection with generation is also an Aristotelian inheritance, since the male's ability to concoct semen from blood (by means of his superior heat) is the *nutritional* feat that distinguishes him from the female, whose inferior generative matter is fit only to be shaped by the semen. See *De Generatione Animalium*, 766b8–15, where semen is defined as "the ultimate secretion of the nutriment."

53 See *Matter of Glory*, pp. 71–77, 83–93. The alchemical process was also compared to pregnancy. See Lyndy Abraham, *Marvell and Alchemy* (Aldershot, England, 1990), p. 50.

54 That Milton should refer to the fruit of the Tree of Life as vegetable gold, capable of conferring immortality, reflects the high value that Renaissance medicine generally placed on gems and precious metals. Marsilio Ficino, for example, recommends drinking out of golden vessels in addition to consuming gold in solution, an earthly approximation of the potable gold that flows in the rivers of Milton's sun (*PL* 3, 608). See Marsilio Ficino, "De Vita," in *Three Books on Life*, ed. and trans. Carol V. Kaske and John R. Clark (Binghamton, NY, 1989), pp. 134–35. Nearly every electuary for which Ficino provides a recipe includes gold as an ingredient. Of gold as a medicinal substance generally, Ficino writes "all writers place gold before everything else" (pp. 194–95). In Milton's heaven, drinking from vessels made of gold and other precious substances is ordinary and presumably part of the regimen that sustains immortal being (5, 634).

55 See J. M. Evans, *Milton and the Genesis Tradition*, p. 45.

56 As various scholars have made clear in tracing the relations between the first and last two books of the poem, the fallen angels in hell bear a relation to humanity that is perversely comparable to that between ideal and instance in Platonism. Eve who in the potency of her womb holds all mankind may thus be seen as analogous to the hollow enclosure of Pandemonium, which holds all the demons.

57 William Shakespeare, *Romeo and Juliet*, ed. Brian Gibhouse (London, 1980), 5.1.64–65. The simile is used to describe the spread of powerful poison through the body, which brings to mind Satan's attempt to poison Eve's mind as she sleeps.

58 Here I draw on Tzvetan Todorov's conception of symbolic thought as the conversion of one set of symbolic terms into another, establishing a pattern of accretion that can go on indefinitely. See *Theories of the Symbol*, trans. Catherine Porter (Ithaca, 1982), p. 245.

6 CULTURE AND ANARCHY

1 "On Angels," *Sixty Stories* (New York, 1981), p. 137.

2 Robert M. Adams, "A Little Look into Chaos," *Illustrious Evidence: Approaches to English Literature of the Early Seventeenth Century*, ed. Earl Miner (Berkeley, 1975), p. 75.

3 A. B. Chambers, Jr., "Chaos in Paradise Lost," *Journal of the History of Ideas* 24 (1963), pp. 65, 69.

4 On the political configuration of Augustinian theology, see Elaine Pagels, *Adam, Eve, and the Serpent* (New York, 1988), pp. 98–126.

5 Peter Brown, *The Body and Society* (New York, 1988), has surveyed writings from the second to the fourth centuries concerning early Christian attitudes toward the body, what it represents, and its place in society. Augustinian doctrine, despite its anti-carnal bias, actually represents a moderation of the dualistic tenets of then thriving cults of asceticism and sexual renunciation. The writings of male Christian ascetics are often centrally concerned with behavior toward women and with government of the appetites they arouse.

6 Even C. S. Lewis admitted that Milton's God possesses the attribute of potentiality. See *A Preface to "Paradise Lost"* (Oxford, 1942), p. 88. For a historically grounded assessment of Milton's theology of matter as it applies to his epic, see Dennis Danielson, *Milton's Good God* (Cambridge, 1982), pp. 26–49. Danielson offers a particularly lucid account of the Augustinian position and its seventeenth-century exponents. His discussion of chaos in *Paradise Lost* stands out from the general confusion on the subject and I am indebted to its insights.

7 Milton's depiction of chaos as the generative ground of existence follows Spenser, for whom chaos was "the wide wombe of the world": "An huge eternall *Chaos*, which supplyes / The substances of natures fruitfull progenyes." Edmund Spenser, *The Faerie Queene*, ed. Thomas P. Roche, Jr.

(New Haven, 1978), III, VI, 36. In *Paradise Lost* chaos contains the "pregnant causes" of the four elements (2, 913). James C. Nohrnberg, *The Analogy of the "Faerie Queene"* (Princeton, 1976), details the philosophical and mythological associations of chaos in Spenser. His work surveys Mesopotamian and scriptural representations of God's battles with Chaos. See for example his account of biblical depictions of the Creator as a dragonslayer or as the fisherman who hooked Leviathan (pp. 182ff).

8 Plato, *Timaeus*, *The Collected Dialogues*, ed. Edith Hamilton and Huntington Cairns (Princeton, 1961), 53b.

9 Regina Schwartz, *Remembering and Repeating: Biblical Creation in "Paradise Lost"* (Cambridge, 1988), pp. 13, 31. Further citations of this work will appear parenthetically in the body of the text.

10 The claim that the logic of Milton's theology is irrelevant to his poetry is, as we have seen, not unprecedented. It was a position most fully articulated by C. A. Patrides in defending the orthodoxy of *Paradise Lost* (see chapter 2, note 37). In this case, it allows Schwartz to insist that Milton's arguments on behalf of the goodness of matter have little bearing on his poetry. For Patrides, the relevant context is that of the "Christian tradition"; for Schwartz, the mythological antecedents of the ceremonial law.

11 Nor is this apocalyptic consciousness unique to *Paradise Lost*. The reward envisioned for the beloved Diodati, for example, is furious with bacchanalian pleasure: "*Cantus ubi, choreisque furit lyra mista beatis, / Festa Sionaeo bacchantur & Orgia Thyrso*" (*Epitaphium Damonis* 218–19). Darbishire translates Milton's Latin: "where there is singing, where the lyre revels madly, mingled with choirs beatific, and festal orgies run riot, in bacchante fashion, with the thyrsus of Zion."

12 Paul Ricoeur, *The Symbolism of Evil*, trans. Emerson Buchanan (Boston, 1967), p. 180. Schwartz cites Ricoeur's discussion. Danielson, *Milton's Good God*, pp.27–28, also discusses the relevance of Babylonian mythology to Milton's representation of chaos. He observes that drawing on these symbolic resources allows Milton to augment "his presentation of evil, including the role of Satan," while nevertheless avoiding dualism (p. 28).

13 Ricoeur, *Symbolism of Evil*, p.180.

14 See James. B. Pritchard, ed., *Ancient Near Eastern Texts Relating to the Old Testament* (Princeton, 1955), pp. 62–64.

15 N. Katherine Hayles, *Chaos Bound* (Ithaca, 1990), has observed that chaos is associated with "aspects of life that have tended to be culturally encoded as feminine" (p. 173).

16 According to Ricoeur, *Symbolism of Evil*, p. 176, the Marduk story of creation was inserted into an already extant mythology as the Mesopotamian system of kingship gained political ascendancy.

17 Mary Daly, *Gyn/Ecology* (Boston, 1978), p. 355. As noted in chapter 4, a similar symbolic imbedding of a social transition may occur in development of the Perseus myth. Catherine Keller, *From a Broken Web* (Boston,

1986), pp. 69–78, uses the Perseus myth and the Marduk myth in setting the context for her account of biblical and philosophical misogyny.

18 N. J. Girardot, "Chaos," *The Encyclopedia of Religion*, ed. Mircea Eliade, 16 vols. (New York, 1987), 3, 214. It may seem that I place too much weight on an encyclopedia entry. Girardot offers an admirable distillation of theological attitudes toward chaos, however, and the easy accessibility of this standard reference underscores the selective insularity of customary Milton scholarship on the subject.

19 Girardot, "Chaos," p. 214. For further discussion of the ironic cultural functions of chaos, see Mircea Eliade, *Mephistopheles and the Androgyne*, trans. J. M. Cohen (New York, 1965), pp. 78–122.

20 Girardot, "Chaos," p. 216.

21 Thomas Hobbes, *Leviathan*, ed. Richard Tuck (Cambridge, 1991), p.299.

22 Unlike nearly everyone else who has written on Milton's chaos, Adams, "A Little Look," p. 74, does comment on the relevance of this passage, as does Stephen M. Fallon, *Milton Among the Philosophers* (Ithaca, 1991), p. 191, to whose analysis I am indebted. See also Fred Hoerner, "Fire to Use," forthcoming in *Representations*, which is a discussion of Augustinian concepts of use and charity in terms of contemporary practice theory. He interprets the construction of the bridge over hell as the attempt of evil to deny the potency for transformation embodied in created structures.

23 Hobbes, *Leviathan*, p.254.

24 Consider a contrary effort at construction envisioned by Milton in *Areopagitica*:

> when every stone is laid artfully together, it cannot be united into a continuity, it can but be contiguous in this world; neither can every peece of the building be of one form; nay rather the perfection consists in this, that out of many moderat varieties and brotherly dissimilitudes that are not vastly disproportionall arises the goodly and the gracefull symmetry that commends the whole pile and structure. (2, 555)

The temple of truth cannot be built without the sects or without tolerance for their differences, even though a tyrant might attempt to impose uniformity on them. Furthermore, Milton insists that the structure cannot be completed before the apocalypse.

25 William Empson, *Milton's God* (1961; Cambridge, 1981), p. 144.

26 Fallon, *Milton Among the Philosophers*, p. 182.

27 Fallon, *Milton Among the Philosophers*, pp. 169–71, 182–83

28 Fallon, *Milton Among the Philosophers*, p. 173.

29 Gordon Teskey, "Irony, Allegory, and Metaphysical Decay," *PMLA* 109 (1994), p. 398.

30 Girardot, "Chaos," p. 214.

31 Homer's verb for battle and lovemaking is *mignumi*. See the *Iliad*, trans. A. T. Murray, 2 vols. (London, 1988), 9, 275; 15, 510.

32 Margaret Drabble, *A Writer's Britain: Landscape in Literature* (New York,

1979) p. 129. Drabble's remarks could be amplified from the writings of many others.

33 Jonathan Swift, *A Tale of a Tub*, ed. Angus Ross and David Wooley (Oxford, 1984), p. 145.

34 Evans, *Paradise Lost and the Genesis Tradition* (Oxford, 1968), pp. 250–51.

35 Andy Troup of California State University, Bakersfield, formerly a student at the University of Texas, addressed the apparent incoherence of topics in book 8 in a seminar paper. I am indebted to his formulation of the problem.

36 My understanding of symbols as evocational markers expressive of what is not currently fathomed depends on the work of Dan Sperber, *Rethinking Symbolism*, trans. Alice Morton (Cambridge, 1975).

37 W. B .C. Watkins, *An Anatomy of Milton's Verse* (Hamden, CT, 1965), p. 63.

38 Plato, *Timaeus* 49b.

39 Denis Saurat, *Milton, Man and Thinker* (1925, 1944; London, 1946), pp. 235-36.

40 Saurat, *Milton*, p. 236.

41 Empson, *Milton's God*, p. 117.

42 Isabel MacCaffrey, *"Paradise Lost" as "Myth"* (Cambridge, MA, 1959), p.164.

43 John Reesing, "The Materiality of God in Milton's *De Doctrina Christiana*," *Harvard Theological Review* 50 (1957), pp. 159–73, finds Milton's claim that God cannot be called "Actus Purus" inconsistent with his insistence on God's immutability (pp. 171–72). This apparent inconsistency is less troublesome when we consider that once God creates out of his infinite material potency, what he creates becomes essentially distinct from him. God always contains infinite material potency. This condition never changes, no matter how much or how often God creates. Hence, God may be said to remain immutable when part of his potency becomes actualized and distinct from him. That this potency can also be actualized in the form of "black tartareous cold infernal dregs / Adverse to life," moreover, need not be taken to suggest that evil is latent in chaos, at least not any more than it is latent in the deity who establishes hell as "A Universe of death … by curse / Created evil" (2, 622–23). Like Dante, Milton describes hell as a work of divine justice; and if justice is good, God's material potency must include the possibility of matter appropriate to such construction.

44 Walter Clyde Curry, *Milton's Ontology, Cosmogony, and Physics*, (Lexington, 1957), pp. 34–35.

45 Curry, *Milton's Ontology*, p. 145.

46 Isaac Newton's beliefs concerning God's substantial omnipresence, as set out in the General Scholium appended to the second edition of the *Principia* (1713), are similar to Milton's: "He is omnipresent not *virtually* only, but also *substantially*; for virtue cannot subsist without substance." The General Scholium was "composed virtually at the end of [Newton's]

active life" according to Richard S. Westfall, *Never at Rest* (Cambridge, 1980), and contains "a vigorous reassertion against the perceived dangers of Cartesian mechanical philosophy" (pp. 748–49).

47 Hayles, *Chaos Bound*, p. 9.
48 Hayles, *Chaos Bound*, p. 16.
49 Hayles, *Chaos Bound*, pp. 22–23.

Index